W9-AHP-334

DATE DUE

618.92
In3p
P748I

DISCARD

BET
COL
LIBR

BRODART, CO.   Cat. No. 23-221-003

INFANTS AND PARENTS

Clinical Case Reports

Clinical Infant Reports:
Series of the National Center for Clinical Infant Programs

Editorial Board

Sally Provence, M.D., Chairman

Kathryn Barnard
Peter Blos, Jr.
T. Berry Brazelton, M.D.
Stanley I. Greenspan, M.D.
Aneliese Korner
Emily Schrag, Associate Director for
Publications and Public
Policy

INFANTS AND PARENTS

Clinical Case Reports

edited by

Sally Provence, M.D.

International Universities Press, Inc.
New York

Copyright © 1983, National Center for Clinical Infant Programs. All rights reserved. No part of this book may be reproduced by any means, nor translated into a machine language, without the written permission of the publisher.

Library of Congress Cataloging in Publication Data
Main entry under title:

Infants and parents.

(Clinical infant reports; report no. 2)
Bibliography: p.
 1. Infant psychiatry—Case studies. 2. Family psychotheapy—Case studies. I. Provence, Sally, 1916-   . [DNLM: 1. Mental health—In infancy and childhood. 2. Parent-child relations. 3. Mental disorders—In infancy and childhood. WS 350 I436]
RJ502.5.I55 1983   618.92′89156   83-18441
ISBN 0-8236-2636-9

Manufactured in the United States of America

For Selma Fraiberg and Leon J. Yarrow
lovingly remembered, sorely missed

618.92
In 3 P

The **National Center for Clinical Infant Programs** is a nonprofit, tax-exempt corporation. It was established in 1977 by outstanding representatives from the fields of mental health, pediatrics, child development, and related fields, as well as community leaders, in order to improve and support professional initiatives in infant mental health and development.

Board of Directors
Kathryn Barnard, University of Washington
Peter Blos, Jr., University of Michigan Medical Center
T. Berry Brazelton, Children's Hospital Medical Center, Boston
Amy S. Cohen, Center for Preventive Psychiatry, White Plains, NY
Robert N. Emde, University of Colorado School of Medicine
William E. Friedman, Baer Marks & Upham, NYC
Morris Green, Indiana University School of Medicine
Stanley I. Greenspan, Mental Health Study Center, NIMH
Irving B. Harris, Pittway Corporation, Chicago
Anneliese Korner, Stanford University Medical Center
J. Ronald Lally, Far West Laboratory, San Francisco
Bernard Levy, Smart Parts, Inc., NYC
Reginald S. Lourie, Mental Health Study Center, NIMH
Robert A. Nover, Mental Health Study Center, NIMH
Jeree Pawl, San Francisco General Hospital
George H. Pollock, Institute for Psychoanalysis, Chicago
Sally Provence, Yale University School of Medicine
Julius B. Richmond, Harvard University Medical School
Mary E. Robinson, Mental Health Study Center, NIMH
Lisbeth B. Schorr, University of North Carolina, School of Public Health
Rebecca Shahmoon Shanok, Jewish Board of Family and Children's Services, NYC
Albert J. Solnit, Yale University School of Medicine
Bernice Weissbourd, Family Focus, Inc., Evanston, IL
Edward Zigler, Yale University

Executive Director: *Eleanor Stokes Szanton*
Associate Director for Publications and Public Policy: *Emily Schrag*
Director of Development: *Carol Berman*

CONTENTS

Contributors ix

Introduction
  Sally Provence, M.D. 1

CHAPTER ONE
Early Intervention in a Pediatric Multidisciplinary
Clinic
T. Berry Brazelton, M.D.
and *Catherine Buttenwieser, M.S.W.* 9

CHAPTER TWO
Infant-Parent Psychotherapy: A Family in Crisis
Jeree H. Pawl, Ph.D. and
Judith H. Pekarsky, Ph.D. 39

CHAPTER THREE
Infant-Parent Psychotherapy During Pregnancy
Alicia F. Lieberman, Ph.D. 85

CHAPTER FOUR
A Family in a Mental Health Day Care Center:
Clinical Assessment Procedures and Services
*Peter B. Neubauer, M.D., Virginia
Flynn, M.S.* and *Christina Sekaer, M.D.* 143

CHAPTER FIVE
Babies Everywhere: Assessing and Treating a
Toddler's Pervasive Developmental Disorder
Kyle D. Pruett, M.D. 177

CHAPTER SIX
The Therapist as Decoder: Psychotherapy with
Toddlers
E. Kirsten Dahl, Ph.D. 213

vii

CHAPTER SEVEN
    Magical Thinking and Destructiveness: A
    Comprehensive Clinical Approach to an Infant
    and Mother with Multiple Affective and
    Developmental Challenges
    Euthymia D. Hibbs, Ph.D., Patricia Findikoglu,
    M.A., Alicia F. Lieberman, Ph.D., Reginald S.
    Lourie, Ph.D., *Robert A. Nover, M.D., Serena*
    Wieder, Ph.D., and *Stanley I. Greenspan, M.D.* . 247

Contributors

T. Berry Brazelton, M.D.—Child Development Unit, Children's Hospital Medical Center; Boston, Massachusetts

Catherine Buttenwieser, M.S.W.—Child Development Unit, Children's Hospital Medical Center; Boston, Massachusetts

E. Kirsten Dahl, Ph.D.—Child Study Center, Yale University School of Medicine; New Haven, Connecticut

Patricia Findikoglu, M.A.—Regional Center for Infants and Young Children of Maryland, Washington, DC and Virginia; Silver Spring, Maryland

Virginia Flynn, M.S.—Infant Care Center, Jewish Board of Family and Children's Services; New York, New York

Stanley I. Greenspan, M.D.—Mental Health Study Center, National Institute of Mental Health, Adelphi, Maryland

Euthymia D. Hibbs, Ph.D.—Intramural Research Program, National Institute of Mental Health, Bethesda, Maryland

Alicia F. Lieberman, Ph.D.—Infant-Parent Program, San Francisco General Hospital, San Francisco, California

Reginald S. Lourie, M.D.—Mental Health Study Center, National Institute of Mental Health, Adelphi, Maryland

Peter B. Neubauer, M.D.—Child Development Center, Jewish Board of Family and Children's Services, New York, New York

Robert A. Nover, M.D.—Mental Health Study Center, National Institute of Mental Health, Adelphi, Maryland

Jeree H. Pawl, Ph.D.—Infant-Parent Program, San Francisco General Hospital, San Francisco, California

Judith H. Pekarsky, Ph.D.—Infant-Parent Program, San Francisco General Hospital, San Francisco, California

Kyle D. Pruett, M.D.—Child Study Center, Yale University School of Medicine, New Haven, Connecticut

Sally Provence, M.D.—Child Study Center, Yale University School of Medicine, New Haven, Connecticut

Christina Sekaer, M.D.—Infant Care Center, Jewish Board of Family and Children's Services, New York, New York

Serena Wieder, Ph.D.—Regional Center for Infants and Young Children of Maryland, Washington, DC and Virginia, Silver Spring, Maryland

Introduction

This volume, the second in the series of Clinical Infant Reports published by the National Center for Clinical Infant Programs, addresses a widely acknowledged need in the literature on infant mental health—a need for detailed case studies illustrating diagnostic and therapeutic issues and methods. As practitioners, we learn most from those we serve and from other clinicians who share their experience with us; telling the stories of individuals who touch, puzzle, challenge, and inevitably instruct us is a time-honored and effective method for such communication. Moreover, the gradual accumulation of individually studied cases, carefully detailed and made available for scrutiny and for information, has led historically not only to greater specificity in treatment but also to the recognition of subgroups and variations in disorders carrying the same label. For rich case material to remain available only to small groups of colleagues or limited numbers of participants in clinical conferences is a tremendous waste. This book, then, can be seen as an effort to widen the circle of sharing.

The case reports in this volume tell us how clinicians work with infants and parents and describe the change, or lack of change, in the lives of the children and parents during the period of their work with those providing services. In some instances, authors are also able to report on the children and families some time after close clinical contact has ended.

While settings, treatment approaches, and infants' pre-

1

senting problems vary considerably from case to case, certain shared beliefs and attitudes can be recognized.

• It is assumed that diagnosis and treatment can best be carried out when parents have an opportunity to become involved in a therapeutic alliance with those who offer help. Such an alliance usually forms gradually, based on professionals' ability to engender feelings of trust in the patient regarding their competence, interest and availability. When care is episodic, discontinuous, or fragmented because of personnel changes—even in settings staffed by competent professionals—work with individual clients and patients is impeded, and many a good beginning lost.

• It is assumed (and has been amply demonstrated) that there is no substitute for the careful individualization of each child and parent in clinical work. Among the more encouraging results of work with disadvantaged families and with parents whose infants are difficult or handicapped are the continuing benefits to the child and parent of having the right kind of help at the time when it is needed. This thread runs through the fabric of this book, as the authors describe the rationale and details of their work.

• It is assumed that parents and their children must be enabled to work actively in their own behalf and that helping them to do so is part of the function of the clinician. Of course some individuals and families are able to do so more promptly, and more fully, than others.

Before introducing the case reports individually, I would like to warn the reader against assuming that clinical work is as easily accomplished as it may appear on these pages. When we write case studies and reports we seldom convey much about how difficult, and often discouraging, the work may be. Little is said, from the therapists' side, about the periods—sometimes long ones—when nothing very good seems to be happening, when things are not going well between them and their clients or patients. It is at these times that colleagues or mentors or consultants may be of some service—not only in helping to rethink and evaluate the case and the work, but also to share in the frustration, anxiety, and perplexity we feel when the therapeutic goals we have set are not in sight. That some infants and parents will not improve as much as we hope and expect is inevitable. But this fact cannot become a reason for avoiding the challenge to mobilize our best resources for each child and to help build services for all children.

T. Berry Brazelton and Catherine Buttenwieser describe a method of early, short-term intervention carried out in a pediatric setting by a multidisciplinary team in which pediatricians taking advanced training in child development assume primary responsibility for the care of patients. Stimulated by the increase in what are now called psychosocial disorders of infancy and childhood, the training of pediatricians in the psychological and social aspects of child health and development has received new emphasis. And after many years of consideration, by pediatric educators and their colleagues in psychiatry, social work, and psychology, of the best ways to provide the most effective training opportunities for young professionals, the clinician's work with the individual child and his parents remains the centrally important learning experience. While the Brazelton and Buttenwieser report is not about training per se, many of the attitudes and approaches which the beginning practitioner must absorb to practice effectively are implicit in its pages.

Dealing with problems commonly brought to a pediatric clinician, the two case histories in the chapter illustrate how such work is done. They clearly demonstrate the practical usefulness of observations of mother-infant interaction, developmental assessment, and sensitive clinical interviewing.

The case of Peter and his mother makes abundantly clear the value of astute evaluation and the provision of care and guidance beginning *at the right time* and continued as needed. In the story of Carol, the pediatrician—with timely assistance from the child psychiatrist—helps a 3-year-old and her parents find a way out of a conflict situation occurring between mother and child and perhaps within the child herself. The report illustrates the pediatrician's need to understand both some of the complexities of the parent-child relationship and the development of the child before giving advice. The importance to outcome of the psychological resources of the parents—of their ability to use and extend the help given by professional—is also well illustrated here.

The report of Peter Neubauer, Virginia Flynn, and Christina Sekaer describes the setting and process of work in an infant mental health day care center developed to meet the needs of infants and parents from the severely disadvantaged, deprived and disorganized segment of the population of a large city. Facilitation of the mother-infant relationship and of the child's development are aims of a day care program staffed by a group of sophisticated, experienced mental health professionals and of educators offering intensive, individualized care and treatment.

The authors sketch for us part of the story of Mathilda, 16 years old and not yet pregnant when the work begins, and her daughter, Claudia, who is 2½ years of age when the report ends. Choosing to share with us details of their work with a very difficult case—a disadvantaged young woman with psychological problems and few resources to meet them, and her child, whose biological predispositions render her especially vulnerable to the risks in her environment—is courageous of the authors and instructive to us. The report focuses on the assessment, evaluation, and treatment planning procedures which guided the intervention, presented in a condensed record of work over three years. As the account unfolds, we recognize the benefits to Mathilda and Claudia of the services provided as well as the limitations of treatment. The account not only tells us about one family but also provides a realistic look at the challenges, satisfactions, and disappointments (and at times the plain tediousness) experienced by dedicated, competent professionals in long-term work with very needy people.

Preventive intervention is one of the goals of those concerned with infant mental health. Alicia Lieberman's report documents the beneficial influence for the parent-infant relationship of therapy begun during the mother's pregnancy and directed toward alleviating the fears and ambivalence associated with the anticipation of parenthood.

As some of the links between the mother's traumatic past, precariously stabilized present, and fantasies of the future emerge with great vividness in the work, the therapist must choose among various ways of defining the therapeutic task. To surmount the emotional conflicts that stand in the way of the patient's "becoming a mother with a positive emotional investment in her baby" becomes the initial focus of treatment.

Four phases in the treatment are then described, each phase determined by parental—especially maternal—needs and readiness. In all phases, attention to the welfare of the baby provides a unifying focus. Lieberman's description of the follow-up visit of the mother and the 2-year-old child is a satisfying and eloquent conclusion which attests the success of the work and improved prospects for the future.

The very high incidence of marital conflict in the families of infants and young children who are not doing well is familiar to early childhood specialists. Although parents are often unaware that their problems with one another are important determinants of their child's difficulty, nevertheless the infant's disturbance—whether psychophysiological, behavioral, or developmental—is the ticket of admission for the family to a therapeutic environment where help may be at hand.

Jeree Pawl and Judith Pekarsky describe such a case. Assessment following a mother's call for assistance with her 16-month-old son revealed that the child's mother and father had problems with each other and in their roles as parents. While the decision was made to work primarily with the boy

Barry's parents, all members of this young family were involved in the treatment; Barry is present in the minds of therapist and parents even when physically absent from the interview.

As the authors point out, the prompt and steady improvement in the family environment over a five-month period appears to have occurred as a result of the parents' willingness to work very hard in a form of intervention combining education, advising, interpretation, and consistent, responsive concern and support. The unfolding story of Barry and his family illustrates how a baby's condition at birth can interfere with his parents' successful adaptation to parenthood and infant care, and can color their relationship to him in ways that markedly influence his behavior and development. Another important lesson is the advantage of a therapeutic approach which is flexible and responsive to the changing needs of parents and child. The sensitivity of the therapeutic process, its timeliness, and the resources in the parents enabling them to help themselves are noteworthy as well.

What strikes one immediately about Kyle Pruett's report is the crisis for the child and the family—an acute, intense disturbance erupting from the depths of a long-term chronic marital and parent-child problem. The treatment of a toddler and his parents begins with a bang, as the mother of 20-month-old Gary, in her poignant plea for help, describes her child as a monster terrorizing the family. That this mother is terrorized by the intensity of her own feelings, and needs much help in mastering them, becomes clear to her only gradually.

As issues and needs were clarified in the work with Gary and his parents, pediatric hospitalization and couples therapy for the marital problems of Mr. and Mrs. Ames were followed by individual treatment of Gary. Pruett spells out the relationship between diagnostic data and therapeutic work in enough detail to permit one to follow his thinking and that of his colleagues as the extent, tenacity, and interrelatedness of the problems of parents and child become apparent over time. Continuing assessment as a part of therapy is clearly illustrated in this case.

The description of the individual treatment of Gary beginning at age 31 months is instructive in its view of a distressed and symptomatic young child and in its discussion of treatment strategies and the interaction between Gary and his therapist.

Kirsten Dahl's report emphasizes the nature of the mental life of the young child and some of the hazards to the smooth unfolding and organization of the emotions and intellect. The role of the child therapist as interpreter, guide, and trustworthy adult is illustrated. And while the value of the child therapist as an object onto whom the young child can transfer the feelings and conflicts he has in regard to his parents and, beyond that, as a new, real, and unique adult who can provide new opportunities for development and conflict solution has long been recognized, this report reminds us that those who work with infants and very young children must meet special requirements for versatility in communication. A willingness to be imaginative about what the child is feeling and thinking and an ability to use that imagination without imposing its products on the child are essential. One is guided in this creative process and search for therapeutic effectiveness by a knowledge of child behavior and development and by clinical theory. The goal is to understand as well as to alleviate suffering, because the process of understanding one child at a time, and adding that understanding to the existing body of knowledge, is one of the most important sources of effective work.

Because it illustrates anew many aspects of the tasks of preventive intervention and therapy, the discussion of the work with Amy and her mother by Hibbs, Findikoglu, and their colleagues was placed last in this selection of clinical encounters with infants and parents. In their own introduction to the chapter, the authors summarize the many issues of this case: the search for appropriate treatment approaches under the pressure of recurring crises; the professional creativity released by a setting in which staff and resources can be deployed according to best clinical judgment with few external constraints; the conflicting views and deep emotions aroused in this able, caring group of clinicians by their feelings of responsibility toward an infant whose very survival often seemed at risk; and the obligations of an infant program to an older child in urgent need of help.

Reading the saga of Amy, her mother, and the many people working so hard to help them reminds us, too, of the shared conviction of all the therapists reporting their work in this volume: that a stable therapeutic alliance based on mutual trust and respect, careful individualization of services available at the time they are needed, and support of parents' and children's active efforts to grow and change are essential elements of sound, effective work with infants and parents.

Sally Provence, M.D.

1

Early Intervention in a Pediatric Multidisciplinary Clinic

T. Berry Brazelton, M.D.
Catherine Buttenwieser, M.S.W.

In order to provide short-term intervention for parents of babies and small children, we have established a multidisciplinary outpatient clinic which meets weekly at the Boston Children's Hospital Medical Center. This clinic, the Early Childhood Program (ECP) (Buttenwieser and Keefer, 1982), provides diagnostic and treatment services to families. The Child Development fellows, who have primary responsibility for the care of patients, are pediatricians; they are helped with diagnostic formulations and treatment plans by a staff from the disciplines of child development, child psychiatry, nursing, pediatrics, psychology, and social work.

Approximately half of the families seen have decided on their own to call Children's Hospital, often after they have explored other resources without satisfaction. Many of these parents are aware of developing failure in their interaction with their small baby, but they feel trapped in their situation and helpless to change it. The rest are referred by local phy-

This work was conducted under the aegis of grants from the Robert Wood Johnson Foundation and the National Institute of Mental Health.

sicians, other departments within Children's Hospital, and social service agencies concerned about issues of custody, preadoptive evaluation, etc.

At least one third of the children referred to the ECP are considered overactive by their parents, who request "a test" for hyperactivity. The children's behavior usually includes aggressive behavior, sleep disturbance, and temper tantrums which interfere with family life and with the baby's ability to function. Other presenting problems include colic and irritability, feeding difficulties with or without poor weight gain, sometimes accompanied by a history of SGA, small for gestational age, questions of normal development, atypical affect and behavior, headbanging, rhythmic behavior, hairpulling, breathholding, and constipation. Parents are feeling desperate by the time they contact the hospital, which they regard as the last hope in their long search for solutions to their problems. We believe that offering parents an early opportunity for evaluation and an understanding of failing interaction, including the infant's contribution to this failure, can mobilize their reserves of energy and caring for reorganization to more successful patterns in the family.

Through the telephone intake and confirmation of the appointment, staff explore the purpose of the clinic visit with parents and attempt to dispel any unrealistic expectations about what will happen at the hospital. After the appointment is scheduled, a medical/social questionnaire and more information about the clinic are mailed to each prospective patient. These verbal and written explanations of the structure of the clinic visits and of the need for follow-up (an average of four to six visits are usually expected) are designed to help the parents understand that there will be no immediate answers, and that they will be involved in the formulation of diagnostic assessments and treatment plans for their children. These early communications with the parents and a review of the medical records and medical/social questionnaires help to shape the focus and the content of the first clinic visit.

The child development specialist, a trained teacher, is usually the first member of the multidisciplinary team to greet the patients and their families in the clinic. Her observations of the child's play and his interactions with family members and with other children in the waiting/play area add an important dimension to the information gathered by the pediatrician. In addition, the child development specialist will spend time alone with the child at a later point in the first visit and during follow-up visits to assess further the child's functioning and to provide the parents an opportunity to discuss issues with the pediatrician when the child is not present.

Setting up an understanding, accepting relationship with the anguished parents is the first and major goal of the initial interview. Collecting historical data and assessment of the child and his use of the parents are all secondary to this first goal. The parents come to a pediatrician with a special interest in child development with particular expectations. Since they assume she will take the physical as well as the psychological aspects of their child's presenting problems into account, her emphasis on a pediatric and neurological evaluation becomes a critical part of her evaluation. Not only is she able, in many instances, to use this evaluation to reassure the parents with regard to any possible underlying organicity, but within the structure of a pediatric examination she can gather important developmental observations. She can assess the child's cognitive and affective responses to his exam, and can see the child and his parents in a situation known to be stressful.

Because the Early Childhood Program is a pediatric clinic, many parents come to the initial visit expecting medical solutions to their child's difficulties. It is a delicate task for the pediatrician to lead the parents away from the search for unilateral organic causes toward a look at the whole child in the context of his environment. To achieve this goal, the pediatrician needs to establish a therapeutic relationship with the parents and to begin to answer the following questions:

1. Whatever the chief complaint is, what is the underlying concern on the part of the parents?

2. How do the parents interpret the child's behavior, and what motivates that interpretation?

3. How do the parents feel about coping with the problem: can they see the problem objectively, or is it seen as somehow part of the child (good or bad) or of the parents (competent or incompetent)?

4. What is the child's temperament? How does the child cope with life situations?

5. How do parents and child interact around such issues as control, nurturance, attachment, and protection?

6. Can the parents' feelings and behavior and the child's behavior be understood in a developmental framework, e.g., in terms of developmental tasks for parents and child around separation?

During the first hour of the visit, the pediatrician explores the problem, observes parent-child interaction, and examines the child developmentally once the child has become comfortable in the new surroundings. The pediatrician's toys are used to ease the child's transition into the physical exam and to assess his developmental functioning. Other members of the multidisciplinary team, including the supervisor, observe the visit through a one-way mirror. The supervisor will be available for consultation at a break after the first hour. Diagnostic and developmental play sessions conducted by the child psychiatrist, visits to the children's day care or preschool programs by the child development specialist, home visits by the nurse practitioner, and contacts with community resources by the social worker will often be used to collect additional information.

Midway through the interview, the pediatrician can consult with the supervisor and other team members. This interval is also an important time for the family to reflect about the information that has been gathered thus far.

During the first half of the session the pediatrician has been listening for clues about the parents' underlying concerns about the child as well as to the parents' expressed reasons for the clinic visit. During the review of the medical and social history and the physical/developmental exam, the pediatrician makes a tentative formulation regarding the problem: is it psychological, organic, or a combination of the two? During the break, the pediatrician exchanges impressions with the observation group and arrives at a tentative diagnosis and treatment plan, defining short- and long-term goals and deciding which issues should be addressed with the parents that day. During the latter part of the visit, the physician shares these thoughts with the family, elicits parental insights and observations in developing a plan of management, and makes a therapeutic contract with the parents.

Throughout the period of working with the family, the pediatrician consults with the team members—the mental health professionals, child development specialists, and other pediatricians—to define, and sometimes to modify, treatment goals. The physician does not attempt to provide simple answers or blanket reassurance, but, sharing observations and impressions, works within the context of a relationship with the parent to explore ways of dealing with the problem. Rarely will she give advice regarding specific behaviors. For example, observations of a colicky infant's particular style and temperament can be used to suggest ways of calming the infant, but only after the doctor has explored with the mother her perceptions of why the colic is occurring (e.g., she might ascribe the child's behavior to her own inadequacy). A mother might need to give up the fantasy of the very different baby she had hoped to have, and to mourn the loss of that idealized baby, before she can mobilize her resources to interact more effectively with the baby she actually has. Colicky babies are often hypersensitive, overactive infants. This information can be shared with a mother to relieve her guilty feelings about failure. As she recognizes the infant's overactivity and can share it with the physician, her anxiety, her anger, her helplessness, and her inevitable depression can surface and also be shared. Then, and only then, can she and the physician begin to explore the baby's "colic" and learn how to deal with it.

During follow-up (an average of four to six visits per patient), the nature of the doctor's contact with the family may change. The focus of the work might shift from the child's symptoms to the interplay between that child's behavior and other areas of family functioning. For example, parents might well demand suggestions for helping their child to sleep through the night although the child's behavior actually reflects *their* inability to separate from their child. Having initially blamed the child, parents may, with the doctor's help, begin to see the behavior as a result of the too-close tie between them. Throughout contact with the family, the pediatric fellow must be sensitive to the level at which parents are ready to work and to pace the treatment according to their understanding of the problem. Within this supportive framework, the child and other family members can modify their interactions with each other and can make use of any of the other services that might be needed.

The Early Childhood Program sees cases ranging from reasonably simple examples of normal parental anxiety, the need for reeducation, or issues which can be referred to local resources to slightly more difficult situations involving parental feelings that lead to problematic misinterpretation of the child's behavior. While parents of a temperamentally difficult child can be worked with in the clinic framework, parents of a developmentally delayed child might require services from other departments of Children's Hospital, with the Early Childhood Program providing a coordinating and supportive role. In some cases, family psychopathology is beyond the skills of a pediatric team and requires psychotherapeutic intervention.

The general principles of approach have then to be modified according to the content of the individual case, as illustrated in the following.

Case 1

Peter, age 3½ months, was first seen with his mother by a pediatrician in our Early Childhood Program clinic, because he was "unhappy—constantly crying and fussing." Mrs. Smith sought help from many sources before she found out about us—from her obstetrician, from her own pediatrician, who called the behavior "colic" and assured her Peter would outgrow it, and from her own parents, who blamed her for the baby's crying. Finally, she came to the emergency ward at our hospital. She was hysterical, weeping and even threatening that she might "hurt the baby" if she were sent home without relief. Although Mrs. Smith was distraught, the baby was assessed by the emergency room pediatrician as perfectly normal physically. Overwhelmed by the woman's anxiety, he referred her to our clinic "as an emergency."

Indeed, Mrs. Smith looked depressed and dishevelled when she first came to the Early Childhood Program clinic. Although she was middle-class in her dress and appearance and seemed to have come from an advantaged, supportive environment, she came in alone. She assured us that her family (including her husband) couldn't see any of this as a problem. She felt thoroughly alone and deserted by them. She felt she had nowhere to turn with this baby—she was afraid of either leaving him or of hurting him in the midst of one of his crying "jags." She knew it was "just" colic and it was all her fault but that didn't help. She still didn't know what to do about it and she was so depressed that she was afraid—for herself and for the baby.

While she talked, Mrs. Smith held the baby out from her as if he were a board or a wooden doll. Peter faced away from her, looking into the room. His little face looked pained and he frowned off into the distance. He held his body stiff, jumping from time to time as his mother talked and as her emotions came to the surface. He winced when the examiner tried to speak directly to him. And when he was, with some difficulty, engaged in eye-to-eye contact, he frowned as the examiner drew close. As their faces became closer, he looked off into the distance, avoiding this close approach. When the examiner made the mistake of trying to hold him, Peter immediately began to scream, in a piercing, hopeless-sounding wail. His mother sighed deeply, took him back into her wooden arms, holding him out from her body. He quieted and resumed his empty staring off into space.

It seemed as if Peter preferred to be left alone to handle his overreactivity by shutting out everything and everyone around him. His mother tossed him around but never looked down at him. When she moved him, he startled and stiffened, maintaining a boardlike posture. When Peter began to cry suddenly in the midst of being handled, his cry was a rather piercing, empty wail, as if he were crying into a vacuum. His mother startled, came to attention, and, as if suddenly conscious of her baby, said, "You see! He does this to me all the time!" Half desperate, half angry, Mrs. Smith pulled out a bottle, and without warming it up pushed it into Peter's mouth. Peter mouthed it for a few moments, then finally began to suck successfully. Meanwhile, his mother sat looking off into the distance. She had set him in her arms looking away from her. Peter, too, was staring off into the distance, sucking hard and automatically, half choking down his milk. It was easy to see that in this cold, automatic feeding situation Peter was choking down a lot of gas with each feeding. That he would spit half of it up later seemed an obvious outcome. The most disturbing aspect of this scene was the complete lack of positive interaction between this mother and child. Both of their faces were strained, tight, and distant.

As she fed him, Mrs. Smith gave the pediatrician Peter's history. He had been the product of a planned pregnancy. Both of his parents were over thirty and wanted a baby very much. Before Peter's birth, Mrs. Smith had been enjoying her work as a computer technician, but she and her husband planned carefully for her to stop work for four months to "give the baby a start." She added, "I never planned on this!" and she looked down at Peter with an angry look.

Mrs. Smith had had to quit her job during the third month of pregnancy because she had morning sickness "all

day long." She began to have misgivings in the fourth month
of pregnancy when she realized that her morning sickness
would never cease. She wondered at times what her inability
to keep food down was doing to her baby, but she kept thinking that "it served him right. Look what he was doing to her."
Mrs. Smith reported that she always thought about Peter as
a "him," long before she knew his sex. When she spoke of
her husband at all, it was as if he were as distant and as remote
as Peter.

At birth Peter weighed 8 pounds, 2 ounces, and seemed
just fine. Apgars were 8–9–9—"almost perfect." But Peter
soon began to have difficulty breathing and had to be put in
oxygen for twenty-four hours. Mrs. Smith said she knew something would be "wrong"—and when it was, this just confirmed
her expectations. Peter had mild hyperbilirubinemia, and his
mother was sure his jaundice was evidence of "something
wrong." He was discharged with her after four days, but one
of the nurses told her he was a "wild man," so she knew she
was headed for trouble.

During his first three months at home, Peter seemed to
have difficulty in virtually every area of functioning. Mrs.
Smith said he had "always been fussy since we got him." It
was always difficult to soothe the baby, though an automatic
swing and bouncing carriage rides seemed to help for a while.
Peter's fussing worsened over the first three months to the
point where he seemed to cry continually except for about
twenty minutes after a feeding.

Feeding and sleeping were difficult for Peter. He
squirmed during feedings, often arching his back. At 1 month,
Peter's formula was switched from Similac to Isomil; the
change seemed to decrease his flatus but not his fussing. Cereal seemed only to worsen the fussing. But despite his difficulties Peter was growing well. Mrs. Smith described his
sleep as restless and his naps as "light." He was not sleeping
through the night at the time of the visit to the Early Childhood Program.

Mrs. Smith was clearly upset by her difficulties in interacting with Peter. She felt he often seemed to ignore her attempts to interact with him.

OBSERVATIONS BY THE PEDIATRICIAN

Observations were made with Peter initially on his mother's lap. He was a well-nourished, healthy-appearing, blond boy of 3½ months, alert and smiling occasionally at me while he looked from a distance of about six feet. He sat quietly but was active, visually exploring the environment while I talked with his mother. His mother was very anxious, both in his care and in conversation with me. She impressed me as concerned, sensitive, intelligent, and open.

As I moved closer to Peter after the initial conversation with his mother, he looked at me intently, occasionally smiling and briefly turning away before fixing his gaze on me again as I gradually approached. My next step was to gently shake a rattle about a foot from his left ear. He immediately became alert, stiffened, and turned to the stimulus. I got a similar response on the right side. I next took a bell, got up, and walked behind him and his mother. I rang the bell a foot from his right ear and he did not turn to it. Instead he stiffened and stared in the opposite direction. This type of response, which his parents had misinterpreted as ignoring or failing to respond to a stimulus, was actually an active aversion.

Throughout the developmental assessment and physical exam, both of which showed him to be entirely normal, Peter demonstrated a hypersensitivity to stimuli, with jerky, startle-type responses to any moderate or loud auditory stimulus. He frequently used the coping strategy of turning away from or "turning off" intrusive stimuli. When he became upset it was very difficult to console him, though he eventually quieted down as his mother held him still in her lap. Walking and rocking and patting did not help at all.

My impression was that Peter clearly evinced the constellation of temperamental characteristics labeled "difficult" by Chess and Thomas (1974). He was hypersensitive to stimuli, easily upset, and difficult to console, and had a history of irregularity in sleeping and feeding schedules. The neonatal intensive care nursery had probably been a very disturbing environment for this already disorganized infant. His mother's concern during the pregnancy, which seemed to be confirmed by his neonatal difficulties, had heightened her anxiety over not being able to mesh well with this temperamentally difficult baby. Mrs. Smith had been blaming herself for what she interpreted as Peter's "unhappiness."

My discussion with the mother focused on Peter's temperament and her tendency to blame herself. A few specific suggestions were made: provide a quiet room for feedings to diminish competing and disturbing stimuli; diminish nearby noises during naps by closing his door and having his sisters play elsewhere; interact with him gently, providing gradually modulated stimuli and looking carefully for signs of overload, like turning away or tension in the extremities.

Mrs. Smith was urged to call as needed, and a follow-up appointment was made for one week later.

Second visit. I didn't get any phone calls from Mrs. Smith between the initial visit and the next visit one week later, when Peter was 4 months old. She told me the child had definitely improved, though he was still difficult. He was sleeping through the night, and she was beginning to have some success in positively interacting with him. She also told me she could often quiet him down merely by touching his back or leg.

My impression was that Peter remained hypersensitive and tense, but had clearly progressed in his ability to cope with stimuli. His face was not as anxious. He could look at you for a short space of time. His mother seemed much less anxious in her handling of him, and she seemed relieved of much of the guilt so manifest in her first visit.

Mrs. Smith's face was softer, less angry-looking. She said repeatedly something like the following: "What you showed

me about him was such a help. I couldn't tell you how guilty
I felt about him. I realized that I'd resented him from the
very first. And I'd been blaming him for all the misery that
I was feeling about our failure together." She went on to tell
me how good she felt about him when he relaxed in her arms
"in the quiet, dark room you told me about." In fact, he
seemed to be able to let her hold him just for fun. She had
gotten herself a rocking chair "like you have here in the clinic."
And she'd found that if she just rocked him quietly for a
period, she could then talk to him gently and feel by his body's
relaxation when he could take her voice. As she got closer to
Peter this way, feeling for his reactions in her arms, she found
she could even turn his body into hers, and he could take it.
However, she said, "He still won't let me look him in the
face." She expressed to me the evolution of her apparently
rejecting wooden posture with the baby. He had been so
unaccepting, so easily overloaded by her face and her voice,
that she had ended by holding him facing away from her as
a compromise. She now expressed her longing to get close to
this baby.

   Discussion. Up to this point, I felt quite confident that
things were going well. I had capsulized the case as "difficult
child with depressed but competent mother who was blaming
herself for the difficult interactions." On the face of it, my
intervention could be boiled down to telling the mother that
Peter was a difficult child, that she shouldn't blame herself,
and that things would improve with time. Yet Mrs. Smith had
been told that already by more than one person and it had
not helped. What had I done differently?

   I asked Mrs. Smith that question, and after some thought
she said that she felt I had not judged her overanxious. It also
became clear as we talked that the observations we shared
about Peter's behavior during my interactions with him, including the physical exam, in the first visit, had increased her
confidence that I was seeing her child as she did. We often
speculate about the effect of this sort of alliance, the formation

of a working relationship with the parents. One of the clear effects in this instance seemed to be that my reassurances were more helpful than those of others who had been consulted. The reassurances were not seen as attempts by me to dismiss the concern altogether. At the follow-up visit, concern about Peter's behavior was still there, but the mother seemed freer to see improvement, and less bound up with guilt and depression.

Mrs. Smith. After she had shared this with me, Mrs. Smith began to tell me that she felt intensely that she needed help with her feelings more than she needed advice about handling Peter. She clearly felt that she was failing with her child. She was unable to accept praise for the excellent developmental gains Peter had made cognitively and socially. She was finding herself getting angry both with friends who tried to downplay Peter's episodes and with those who tried to be sympathetic. Both situations seemed to point up that she was not doing well with him. She had had thoughts of running away and deep anger that had further increased her guilt and loss of self esteem. Relationships with her husband and other relatives and friends were becoming strained.

During her discussion, Mrs. Smith began to talk about her childhood, her feelings that her parents were not close to her, and her determination to reverse that with her own children. She talked about petit mal episodes she had had throughout childhood. These episodes were not recognized as seizures until as a teenager she was almost run over by a car. She had been the subject of jokes and ridicule at home and in school because of these episodes, and she was concerned not to neglect Peter's symptoms as she felt hers had been.

Mrs. Smith felt neglected and rejected as a child. She longed to be like an older sister who was so pretty and "with it." But she knew her parents hated her. And now with Peter she was feeling the same longing, the same hatred she had felt as a child. What a failure she was! As she unloaded this in a real surge of emotion, her eyes filled with tears. She said, "I know I'm unreasonable, but I don't know how to handle the feelings that come up in me when Peter cries."

It became clear to Mrs. Smith that at least some of the fussing represented a sort of distress from overstimulation, exogenous or endogenous, but she also felt that Peter was using his distress manipulatively to gain her attention. This made her feel more guilt. We talked about that openly, which was fortunate, because without any input from me, Mrs. Smith had assumed that I too had labeled her overanxious. This led us to a discussion of feelings she had had during one of Peter's episodes of prolonged crying. The frequency of these episodes was not the important factor. The monumental impact each episode had on Mrs. Smith was more to the point.

I was confused about why a mother's confidence would be so shaken by a crying episode. I expect that the benefit to Mrs. Smith came not from what *I* understood or didn't understand, though, but from what *she* came to understand about her feelings during our conversations and in the work she did to bring these feelings to the surface.

I did offer two suggestions that at the time seemed small stabs at the problem; to Mrs. Smith's credit she was eventually able to incorporate both of them into her interactions with Peter and found them of some benefit. One was based on my observation in the clinic, and on assumptions from the history taken, that Mrs. Smith was responding primarily to negative, fussy eliciting behavior from Peter. I hoped to break into this vicious circle by instituting regular play sessions, of about ten minutes each, several times a day when Peter had her undivided attention. In these sessions she was to respond only to positive eliciting behavior from him. The purpose was twofold: (1) to give Mrs. Smith confidence that she could have positive interactions with Peter; and (2) to teach Peter that behaviors other than fussing could elicit attention. The second suggestion was that Mrs. Smith step back when she felt the desperate feelings of guilt or helplessness overwhelming her, and get some control over them before interacting with Peter to comfort his distress. Intellectually, she was already aware of the aggravating effect of her tension on Peter at these times. Her ability to put these feelings in perspective was presumably helped by our conversations and the further work of understanding that she did herself.

Third visit. By the time they came in one month later, Mrs. Smith and Peter were in much better shape. Peter's bewildering crying episodes had ended. When he cried now, "it was always for a purpose." His mother said she could take my suggestions and put them to work when he did cry. She could step back from him "and from herself" to see what he was crying about. Usually, he'd gotten overloaded with too much stimulation. She could then sit down with him in a quiet room, rock him, talk quietly to him, and "teach" him how to accept her and her ways of reaching him. As she talked this way, I felt she assumed an almost childlike voice and look, as if she needed for me to approve of her. I pointed this out to her. She said, "I've wished so much for someone to tell me I'm doing a good job for Peter." I asked her whether Peter's responses helped in this way. "They certainly do let me know I'm on track with him, but I need more." I asked her how her husband responded. She said, "Now that things are better with Peter, I feel better when he reassures me. Before, it just seemed as if he were trying to talk me out of how bad I felt about our failure."

I wondered aloud whether she was looking for reassurance from someone we hadn't spoken of yet. At this, Mrs. Smith broke down in deep sobs, saying how she longed for her mother, who had stayed away from her and the baby. She felt her mother was staying away in exactly the same way she'd grown up, with rejection of her for her failures. Suddenly she sat up, holding Peter closer to her, looked down at him tenderly, and said, "But I do think you understand, and that's a big help." She seemed to be talking to the baby and to me at the same time.

Hospitalization. I did not see the Smiths again until much later. How well they'd done was apparent at Peter's hospitalization for pneumonia at age 8 months. Mrs. Smith called early in the illness, before the hospitalization. She was concerned that he was regressing after a very encouraging period of "marvelous" behavior before the illness. I expected the illness to be difficult for him and we discussed his likely regression. Shortly thereafter he was hospitalized. His first night in the hospital was difficult; he cried almost constantly in his mist tent. Mrs. Smith was apparently frustrated and exhausted and went home to rest on subsequent days. Peter settled down the second day of hospitalization and surprised his mother by acting "like an angel" upon his return home after three days in the hospital.

I saw the family one week after discharge. Peter had been sleeping through the night and was amusing himself for longer periods of time; according to Mrs. Smith, he seemed much easier to interact with. She seemed calm and more self-confident in this visit than in previous ones, but was still uneasy with his improved behavior because she didn't know why it had happened.

Summary. To summarize briefly, Peter is a temperamentally difficult infant whom we have seen three times between 3½ and 8 months of age. During this period he has shown marked improvement in his ability to cope with stimuli and to interact with his mother. His mother's self-blame and feelings of helplessness could not be dismissed by reassurances, however. Harder work to understand these feelings was required on her part and ours before she could begin to have confidence in her interactions with him and to see his improvement. The importance of reflection by the physician between visits about aspects of the case that don't quite fit the formulation, or about communications with the parents that don't seem to be mutually understood, is well illustrated by this case. There seems to be a synergistic relationship between Peter's maturational improvements and his development of better coping strategies and Mrs. Smith's improving self-image as a mother. Obviously, only follow-up will tell us if this hypothesis is correct.

I might add as a final note that the amount of time I spent with this family was not excessive. The first visit took two hours, half of which was history-gathering which would have been unnecessary had I been the family's primary physician. The subsequent two visits each took one hour or less, and phone conversations have together amounted to less than one hour.

This case is an example of a somewhat superficial but critical pediatric involvement in the developing mother-infant relationship. Mrs. Smith had had negative feelings about her developing fetus during pregnancy, and separation from her infant during the perinatal period confirmed her sense of herself as a failure who had damaged her baby. These experiences led the new mother to overreact to Peter's crying and "negative" behavior. Fortunately, Mrs. Smith's mounting desperation led her to seek help early; she also had the ability to look below the surface for the reasons for her reactions to Peter's symptoms. Early intervention gave the family the chance to reorganize itself early, before failures in the relationship could cause lasting damage.

The child's own hypersensitivity to external stimuli was a critical issue in the failure of the mother-child relationship. As we shared it, Mrs. Smith could begin to see Peter as a reactive individual, separate from herself. As long as she saw the hypersensitivity and the crying as symptoms of *her* failure, she was unable to see her child as a person. Her symbiotic overreaction tended to build on itself, increasing her anxious handling of the baby and her reinforcing responses to his "negativistic" or guarded behavior. Peter, in turn, became more likely to respond to such "overloading" by not looking, by shutting his mother out, by crying. As soon as Mrs. Smith could recognize these signals, and could begin to look for more positive patterns in her son which accompanied her efforts to reduce her stimulation, Peter could become responsive to her. She then found that Peter could build upon positive experiences if she used one sensory modality at a time for interaction. She could talk, or look, or rock Peter—but not all at once. As his nervous system matured, as he learned to adapt to and use his mother's stimulation, the need for crying decreased. Success between mother and son nurtured them both. Each learned from the other, and indeed Mrs. Smith began to feel that Peter was a source of the nurturing and of the sense of herself as a successful person that she had always longed for.

Peter's illness and his mother's mature handling of it seemed to confirm the growing success of their interaction. Although the father's role is not clearly understood or brought out in this case, his involvement with his wife and son will be critical along the way, particularly at times of crisis.

Case 2

Carol was a 3-year-old girl who was first seen in a medical diagnostic evaluation at Children's Hospital for constipation of nine months' duration. She was found to have no physical problems and responded reasonably well to a regimen of laxatives. However, because her parents continued to be perplexed by her resistance to bowel training (bladder training had been achieved for several months), she was referred to the early childhood program for further evaluation.

One month after the initial evaluation, Carol and her mother, Mrs. Ford, were seen in the ECP clinic by Dr. M., a Child Development Fellow. By this time, Mrs. Ford's relief that Carol's constipation had been ameliorated through laxative had been replaced by anger at her daughter's daily bowel movements in her underwear.

Mrs. Ford spoke with a rush of feeling about her efforts to toilet train Carol over the past year. Carol had clearly understood the purpose of the toilet and had immediately been cooperative about urinating there. However, she "hung on" to her bowel movements after her mother had placed her on the pot and until she was allowed to get off. Then she had them in her underpants. More recently, she stopped having them altogether and withheld her bowel movements for days at a time. Mrs. Ford felt it was time for Carol to be more "grown up"; she was the oldest of three children, and Mrs. Ford was tired of diapering all of her offspring. Carol did not appear to be jealous of her brother (age 2) and her sister (age 9 months), but her mother had expected her to be more helpful with the care of her siblings than she was.

Mrs. Ford looked intently at Dr. M. while she related these concerns, rushing along without stopping between sentences. Meanwhile, Carol was sitting quietly at the play table, continuously fingering some of the toys that Dr. M. had placed there. She had brought no toys of her own with her. While Mrs. Ford continued to talk, Dr. M. began to play with Carol. With Dr. M.'s encouragement, Carol became involved with the toys and demonstrated her fine motor, verbal, and intellectual skills through her stacking of cubes, identifying their colors, and stacking them expertly to fit each other. Quickly she completed all of the puzzles available, and she identified the objects in the picture book. However, Carol did not respond to Dr. M.'s initiative around fantasy play with the dollhouse figures and went back to fingering the blocks solemnly when Dr. M. stopped playing with her. Mrs. Ford took obvious pleasure in Carol's achievements with the toys, but criticized her when the first cube tower collapsed, telling her to pick up the cubes immediately.

By this time Dr. M. had observed enough of the interaction between Carol and her mother to realize that this bright little girl was extremely sensitive to her mother's feelings about her. Dr. M. also wanted to give Mrs. Ford an opportunity to ventilate some of the negative emotion that had clearly been gathering momentum over the period of time her daughter had been playing. Carol readily accepted Dr. M.'s suggestion that she play in the waiting room with the

child development specialist, who had met her earlier and
who was observing now through the one-way mirror. Carol
went happily to play in the other room, as if relieved to be
out of the tense situation.

After Carol had left the examining room, Dr. M. said
that she would like to ask Mrs. Ford questions about herself
and other members of the family, what her pegnancy with
Carol had been like, etc. Mrs. Ford, age 28, related that she
had become pregnant soon after her marriage to her husband,
now 30 years old. She had been pleased about the pregnancy,
as she had no particular career aspirations and was eager to
have a family. She had felt fine during the pregnancy and
continued to work as a secretary until the time of delivery.
Carol was a full-term baby, weighing 6 pounds, 14 ounces,
and had been delivered vaginally. Mrs. Ford talked with
pleasure about Carol's first few months of life. She had been
a quiet baby who took her bottle at regular intervals and was
sleeping through the night by the age of 6 weeks. She and
Carol had had a lovely time, and Mrs. Ford's longing for this
period was reflected in her softened voice as she told about
it.

When Carol was 6 months old, Mrs. Ford discovered
that her increasing fatigue was not related to postpartum recovery, but to the fact that she was again pregnant. Mrs.
Ford's facial expression changed as she described this second
pregnancy. She and her husband had wanted three children,
and he did not share her dismay at having them so close
together. He worked long hours as a computer technician and
did not appreciate what it was like to care for three young
children. Mrs. Ford was so tired throughout her second pregnancy that she remembers little regarding Carol's developmental milestones. However, she sadly recalled that she
missed Carol's taking her first steps at the age of 13 months.
At that time, Carol was staying with her maternal grandmother
while her mother was in the hospital giving birth to her
younger brother.

As she said this, Mrs. Ford's voice hardened. While the labor and the delivery of her second child were also normal, Mrs. Ford described his first six months of life as "a nightmare." Charlie, the new baby, seemed to cry almost constantly and required several formula changes before one was found that agreed with him. Eventually, however, he did thrive and is now almost the same size as Carol. He is the most active of the three children and requires constant supervision. Charles's first year of life was so chaotic that it was not surprising to Mrs. Ford that she was "careless" about birth control and became pregnant once again. After the delivery of her third child she had a tubal ligation to make sure this pattern would not be repeated.

Mrs. Ford thought she should feel grateful that she had three healthy youngsters when so many people who wanted children couldn't have them. But she really couldn't—she felt too overwhelmed. She felt caught up in the whirlwind of her children's physical care and couldn't really enjoy them. It had been far too long since her household had been run with the order and routine that were once so important to her. She rarely had supper prepared when her husband came home from work in the evening and had no time or energy for adult communication; when Dr. M. asked what Mr. Ford thought about Carol, Mrs. Ford said that he was even more upset than she was about Carol's constipation and soiling. Each evening he asked for a report about her soiling episodes and was often too angry to spend time with her (as he once did) before she went to bed. When Dr. M. suggested that he come to a clinic visit in the future, Mrs. Ford thought that he would be too busy to take time off from work. Dr. M. sensed that she was protective of him and that the suggestion had not been well timed.

Dr. M. observed that Mrs. Ford appeared well groomed but tired and asked her if she ever had time to herself or relief from child care. She said that her mother, who lives in a nearby community, sometimes took Carol, but was not strong enough to keep pace with the younger two. She used to get together with friends, but conversation with other adults was almost impossible when she was with all three or even two of her children. She could sometimes persuade Mr. Ford to go out in the evening, but he preferred to be home after a long working day. Carol used to be reluctant to separate from her mother, but was just beginning to play with children in the neighborhood.

As she spoke, Mrs. Ford suddenly realized that she almost never had time alone with Carol, who had once been the "easiest" of her three children. Dr. M. recognized the sadness that underlay Mrs. Ford's anger at Carol and helped her to identify her yearning to go back and relive Carol's first year of life, which had held such promise. Mrs. Ford's face softened and her longing came through. She said, "Yes, I know it's my fault that Carol is having problems but that doesn't help me; I just get angrier when I realize it. I need help with handling my anger." Mrs. Ford looked rather child-like as she said this, and Dr. M. agreed. She assured her she could help and would.

Dr. M. said that it was time for a short break so that she could discuss the evaluation with the observing team members and so that Mrs. Ford would have a chance to think about their discussion thus far. Dr. M. reviewed the purpose of the visit with Mrs. Ford and made certain she had no concerns about Carol's health and understood that her soiling and constipation were related to "stubbornness."

During the break, the child development specialist reported that Carol's play in the waiting area had been as constricted as it was in the examining room. With a good deal of encouragement she had approached the slide but had preferred to be at the blackboard, copying the figures and letters that were made by the child development specialist rather than drawing freely. The other team members—a child psychiatrist, a nurse practitioner, and a social worker—agreed that this theme of "withholding" was evident in much of

Carol's behavior, possibly in response to her mother's expectations that Carol "grow up" and her inability to see the child's
need for autonomy regarding when and where she moved her
bowels.

The group also wondered about Carol's fantasies with
regard to babies and stools and thought it would be helpful
to know what she had been told about the birth of her siblings.
That her constipation coincided with her sister's birth suggested that Carol might be confused about these issues. Staff
members disagreed about Mrs. Ford's readiness to hear about
Carol's fantasies regarding the origins of babies and bowel
movements and to recognize that she was in a power struggle
with Carol around independence (wanting her to be more
"grown up") and dependence (not allowing her to be in charge
of her own toileting). These issues could be postponed for
future interviews. Everyone concluded that Dr. M. should
continue to empathize with Mrs. Ford in the demanding task
she has in caring for three small children with little support
from others. It was felt that she needed to mourn the loss of
the all-too-brief period alone with Carol that ended when she
became preoccupied with subsequent pregnancies and infants. The group decided that if Mrs. Ford had an opportunity
to talk about these issues first, she might be able to perceive
her developmentally inappropriate expectations of Carol and
to interact with her in a more positive way. They also felt that
Mrs. Ford needed to ventilate her anger and her feelings of
being so isolated and lonely in her child-rearing tasks.

When Dr. M. rejoined Carol and her mother in the examination room, she asked Mrs. Ford if she'd thought of any
other concerns or questions during the break. Mrs. Ford said
that she hadn't and that she had just enjoyed having a snack
with Carol in the cafeteria. She observed that her only time
alone with Carol was during these recent visits to the hospital.
She willingly held Carol in her lap while Dr. M. performed
the physical exam. Carol stiffened as Dr. M. approached her,
but visibly relaxed after Dr. M. told her what she was going

to do and that there was to be no rectal exam. She seemed to understand this statement. Carol enjoyed playing with the stethoscope and otoscope and was cooperative when they were used to examine her. Mrs. Ford smiled as Dr. M. made positive comments about Carol's cooperation, health, and developmental accomplishments. Carol then returned willingly to the waiting area to play with the child development specialist while Dr. M. formulated her impressions and recommendations.

Mrs. Ford nodded vigorously when Dr. M. talked about her lack of support in caring for three small children and said that she must have felt robbed of the experience of enjoying each of them individually as babies. Mrs. Ford looked a little skeptical when Dr. M. suggested that Carol might also wish to go back to infancy and recapture that time alone with her mother. Dr. M. asked what Carol had been told about the births of her siblings, especially her 9-month-old sister. Mrs. Ford said that she had not told her anything, thinking that she was too young to understand what was happening. Mrs. Ford expressed surprise when Dr. M. suggested that Carol was at an age where she was very curious about where babies come from and might have some confusions about their origin and that of stools. Mrs. Ford agreed to give these ideas some thought before the next appointment. She seemed happier already and was eager to return.

Although Mrs. Ford asked what she was to do about her daughter's constipation, she seemed ready to accept Dr. M.'s statement that they needed to do more talking to understand what was behind it. Mrs. Ford seemed relieved to be "heard" and understood, and as she left, she thanked Dr. M. for her understanding of her and Carol. As they walked away together, Mrs. Ford held Carol's hand; they talked together all the way to the elevator.

Within two weeks after this first visit to the clinic, Mrs. Ford telephoned Dr. M. to report that her neighbor had overheard Carol telling her 2-year-old companion that babies

and "stinkers" come out of the "bum" and that she didn't want
to "drop her baby." Mrs. Ford said she had initially thought
that Dr. M.'s suggestion regarding Carol's confusion about
babies and stools was "farfetched," but she now realized that
Carol clearly had some of her own ideas about this matter.
Mrs. Ford was eager to know what books about the human
body and reproduction would be appropriate for Carol. Dr.
M. suggested one for Mrs. Ford to read and a simple one that
she could read to Carol.

Mrs. Ford came alone to the next visit, several days later,
and described the books she had been reading to Carol, who
was asking many questions about her body and why it was
different from her brother's. Mrs. Ford was somewhat hesitant
about how "thoroughly" she should answer Carol's questions,
and Dr. M. encouraged her to express her discomfort about
approaching this subject, which had never been discussed
openly in her household when she was a child. Carol was
responding well to her mother's openness and had been free
of constipation for several weeks. However, to her mother's
dismay, she continued to soil herself daily. Mrs. Ford was
receptive to Dr. M.'s observation that Carol seemed upset
about doing this to her mother. Mrs. Ford readily acknowledged this and said, "Yes. I think Carol and I have become
so close again that it is really painful for her to do this to me."
As she talked about Carol now, Dr. M. felt that Mrs. Ford
was describing a warmer and more understanding relationship.

Mrs. Ford said, "Carol's so upset now when she needs
to have a bowel movement that she almost has a temper
tantrum. She holds her legs together and jumps up and down,
screaming and getting red in the face. She seems to want to
have the bowel movement but she won't go to the toilet for
me, and she hates to do it to me by having the bowel movement in her pants. She's caught. I can't help her."

As Mrs. Ford and Dr. M. talked about how upset Carol
was about "doing it" to her mother, Mrs. Ford began to weep.

"She needs me as much as I need her. Now we are getting close again, and we both love it. It almost seems as if she knows her bowel movements are still between us, but she doesn't know what to do about it. I feel helpless to help her."

At this point, Dr. M. suggested that a diagnostic play session with the child psychiatrist on the team could help clarify the meaning of Carol's withholding and soiling. Mrs. Ford seemed receptive to the suggestion. As before, Dr. M. invited Mr. Ford to accompany his wife and daughter to the next visit. Mrs. Ford said that she would stress the importance of his presence.

At the next clinic visit, Dr. M. and Dr. H., the child psychiatrist, met with Carol and her parents together. Carol then had a play session alone with Dr. H., while Dr. M. talked with both of her parents and confirmed that Mr. Ford shared his wife's concern and anger regarding Carol's behavior. Dr. H. then told Mr. and Mrs. Ford that through her play and conversation with him Carol expressed her confusion about babies and their origins and her conflicts about "growing up." Her play appeared less constricted than it had at the first session, and Mr. and Mrs. Ford were encouraged to continue helping her explore the subject of reproduction and her own body.

The Fords explored with Dr. M. their feelings about talking so openly with Carol. Mrs. Ford said, "No one ever talked that way to me and I had a terrible time understanding about babies and my own body." Mr. Ford said, "Maybe that's why we got caught with three so soon." Mrs. Ford expressed her anger at him for having gotten her pregnant. He accepted this and said to Dr. M., "I've felt so guilty and upset that I've really pulled out on Carol and her mother. If I come home to all of their turmoil, I just want to run away. So I walk in the door, pick up my boy or the baby and get out as fast as I can. Maybe I'm the reason for all this upset." He put a hand on Mrs. Ford's arm. She took his hand, looked up at him with a softening face and said, "Carol and I need you."

After this interchange, the Fords began to question Dr. M. as to what to say and do to help Carol. They seemed to have entered a new level of readiness to work with each other. Dr. M. talked to them about Carol's questions about herself and the babies and about the questions she must have about her failure in the toileting area. But she also stressed the fact that both parents seemed to be longing for Carol and she for them. She suggested to each of them that they set apart a special time each week just for Carol. Each of them could refer to it all week and, then, when "their" time with her came, Carol and her father or Carol and her mother could heighten the occasion by getting away from all the rest of the family. In this way, they might re-create the closeness they all longed for, and could see whether Carol would ask questions about herself, and whether she could accept the interpretations they'd talked about. In closing, Dr. M. said, "And couldn't you two get a sitter once in a while so you could go off by yourselves and be together, too?" The Fords both smiled at this suggestion, as if they had not dared to bring it up themselves. A real feeling of relief was in the air as Carol and her parents left the clinic.

At the next visit, Mrs. Ford seemed jaunty. She brought her baby in with Carol, as if to show how "motherly" Carol had become. Although he did not come at first, Mr. Ford appeared fifteen minutes after the interview began, "to help his wife with all the babies." Mrs. Ford handed him the baby proudly and said, "He's a new man. He helps all the time, and seems to love it. And Carol is just grown up. She not only loves to help me with the baby, but she has completely solved her problems with her bowel movements. She goes to the pot herself, flushes it after her. I never have to help her."

Dr. M. accepted all this with real pleasure but wondered whether Carol was just trying very hard to please her parents, and whether she was indeed ready for all this responsibility. Mrs. Ford assured her that Carol was "getting in her innings." She still had bouts of stubbornness and of negativism but Mrs.

Ford didn't get so upset about them. Both parents could see that Carol was "just a child," one who had ideas and needs of her own. Indeed, as they talked about her, Dr. M. did have the feeling that her parents had come to understand Carol, and to accept her as she was. They credited their times alone with her as times for "learning about each other" as well as for times of closeness.

The crisis around her constipation and soiling had indeed passed, and Carol had regained a closeness and understanding from her parents which allowed her to start to grow up again. Her obvious self-confidence and her pleasure in her achievements as her parents commended her seemed to cap the result of this short-term intervention. Dr. M. terminated the Fords' visits with a request to call her if problems with Carol or with the rest of the family did arise.

In summary, Dr. M. and her colleagues decided that Mr. and Mrs. Ford were well-meaning, anxious parents who had high expectations of themselves and their children. It appeared that they had experienced a very positive first year with Carol, but they had become so overwhelmed by caring for three small children that they had pressed her to become more independent than was appropriate to her developmental needs. The first level of intervention was to develop a supportive relationship with the parents (in this case, primarily with Mrs. Ford), identifying and empathizing with their feelings of anger about Carol's behavior and their grief about the loss of the relationship that they once had with her as their only child. Other methods of intervention included clarification of the reasons for Carol's withholding and soiling, and education about the developmental tasks she was facing: her conflicts about autonomy were heightened by the births of two younger siblings by the time she was 2 years old; her confusion about babies and stools had not been understood by her parents.

As our culture does little to prepare families for child-rearing, a pediatrician can play a very important role in helping parents establish age-appropriate expectations of their children. Ultimately, Carol's symptomatology required a brief psychotherapeutic intervention, to be continued by the parents' work with Carol at home. By uncovering and exposing their need for each other, and by making concrete suggestions as to how to find time for each other in a busy schedule, Dr. M. had supported each parent's strengths and ability to work this out independently. The exposure and use of Carol's unconscious material could become a goal for their own work with her, after they had provided her with their closeness. In the context of the renewed relationships, Carol's symptoms could be given up. This brief and rather superficial intervention affected the entire family—the parents' relationship as much as Carol's adjustment.

References

Buttenwieser, C., & Keefer, C. (1982), *Behavior problems of infants and young children: Management and follow-up study of care in a pediatric clinic.* Paper presented at 10th International Congress of the Association of Child and Adolescent Psychiatry, Dublin, July.

Brazelton, T.B. (1981), The use of neonatal assessment as an intervention. *Zero to Three: Bulletin of the National Center for Clinical Infant Programs,* October.

———— (1982), Early intervention: What does it mean? In: *Theory and Research in Behavioral Pediatrics,* Vol. I, ed. H.E. Fitzgerald, B.M. Lester, & M.W. Yogman. New York: Plenum Press.

Chess, S., & Thomas, A. (1974), Temperament in the normal infant. In: *Individual Differences in Children,* ed. J. Westman. New York: Wiley.

2
Infant-Parent Psychotherapy: A Family in Crisis

Jeree H. Pawl, Ph.D.
Judith H. Pekarsky, Ph.D.

The following case illustrates the complex application of a set of intervention techniques developed by Selma Fraiberg and her staff (Fraiberg, 1980) to deal with the myriad factors which interfere with the development of the relationship between parents and infants.

Using detailed descriptions of selected therapeutic interviews, this presentation attempts to illustrate the several kinds of intervention necessary to free parents' positive feelings and essentially sound judgment from current destructive interaction, negative influences stemming from their pasts, and the effects of a difficult birth on both parents and child. In this case a traumatic delivery and the parents' own problems around separation, mutuality, and trust had resulted in a dangerously strained marriage and alternating anger and helplessness in parent-child relations.

We are convinced that timely intervention prevented a divorce that seemed imminent, interrupted destructive and ambivalently overindulgent aspects of a mother-son relationship, and helped a withdrawn and angry father modify a harsh and punishing stance toward his child.

The therapist gave this family support, provided developmental information and advice, and interpreted both parental conflicts and the child's behavior in a flexible schedule of meetings with the whole family, with the marital couple, or with one parent alone. The therapist chose to intervene as little as possible and to respond only to those aspects of parental difficulty which were most clearly affecting the relationship with their son. Many difficulties which might have been explored in individual treatment were neither probed nor engaged; the choice to pursue further understanding through individual treatment was left to the parents.

This case demonstrates the effectiveness of early intervention in halting the spreading effects of well-established destructive patterns of interaction and in undoing these patterns so that positive relationships can take root and begin to flourish. This process is a complex one, and our report will particularly note the blend of intervention techniques used in the work.

Intake and Assessment

The mother of the family made the initial contact with our service. Mrs. Woodruff called to request a consultation about her 16-month-old baby, who, she reported, had an attachment to his bottle that was "unreal." Barry would eat no solid foods unless his parents thoroughly distracted him, and even that tactic failed most of the time. At 16 months, Barry was taking a bottle almost every two hours. Mrs. Woodruff was infuriated with her son.

Following this initial call, we agreed to do an assessment for the family in order to understand with them what the sources of the difficulty might be. The assessment would consist of six meetings with the parents and their baby over a period of four to five weeks. A formal developmental assessment of the baby would be included if it seemed appropriate. At the end of the assessment period we would attempt to understand both what was happening within the family and what possibilities existed for dealing with problems revealed by the assessment. The Woodruffs chose to have home visits during this period but were willing to come to the office if the developmental assessment were to be done.

During the course of this assessment we learned that the Woodruffs had been married five years. Barry, now 16 months old, was a sturdy, handsome brown-haired boy. His dark eyes had a lively, intelligent expression, though he was rather quiet and seemed muted in affect. He played well with his toys, becoming absorbed in small details, but he rarely left his mother's very immediate presence. Barry seemed to take for granted his mother's quick and unhesitating response to his every expression.

Mr. Woodruff, age 32, was a tall blond man, thin and very wiry. He appeared strong and comfortable with his body. Although Mr. Woodruff had a master's degree in history, he had not succeeded in finding any work that sustained his interest or satisfied him. He was intelligent, very articulate, and extremely witty, though often bitterly so. Although he was depressed, Mr. Woodruff could at times exhibit great warmth and concern.

Mrs. Woodruff, age 30, was small, dark, and very pretty. She had a bachelor's degree in English and, like her husband, had done some teaching. She was unusually agreeable and pleasant, but laughed too readily and seemed quite anxious. Mrs. Woodruff impressed us as very intelligent, warm, and reflective. She was strikingly responsive to her son.

The Woodruffs had recently returned to the city after a year and a half in rural South Dakota. During that time, Mr. Woodruff had had a temporary teaching job in a small high school, and the couple had attempted to supplement their income by raising rabbits. Barry had been born in South Dakota.

Contrary to any expectation, Barry's birth had been very difficult. During a traumatic delivery witnessed by his father, Barry had sustained skull fractures. The baby needed two

surgical operations and was immediately sent to a distant hospital, where he remained for a period of more than three
weeks. Within two weeks, successful operations on the sides
of his skull were performed. The distance to the hospital made
only the most infrequent visiting possible for Mr. and Mrs.
Woodruff. The therapist was able to elicit a great deal of
painful and difficult material regarding Barry's birth and the
legacy of fear it had left the parents.

At nine months, Barry was again hospitalized, this time
for four days with a respiratory illness. During this period he
refused solid food and resisted bottle feedings by the nurses.
Once home, he refused solid food, according to his mother,
and began demanding more and more bottles. This pattern
persisted for seven months up to the present.

It was clear that Mr. Woodruff was seriously depressed
and had been so before the delivery. Extreme anger alternated
with depression. The experience in South Dakota had been
an utter disaster for him, and for months afterwards he had
not worked at anything. Mrs. Woodruff, driven to attend to
Barry constantly, was at her wits' end. The small house in
which the family lived and which they were purchasing was
markedly and unmistakably unloved and unlovely. The Woodruffs were seriously discussing separation and divorce.

During the initial assessment period, the family's problems appeared to involve much more than a feeding difficulty.
The therapist was sensitive to Mr. Woodruff's rage, barely
disguised and occasionally witnessed. On one occasion, Mr.
Woodruff clamped a large, heavy wrench to the bottom of
Barry's shirt and announced to him, "This will drive you
crazy." In a videotaped free play session which was included
in the assessment procedure, Mr. Woodruff initiated a lengthy
sequence of aggressive play between himself and Barry in
which he knocked the baby down with a pillow over and over
again. Although Mr. Woodruff's aggression was well-con-
trolled, and although Barry was able to respond to this as a
"game," the therapist felt real concern. In part, Mr. Wood-

ruff's aggressivity was seen as a wish to end the waiting for the ultimate, horrifying loss to occur. Conversely, it seemed to represent a need to see Barry as strong and reassuringly sturdy. It also seemed likely that the intensity and constant interaction between Mrs. Woodruff and Barry had led Mr. Woodruff to experience both a tremendous loss of his wife's attention and an enormous resentment toward Barry.

The therapist also felt that Mrs. Woodruff's personal anguish and difficulty in separating from Barry underlay the baby's difficulties; these did not as yet seem to be internalized problems of Barry's own. The last assessment session was revealing.

The Woodruffs reported experiencing a sense that things had improved and that they had gained a new perspective. Mrs. Woodruff had begun spending small amounts of time away from Barry, and the couple said they hoped to solve their acknowledged problems around separation by having the mother spend more and more time away from Barry.

In the last session of the assessment period, the Woodruffs told the therapist that they had been so impressed the previous week by Barry's having elected to leave the room briefly with the therapist that Mrs. Woodruff had gone away for the weekend, leaving the house while Barry and his father were on an excursion to the zoo. Mrs. Woodruff had been surprised that Barry was not happy to see her when she returned. This lack of response had bothered her a bit, she reported, but she was beginning to feel like herself again now that she had been able to spend some time away from Barry. A few days following this meeting, Mrs. Woodruff called to say that Barry was having terrible nightmares, waking up and crying for long periods. The therapist attempted on the phone to suggest possible links between Barry's nightmares, Mrs. Woodruff's recent sudden absences, and her technique of "disappearing" rather than saying goodbye to Barry. Mrs. Woodruff maintained, however, that she had no choice about how to manage separations because Barry cried and protested so vehemently when she attempted to leave him after a direct goodbye.

In the midst of these parental conflicts, Barry was functioning within the average range as assessed by the Bayley Scales. Nevertheless, he demonstrated quite muted affect, a consistently restricted range of affect, and a marked language lag. Although he had a word for his father, he had none for his mother at all. No physical sequelae of the birth trauma were apparent, an impression confirmed by Barry's medical records.

By the close of the assessment period, both the therapist and the Woodruffs felt sufficient concern about the latter's relationship with Barry to proceed with an open-ended treatment.

The next five months of work saw changes in the family environment, in Barry's relationship with each of his parents, between Mr. and Mrs. Woodruff, and within each parent. These changes appear to have occurred as a result of the parents' desperation and their readiness to work extraordinarily hard in a form of intervention combining education, advising, interpretation, and consistent responsive concern and support.

The structure of the sessions, which were all home based, responded flexibly to the dynamic needs of the family. The Woodruffs were always seen at least once a week. In addition, during one five-week period Mrs. Woodruff was seen in weekly individual sessions. Initially all regular meetings included Barry and the parents, but after the first three weeks Barry was present only once every three weeks. In the last three months of this reported period, Mrs. Woodruff and the therapist began the home visits, while Mr. Woodruff delivered Barry to a friend's apartment and joined the group after twenty or twenty-five minutes. Sessions typically lasted between an hour and a half and two hours and were terminated by mutual agreement within that time frame, according to the natural rhythm of the session. The five-month period described in this report was followed by an additional four months of treatment, during which gains were consolidated and further progress made.

The Beginning of Treatment

During the first home visit after their decision to pursue treatment, the Woodruffs supplied both details of their attempts to separate from Barry and descriptions of Barry's feeding problem. They also continued to discuss their experiences in South Dakota, with Mr. Woodruff offering many of the details. Barry's birth was also discussed.

During this session, the Woodruffs and the therapist together devised a structure for future meetings. It was felt that although the focus of the work was on the parents' relationship with Barry, there were aspects of the Woodruffs' own relationship and elements from their own histories relevant to the relationship with their son which were inappropriate to discuss in front of Barry. Both parents experienced Barry's presence as an inhibition and a distraction. As Mrs. Woodruff said, "Barry is at an age now—just recently—when I can't even feel free to talk about the things surrounding his birth in front of him that I would like to. It doesn't seem right." She also added, with Mr. Woodruff's agreement, "There are times when I want to be free of having to respond to him and I know I will resent it—I already have—those times when I am very much involved in my own feelings and then he needs something." It was clear to the therapist that for Mrs. Woodruff to stake a claim to her own rights already represented progress, and there was general agreement that discussion of some topics could be inappropriately disturbing for Barry. On the other hand, everyone agreed that the richness and affective immediacy that the child's presence provided added something vital to the process. It was also true that everyone wanted to observe together. For these reasons an arrangement was agreed to in which two out of three meetings would occur *without* Barry. The Woodruffs and the therapist agreed to conduct the second meeting without Barry, and the details of how that separation might be accomplished were worked out.

At the next home visit, during which Barry stayed at a friend's apartment, the subject of Barry's nighttime waking came immediately into focus. Waking and crying had occurred even though, at the therapist's suggestion, the Woodruffs had been very careful with their goodbyes and explanations. Some new difficulties had also appeared. Barry had become attached to a particular blanket during his hospitalization at nine months, and he now had begun to throw it out of his bed and then howl until it was returned.

The therapist learned that Barry had first awakened the very night that his mother had "disappeared" for her weekend alone, that Mr. Woodruff had not mentioned her absence to Barry then, even though he had taken Barry into the parental bed, and that Barry had awakened every night since. Mr. Woodruff considered this nighttime activity a simple manipulative ploy on Barry's part to get someone into his room, and the behavior enraged him. Mrs. Woodruff was not so sure. She recognized that she and her husband had—unintentionally, to be sure—been extremely inconsistent about taking Barry into their bed.

Mr. Woodruff delivered one of the first of a series of lengthy intellectual discourses: in this case he theorized that wrestling with a new developmental stage was causing Barry's upset, manifested in a sleep disturbance. Mr. Woodruff had in mind the fact that Barry was learning many new words.

The therapist was able to determine that it was Mr. Woodruff, rather than his wife, who went to Barry at night. In the course of further discussion Mrs. Woodruff mentioned that Barry was also recently spending rather a great deal of time in his crib during the day, when she was upstairs with him. He would want to get into his crib to play and would have a marvelous time. She didn't understand that at all, as Barry hated his crib so much at night.

The therapist first asked why it was that only Mr. Woodruff went into Barry. Mrs. Woodruff said that she had difficulty extricating herself from the situation and always was tempted to bring Barry into their bed. Her husband, she said, could be firmer. The therapist asked if Barry's crying bothered Mrs. Woodruff, and she said yes, it bothered her but "not so much then." The therapist asked if that meant that Barry's crying bothered her less at night than during the day when, for example, she had said that she had to avoid his crying at separation by disappearing. Mrs. Woodruff said it felt very different but she didn't know why; she attempted to turn the question back to the therapist. Mr. Woodruff commented he thought it was a very good question. Mrs. Woodruff laughed and said that was precisely why she was trying to get the therapist to answer it. The therapist waited and then said, "Well, in his crib when he's crying you can tolerate it more, but when you are leaving him and he . . ." The sentence got only that far before Mrs. Woodruff began to cry.

After a time, Mrs. Woodruff talked about her fear in the situation of leave-taking that something would happen to Barry. Although his crying always bothered her, his crying when she was leaving him made her feel that there was something terrible about her leaving and that she was somehow going to allow something dreadful to happen to her son. She described vividly how she felt when she returned after an absence. There was always the sense that she would come back to a disaster. "If I let him see me leave and he cries—then I can't leave. I feel too guilty. Even when I sneak away—it's terrible when I get close to home again."

Crying hard, Mrs. Woodruff began to talk about her fantasies about ambulances and frightening emergencies and terrible things happening. This led her back to the subject of Barry's birth and the overwhelming fear she had that he would die. She reflected that she knew now that Barry was really all right at night and could bear his crying even though she would have great trouble leaving him if she, rather than Mr.

Woodruff, went to him. It was clear, however, that when
Barry was really apart from her, Mrs. Woodruff was truly
frightened that something would happen to him. She was able
to talk about the fact that the first time Barry was, quite
literally, separated from her—at his birth—something terrible
had happened to him. In addition, he had been taken far away
from her where she could neither care for him nor even know
how he was being cared for or how he was doing. Mrs. Woodruff then recalled that each time she had visited the newborn
Barry in the hospital she was afraid that she would learn that
something terrible had happened. With great difficulty Mrs.
Woodruff was finally able to say that her fear had been that
she would arrive at the hospital and that Barry would be dead.
Mr. Woodruff was surprised and concerned upon learning the
depth of his wife's fears and was very comforting. He said he
had not realized it had been quite that way for her. He said
he knew that the birth had been terrible for him, terrible for
both of them, but he had simply never realized the kind of
fears that had remained with his wife. He wondered aloud if
he were so free of these fears himself.

Gradually the discussion moved back to an exploration
of the meaning of Barry's behavior. The therapist recalled to
the Woodruffs the playful control of his blanket that they had
observed in Barry the week before. Everyone remembered
how he had spent a large part of the session throwing his
blanket, hiding it, and retrieving it, and what enormous pleasure he had taken in this game. Both Mr. and Mrs. Woodruff
recalled that the therapist had commented at the time to Barry
that he probably would think it very nice if he could do that
same thing to his mommy and daddy—hide them, find them,
take them out, send them away, and bring them back when
he wanted them. They remembered how much Barry had
giggled and laughed at this idea. At the time there had followed a general discussion of Barry's wish to have that same
control over the comings and goings of his parents.

Now the therapist asked the Woodruffs to imagine how

it might feel if people simply disappeared. Both of the parents, with Mrs. Woodruff in the lead, were able to describe that they imagined that the experience would be frightening and that Barry would probably feel very anxious and worried. The therapist then asked them to imagine how Barry might feel if he awoke and Mr. Woodruff took him into a bed where there was no mommy and no explanation or reassurance about where she was or when he would ever see her again. Mrs. Woodruff particularly was able to be extremely empathic in this regard. The therapist suggested that there was probably a message in Barry's play and that although one could not be sure, it seemed that Barry's play in the crib during the day in his mother's presence was a 17-month-old's attempt to master the terror and anxiety of being in his crib alone at night and his fear that again, as on the night she had disappeared, mommy would be gone—all gone.

Mr. Woodruff responded with a gaze of open admiration and a wondering "Far out!" He said he believed what the therapist had suggested was true and announced that he was very impressed with his son. Mrs. Woodruff said that it made perfect sense and fit in with everything else discussed. She added, "I guess it convinces me that what it means is that it should be me that goes in when he wakes up at night—at least for a while." The therapist said that this seemed a good approach and that it might be the easiest situation in which to separate from Barry, as Mrs. Woodruff was not so bothered by his crying at night and not so concerned for his safety. Mrs. Woodruff reflected that she already felt somewhat better about Barry's safety—somehow saying it all aloud made it seem more manageable. It made sense to her that Barry's difficult beginning had left her not only bad memories but also a great deal of fear.

A silence followed this discussion. Mr. Woodruff then began a lengthy lecture on fatherhood. He spoke of the conspiracy of silence about the magnitude of the negative changes that parenthood entails, hastily adding, however, that he was very excited about the prospect of Barry's developing language. This sudden shift seemed to be Mr. Woodruff's way of saying, "All of this has meant some very negative changes for me and at the very most I have only been able to take the most distant intellectual pleasure in Barry."

Mr. Woodruff quickly went on, though, to change the subject to a discussion of Mrs. Woodruff's pregnancy and the time when there were only happy fantasies about how parenthood might be. Both parents spent the next part of the session talking about those vivid fantasies, particularly Mr. Woodruff's, surrounding the unborn child, who was to be a girl named Jenny. Toward the end of the session the Woodruffs discussed Barry's birth and its aftermath in considerable detail and with a great deal of feeling. They also talked again to one another about what the experience had been for each of them. Mr. Woodruff recalled feeling guilty during the delivery because it seemed to him that he had caused, but not had to suffer the consequences of, the pregnancy. Mrs. Woodruff spoke of a sense that she had let everyone down by being unable to deliver the baby "right." During these exchanges, the couple provided each other a great deal of mutual comfort and understanding.

The Woodruffs talked briefly about the separation from Barry when he was hospitalized at nine months and Mrs. Woodruff's guilt about not rooming-in with him during that time. Mr. Woodruff reassured her that she herself was ill at the time and should not blame herself for not being able to stay with Barry. In passing, the Woodruffs mentioned that their cat was now ill and that they were delighted to see Barry's imaginative imitation of Mrs. Woodruff's medicinal ministrations to the cat. Barry was using a small, empty sewing case his mother had given him to play with; with that he pretended to doctor the cat's ears.

Before the next visit Mrs. Woodruff called to say that Mr. Woodruff had taken a job and that we would have to change our appointment time. She told the therapist that

Barry's nighttime waking had totally ceased now that she had begun going in (she guessed, by the way, that our understanding must have been correct). Perhaps a visit from the therapist at a dinner hour would now be appropriate, so that the eating problem could be observed firsthand. The coming visit was therefore scheduled for dinnertime.

Predictably, no eating problem was evident during the visit. As everyone talked and attended only occasionally to him, Barry ate happily. Mrs. Woodruff seemed excessively aware of what Barry ate and commented on how good he was to eat his meal rather than on how good the food was to eat. In addition, the portions were extremely large. The Woodruffs explained that eating time in their house was typically no fun. Based on her childhood experiences, Mrs. Woodruff expected mealtime to be a time of general, if only superficial, sharing. By contrast, Mr. Woodruff's history led him to consider a meal a triumph if the fights were kept to a minimum of ten in as many minutes; he rushed through the whole thing as fast as possible.

During dinner Mrs. Woodruff announced to the therapist that two nights previous she had actually refused Barry a bottle for the first time. Questioning gradually revealed that she had been enraged at his refusal to eat a lovingly prepared meal. Although he had screamed for his bottle steadily for forty-five minutes, Mrs. Woodruff had remained adamant. During this conversation, Barry got down from the table and moved back and forth between the three adults and a box of toys near the table, primarily bringing toys to his mother. It became clear that Mrs. Woodruff had experienced Barry's refusal to eat her dinner as a personal rejection. This had infuriated her and she had retaliated by refusing to give him the bottle. Of concern to her now was the anger with which she had acted, and the fact that she had followed her refusal by reverting to her pattern of giving Barry bottles on demand.

The therapist suggested that Mrs. Woodruff's sudden explosion of anger might be related to frequent feelings of

being exploited. Mrs. Woodruff guessed she did, but knowing
how terrible Barry would feel to have her refuse him made
it very hard for her to do so. One good thing to report, Mrs.
Woodruff said, was that Barry had remained downstairs twice
recently while she was upstairs; this had never happened
before. A continuing problem was Barry's tantrums at the
icebox. Mrs. Woodruff reported that Barry wanted it open
and shut a hundred times a day and would fling himself on
the floor if his wish were denied.

During this part of the session Barry occasionally moved
around and enjoyed himself, but more frequently he remained
very near his mother or actually climbed on her lap or clung
to her. Mrs. Woodruff began to complain with increasing
bitterness about Barry's attachment to her; it was driving her
mad. At times, she said, she would read to him for an hour
or an hour and a half at a stretch. Asked why she didn't stop,
Mrs. Woodruff replied that she didn't know, but it made her
feel that somehow she would be a bad mother if she did. This
week, she said, she had just wanted to run away because she
had felt so worthless.

The therapist and the Woodruffs were just agreeing that
it was time to bring the visit to an end when Mr. Woodruff
asked his wife if she had decided whether she wanted to see
the therapist alone. As she said yes, Mrs. Woodruff's face took
on a tight, controlled expression at this question and her skin
flushed. The therapist noted Mrs. Woodruff's expression and
brought it to her attention, but she denied she was experiencing anything unusual. The therapist and Mrs. Woodruff
set up an extra home visit that would not disrupt the schedule
of the continuing joint appointments.

Individual and Joint Sessions

In the first individual session with Mrs. Woodruff, the
therapist raised the issue of her husband's suggesting individual sessions and Mrs. Woodruff's response. Mrs. Woodruff
said she and her husband had discussed the possibility and

she thought individual sessions might help her separate from Barry. A great deal of material emerged during the first hour, some involving childhood separations and moves and what these had meant to Mrs. Woodruff at the time. She recounted two recurring dreams from her childhood, which the therapist listened to without comment. She also presented in some detail her view of Mr. Woodruff, which coincided with the therapist's impression of a man so highly involved in his fantasies that the real world rarely seemed as vivid as his fantasy life. The time in South Dakota was agonizing for Mrs. Woodruff, and her disappointment in her husband was very deep. She was having trouble forgiving him and believing in him again, although she continued to love her husband and value him more than anyone.

In the following joint session it was clear that the meeting with Mrs. Woodruff had precipitated some more honest discussion between the Woodruffs, who were talking together much more openly of their mutual disappointment with one another in South Dakota. Mr. Woodruff was able to say that he had been looking for a home for many years. He realized that, like his wife, he could separate only in very abrupt and denying ways. Separation was an issue for both of the Woodruffs.

Each parent was now involved in a recently created, rather vivid fantasy of Mr. Woodruff's regarding a new undertaking in the northern part of the state. The Woodruffs were exploring the possibilities of arranging financing for a small newspaper and were very excited about it.

The most important development in this session was Mr. Woodruff's ability, with considerable support, to begin to verbalize his anger at what he had experienced as the loss of his wife during the past eighteen months. A picture emerged of two people essentially cut off from one another: since Barry's birth, the Woodruffs had never, for any reason, been out together without their child. Mrs. Woodruff tentatively suggested that maybe she was ready to go out with Mr. Woodruff to a movie or to dinner. As the therapist left, the couple were excited about their plan for a Friday night movie "date."

The next joint session was vital to the relationship between Mr. and Mrs. Woodruff. The appointment began with Mrs. Woodruff's meeting the therapist on the street as the former returned from taking Barry to a friend's apartment. Entering the house, she handed her husband a newspaper she had been holding with the comment, "This will drive you crazy. You won't be able to read it for an hour." Mr. Woodruff then announced that he had to go back to work after the meeting; although the couple had just had dinner together, this had not been mentioned before.

Mr. Woodruff launched into an entertaining and very personalized lecture on the newspaper business and how it should function. After some minutes Mrs. Woodruff began to laugh to herself. When Mr. Woodruff asked why she was laughing, she explained, "Here you are, talking and talking, and you haven't said a word to me all day—except that you went off with one of your phrases this morning, one of your poignant phrases." Turning to the therapist, Mrs. Woodruff said, "He left saying, 'Maybe there will come a day when I can be a man in my own house,' something like that." At this, Mr. Woodruff exclaimed, "Oh, Christ! The day just started bad and got worse." Mrs. Woodruff said, "The problem was that Barry woke up at six o'clock this morning. He was wide awake and ready to get up; we weren't. Barry stayed in his crib for a while, but finally I got up and brought him into bed with us. And then finally Dan [Mr. Woodruff] got up and then he kind of grouched around the house and didn't speak to anybody and he sat and read a book until it was time for him to leave for work." Mr. Woodruff said with some anger, "Look, I like to have my wife to myself sometimes. Now God knows I don't expect sex in the morning, but I would like perhaps to hug her." He said, "I need physical contact, that's the kind of person I am."

Mrs. Woodruff's face became a mask. She made no direct

response to her husband's remark but said, "Well, it has been a rotten week." Looking almost cheerful, she continued: "Since last Friday night, as a matter of fact. Our great date was an absolute disaster." She laughed nervously, and Mr. Woodruff looked very tense and angry. Then they began to fight. Mr. Woodruff said he had enjoyed Friday evening. Mrs. Woodruff was incredulous. The therapist asked when Mr. Woodruff realized his wife wasn't enjoying herself. This question revealed that even now he was stunned that she hadn't had a good time, while Mrs. Woodruff could not believe that he could ever have imagined she had. The therapist wondered if his wife's reaction hurt Mr. Woodruff. He softened a bit, but replied that he was "inured"; it was "just part of a pattern"; "it wasn't important."

Mrs. Woodruff said she had thought Friday evening would be more romantic, more like when they were first dating. Mr. Woodruff snorted. "Dated? My God! When did we ever date?" Mrs. Woodruff, chagrined, amended this: "Well, I mean when we first started abruptly living together." They then gave the therapist some new information. The Woodruffs had known one another nearly ten years. Mrs. Woodruff had been working with Mr. Woodruff at the time she had made the decision to marry someone else. This marriage, described as a debacle from the beginning, had lasted only a relatively short time. A brief, tempestuous affair with Mr. Woodruff had followed; recalling this period caused them both to become conspiratorially relaxed and cheerful. Initially, the affair didn't work out and the couple went their separate ways. After several years, however, they met again, began living together, and quickly married.

As the Woodruffs began to discuss what had gone wrong since then, the jolly feelings of the past moments gradually receded. They began to fight again. Mrs. Woodruff gave a devastating description of her husband in South Dakota, and he withered. They continued to fight.

Mrs. Woodruff furiously accused Mr. Woodruff of not

wanting to pick apricots with her. He wondered what was so "madly wonderful" about apricots. He was sick of talking about it. She said they must; it was getting worse. He said, "Of course it is. Look at this house—a goddamned motel. It's hideous and we're miserable."

Suddenly aware of the therapist, Mrs. Woodruff asked wryly if the therapist did marital counseling. They reply was that they would see. The therapist was concerned about anything that was impinging on Barry but was also concerned for them. The therapist said that although the Woodruffs were fighting, one could hear that they were two people who very much wanted one another, but were passing like ships in the night even as they tried to meet. Mr. Woodruff said, "That's right. I love you, Jane, but I don't know who the hell you are anymore. Our sex life is all but nonexistent—*is* nonexistent, and we talk about it, but it doesn't do any good."

Mrs. Woodruff ignored most of these comments and said, "I don't know you anymore either—but we can try—at least we can try." Mr. Woodruff said he was "sick of it" and then referred to Barry and the problems with him. He said that he understood, but still, "I want a wife; I don't want just Barry's mother—it makes me angry." Mrs. Woodruff accused him of being vengeful, of blaming her. He said that he wasn't and didn't, but that "in the abstract" Barry was a pain in the ass and he shouldn't be. He hated it. He absolutely hated it!

The Woodruffs moved from this exchange to speaking of South Dakota and then again of their ugly house, while Mrs. Woodruff made a plea to notice the good things—like the country fair last week, and how much she had enjoyed that; it was lovely to watch Mr. Woodruff and Barry roll in the grass. Mr. Woodruff, enraged, shouted that she couldn't just observe, she had to participate. He screamed at her that she didn't go on the merry-go-round. She screamed at him that merry-go-rounds made her sick. They continued to fight.

The therapist recognized that Mrs. Woodruff had initiated the session's series of arguments by taunting her husband

with the newspaper. Mrs. Woodruff was also steadfastly refusing to acknowledge his reference to the couple's sexual
relationship. During a pause, the therapist said that she wasn't
sure Mrs. Woodruff wanted to talk about the subject and that
she need not, but that she had seemed to respond to everything else her husband had said. A very tense silence followed.
Mr. Woodruff said, "It is a problem." Mrs. Woodruff said in
a very quiet, soft voice, "We do sort of discuss it—sort of—but
we never get anywhere."

In the following discussion, the Woodruffs dated the
problem from the time of Barry's birth and described some
physical difficulties of Mrs. Woodruff. Both parents had
calmed down, but they were still tense and edgy and appeared
to be gearing up for another argument. The therapist said,
"As complicated as it all is—and there are many things of
great importance—it does seem that losing what there was
between you has put many things out of perspective. I have
the feeling, Mr. Woodruff, that if you had one another it
wouldn't matter to you if Jane rolled in the leaves or rode on
the merry-go-round, and I don't think, Mrs. Woodruff, it
would matter much if Dan wanted to pick apricots or not. It
seems to me very sad that you have both lost so much."

The Woodruffs were very quiet. Then their affect shifted
dramatically. Mrs. Woodruff began to cry and Mr. Woodruff's
face, with tears in his eyes, worked busily at arranging itself.
Shortly afterward he said, "I have to go to work." He came
and stood by the therapist saying, "If you don't have to rush
off, maybe you could stay with Jane a bit." His voice was very
husky and he said to the therapist, "You are good." The therapist acknowledged his comment with a nod at him and at
Mrs. Woodruff and commented in turn that "they were good."
Mr. Woodruff walked over and hugged his wife, rumpled her
hair and, snuffling, bid everyone goodbye.

Mrs. Woodruff then began to tell the therapist of a history
of sexual difficulties which had occurred with her first husband
but had never been a problem with Mr. Woodruff until Barry's

birth. Earlier she had had a year and a half of treatment with a therapist, but all to no avail, as far as she could see. She wondered if she should seek individual treatment again. She and the therapist agreed that treatment should certainly be considered. Mrs. Woodruff said she didn't mind so much the poor sexual relationship for herself but she knew it was terribly hard for her husband. The therapist said that seemed doubly painful for him and an utter cheat for her. Mrs. Woodruff looked puzzled and surprised. The therapist explained, "Not only do you not have one another, but you are saying you don't care in the way that he does. And it is as if you have no right to care for yourself." Mrs. Woodruff first looked astonished and then comprehending and thoughtful. She agreed to meet for another individual session.

During the next individual appointment, Mrs. Woodruff told the therapist that separation from Barry was going more easily, and it felt very good. She was far less frightened about something happening to him, and she no longer had fantasies of disasters awaiting her when she got home. After a pause, Mrs. Woodruff said that she had felt both relieved and distressed after the last joint meeting. She said she hadn't realized how painful it all was for Dan, and she felt terrible. She also realized that the therapist was right: she really didn't think of their limited sexual relationship as a deprivation for herself at all. She mentioned feeling upset the following day and calling her parents, and then focused on how she and Dan had begun the next night really talking. That was so in contrast to her own family, in which nothing that mattered was ever mentioned.

Mrs. Woodruff went on to say that she and her husband had a beautiful Sunday. They had had a most satisfactory sexual experience and had both felt it was a very perfect day. Since then, she said she felt very good. She continued that she had learned from her earlier psychotherapy that her problem with sex was that she needed to be in control and couldn't risk giving that up. She supposed it was true, her recurring dreams supported that insight, but it all never seemed to make any difference. Besides, she added, sex was never any problem with Dan until Barry's birth. She repeated the two childhood recurring dreams that she had told the therapist in another context, and explained the sexual meanings of those dreams, but with virtually no affective investment.

The therapist chose to shift the focus and reminded Mrs. Woodruff that the first time she had recounted those dreams it had been in the context of talking about moving so much and about all of the separations she had experienced. The therapist suggested that Mrs. Woodruff had indeed had very little control over those separations. Very possibly, the moves had been barely discussed in her home and she had received no help in dealing with her feelings. Mrs. Woodruff responded with a flood of memories, registering her struggles to get hold of them with a mixture of amazement and excitement at meeting something so familiar but long unrecalled. These memories again had to do with painful separations and with specific threats of separation. Mrs. Woodruff's mother had often threatened to leave if she and her brother didn't do what they were told. Her brother would laugh, but Mrs. Woodruff would rush off to do whatever it was she was being asked. The therapist asked why. Mrs. Woodruff looked at the therapist as if she were not quite bright and said, "Well, so that she wouldn't leave." The therapist said, "But you believed her, that's the why I'm asking about." Mrs. Woodruff looked surprised and said, "I guess I would have never have wondered about that why. I would just have taken it for granted. I don't know why."

A description of Mrs. Woodruff's mother emerged: distant and unemotional, unsatisfied and unhappy. Recent and less recent disappointments were intermingled for Mrs. Woodruff; her parents' crushingly unexcited response to Barry's birth: the fact that when she had called them last week her father had not recognized her voice—just as when she had made a collect call from South Dakota to tell them about

Barry's birth her father had said, "A collect call from who? Jane who?" "Dan's parents fight a lot," Mrs. Woodruff said, "but you have a feeling that at least they are . . ." She paused. The therapist offered, "Connected?" "Yes," Mrs. Woodruff said, "connected."

She wondered why she had called her parents last week after that difficult session and she began to talk more about them. "My own parents—my God—I never even heard from them for a month after Barry was born." She started to say, "They never . . . ," and then she said, "I want them to love me," and she began to cry. "Why do I care so much? Why do I still want their approval and love? But I do. I want my mother to hug me, to tell me I'm okay, that I'm a good person. Why should I care?"

Mrs. Woodruff said, "I hate to cry." The therapist asked why. "Well, I can cry but I hate to cry in front of anyone." The therapist wondered how that made her feel. She answered, "Foolish, because it won't do any good. And there's no point in it." The therapist asked, "Because no one will care or understand or comfort you?" Mrs. Woodruff said "yes" and cried harder. She said that she couldn't cry in front of Dan and remembered always running away to cry. "It makes me feel so little and helpless and afraid."

The therapist then asked, "What do you think I will do?" Mrs. Woodruff gave a lengthy answer: "Leave me. Get up and go. It's like I have some awful cardboard figure that I show everybody, and really I'm sitting over here and I dare not let you see. You'll see that I'm no good, and bad, and you will leave me. I'm afraid of it right now." She cried for some time and then said, "No one would ever help me. No one was ever there. I think I thought it was because I didn't deserve it, because I was bad." As Mrs. Woodruff began to compose herself, the therapist asked if she had lost all of the good feeling that there had been at the beginning of the hour. She replied, "No, that is still there, that is okay."

Somewhat later Mrs. Woodruff said that she did not want

to go into individual treatment. The therapist responded that she could take all the time she needed to decide about that. Mrs. Woodruff then explained that she and Dan had talked about it and decided that maybe they could work together with the therapist. Already it had seemed they had made changes together; if it had not been for the other night with the therapist they knew Sunday could not have happened. They were both so relieved to get that all out in the open. The therapist said, "It is up to you about individual treatment and you will certainly be in control. I think that's important." Mrs. Woodruff said, "So do I, and I don't want to leave you. I don't think I could face another separation. I don't want to go from you to somebody new." The therapist then clarified that this would not be the case no matter what and explained that their involvement would continue even if Mrs. Woodruff decided to pursue individual treatment. The therapist assured Mrs. Woodruff that she wasn't going to leave her or insist that she do anything she did not want to do: the choice was hers.

The first thing mentioned in the next visit with Mr. and Mrs. Woodruff was that the cat's bladder infection had spread and that the vet said there was absolutely nothing to be done. Mrs. Woodruff said that she would miss the cat, that she was such a nice cat. She continued that she didn't know what to tell Barry. Everyone agreed that Barry needed to be told that the cat was very sick, that the doctor couldn't make her better, and, eventually, that the cat was dead and they wouldn't be able to see the cat anymore. Everyone also focused on the issue Mrs. Woodruff had alluded to at the very first: missing the cat. It was important to talk to Barry about her feeling.

The Woodruffs then moved to a discussion of the refrigerator problem, which was becoming unbearable. Barry was now spending long periods of time demanding that the refrigerator be opened. He cried and screamed if his parents refused to keep opening and closing it. The therapist repeatedly tried to help the Woodruffs stop focusing on the "wickedness" of Barry's behavior and instead try to imagine what

Barry was doing when he demanded that the refrigerator be opened again after it had been closed. Finally, the Woodruffs were able to decide that perhaps he was trying to find something out. They discussed with the therapist the possibility that Barry experienced some similarity between his mother and food and then considered the work he was still doing on the disappearance and reappearance of his mother and others.

Once all this made some sense to the Woodruffs, the therapist suggested verbalizing to Barry that when you opened and closed the refrigerator, the food was still there even if you couldn't see it. They could demonstrate that. The therapist told the parents that they couldn't be sure this was the issue of concern to Barry, but suggested that it might be useful to make Barry a cardboard refrigerator and provide him boxes and "toy food" so that he could experiment for himself. The Woodruffs decided that it was worth a try and, besides, it would be rather fun for Mr. Woodruff to arrange this.

Mr. and Mrs. Woodruff were obviously relaxed and happy with one another. They were smiling, interacting, and touching one another in a way that was quite different from any way they had behaved toward one another earlier in the treatment.

Mrs. Woodruff was seen alone for another individual appointment. She began spontaneously to discuss her early sexual history, speaking in considerable detail. The therapist responded throughout with support and concern but picked up on no specifics and asked nothing. Although there was an abundance of material suggesting troublesome sexual feelings and their effects, the therapist chose to respond only to the themes which seemed most relevent to Barry. The therapist, for example, pointed out to Mrs. Woodruff both her consistent inability to claim or to even feel she had a right to claim whatever she might want and also her very strong tendency to "need to be approved of," as she put it. Mrs. Woodruff said that she was very aware also of an enormous need for the therapist's approval and that she had wondered what relation that need might have to her having become such an interesting sexual companion of late. She perceived that the therapist's attitude toward sex was in contrast to that of her mother, who, she felt, totally disapproved of sexual activity.

Mrs. Woodruff was also able to recognize a tendency, frequent in her relationships with men, to attract and hold them by deliberately giving everything until she was sure that they loved her, at which point she would often abandon them. As she described these relationships, Mrs. Woodruff used many words and phrases that she had also applied in speaking of her parents. The therapist needed only to underline these for Mrs. Woodruff to begin to recognize a series of people in her life she had experienced as substitutes for her parents. She said that it wasn't clear to her how she could really change this pattern, but that recognizing it gave her some sense of control. The therapist replied that Mrs. Woodruff would have to decide how much she felt she needed to understand and how much old patterns interfered with her current life. The work Mrs. Woodruff and the therapist would do had a definite focus and would be rather limited. The therapist emphasized that Mrs. Woodruff did not need to decide immediately about further treatment.

Mrs. Woodruff then related more incidents involving her family and others. Again the therapist pointed out Mrs. Woodruff's general need to be loved and approved of, to the exclusion of her other needs. Finally the therapist said, "You know, some of that reminds me of Barry." This connection produced a great flood of affect. Among other things, Mrs. Woodruff said, "I think I am afraid that Barry won't love me, that he won't think I'm a wonderful mother." The therapist agreed that Mrs. Woodruff did seem to need to be a super-mother to Barry—all giving, perfect, almost a martyr, with no independent needs and certainly no rights. Mrs. Woodruff said wonderingly, "My God, I've spent so much time lately thinking about one side of it—the amount that I project onto Barry and caring for him the way I wish I had been cared for—that

I never saw the part of me that needed so much for him to love me and approve of me that I was ready to be whatever he needed or wanted me to be." The therapist underlined the degree to which such stress interfered with Mrs. Woodruff's natural good sense and good mothering.

After these exchanges, many details of daily routines emerged which highlighted Mrs. Woodruff's difficulty in responding appropriately to Barry's demands and in allowing satisfaction of her own needs. It became somewhat clearer to Mrs. Woodruff that emotional explosions resulted when her resentment had built up over time. By the close of the session, Mrs. Woodruff was acutely aware of how destructive this situation was and herself recalled the sudden, rageful denial of the bottle to Barry which had occurred and been discussed earlier.

The next session was a joint one and included Barry. Now 20 months old, he had made many strides over the past months. His affect seemed less muted and his whole range of expression had expanded and grown freer. He could operate for longer intervals apart from, and at greater distances from, his mother. His vocabulary had increased considerably and a sufficient degree of separateness from his mother had developed to make a word for her a necessity; Barry was calling his mother "mommy." The Woodruffs described their son's many accomplishments and were very proud of him. The problem with the refrigerator was rapidly disappearing. They did report, however, that Barry was "giving them fits" about the family dog, whom he never wanted out of his sight. Mrs. Woodruff thought this behavior might be related to separation from her, and Mr. Woodruff thought it was just one of those "developmental" things. While Barry was busy in the kitchen, the therapist suggested that his concern might be connected to the cat's disappearance. After some discussion and suggestions, Mrs. Woodruff decided that she should begin by simply reassuring Barry that the dog was fine, that he could go out and come back and nothing would happen to him.

The next, and last, individual session with Mrs. Woodruff focused almost entirely on Barry. At the end, the therapist commented that there had been three sessions in which Barry was barely mentioned, that the focus had been returned to him at the end of their last appointment, and that the joint session and this meeting had again concentrated on Barry.

Mrs. Woodruff replied that three things seemed to have changed. Her relationship with her husband was much better in every way; sexually, it was better than it had ever been. She was also beginning to separate from Barry comfortably and without anxiety, and she thought that recognizing the fears left over from his birth had helped. Finally, her realization that she was responding to Barry as she had reacted to her parents, her family, and a whole series of other people had helped her interrupt this pattern to some degree. Mrs. Woodruff felt she was ready to end individual sessions and resume meetings with everyone present. The therapist said that this was Mrs. Woodruff's decision to make and that the Woodruffs could certainly do that and see how things went. Mrs. Woodruff said she felt comfortable enough to let the therapist know if things started going badly and if she felt she needed more help of another kind.

Return to Joint Sessions

While Barry remained of central concern, at this point in the treatment Mr. Woodruff became a focus as well. He began to talk about himself, not through a detailed history but through descriptions of himself in the world and his feeling that there was no place for him in it. Though extremely articulate and colorful, Mr. Woodruff was also in great pain. His anguish came dramatically to the fore as his newest fantasy—the possibility of moving up north—collapsed. That night Mr. Woodruff delivered a monologue lasting nearly forty-five minutes in which he described those rare times when he had felt really alive. Those moments always involved a remote fantasy and were always experienced alone. Mr. Woodruff contrasted these moments with the ugliness of the real world, which he illustrated with accounts of world crises and problems.

The therapist chose to let Mr. Woodruff know she understood he was speaking about himself. Toward the end of the session, the therapist commented that although his analysis of world problems was true, what was more impressive was the terrible personal pain in it—as if there was a defense that was not there in him, or a wound that was. Mr. Woodruff agreed but said that he really enjoyed being raw. He discoursed on the virtues of that and then asserted, "Besides, there isn't anything to be done." The therapist said that this wasn't necessarily so, and that these feelings seemed at times to immobilize him. Mr. Woodruff agreed, "Yes, whenever a deal collapses." The therapist inquired if that was the feeling in South Dakota. "Yes," he said, "when the world rejects me." "The world?" asked the therapist. Mr. Woodruff thought a long time and then said, "I know some of it is personal and that there is another rejection," and then he grinned at the therapist as if he were simultaneously acknowledging the truth of her suggestion and asking that this not be pursued. Mr. Woodruff gave the therapist the gift of his admission, but he trusted that the discussion would not go further than he could tolerate. Acknowledging this subtle communication, the therapist smiled back at him and said, "Thank you." Mr. Woodruff grinned even more widely and said, "You're welcome."

For Mr. Woodruff to experience and to suggest, even obliquely, any personal vulnerability was indeed progress. Then Mr. Woodruff was moved to explain more. He had decided at age 25, he recounted, that he did have some "hangups" and "some kind of crap" from his early life, but he decided to turn all of that into something he could use. It would become a tool and he would use it like any other tool. The therapist said, "But right now you're having trouble using it." He nodded, "I'm having trouble using it—right now."

During the following session, Mrs. Woodruff reported that on the strength of a pediatrician's suggestion that it would not harm Barry to cut back on his bottles, she had moved ahead to try to accomplish this. It was clear, from her account, that it was not Mrs. Woodruff who was depriving Barry of his bottle, but the expert. In the next visit the following issue was discussed: the external permission, and, in a sense, authoritative directive, that Mrs. Woodruff needed to limit Barry's demands. Again she and the therapist followed the thread of her difficulty in depriving Barry in any way and in following her own good instincts. From this discussion emerged material about Mrs. Woodruff's fears that Barry would be very angry at her. It was not simply that he would not approve; he would be angry.

What would he do? What did she mean, angry? Mrs. Woodruff said she guessed Barry couldn't do anything, really. After all he was just little. Perhaps she just didn't want him to feel so bad.

The therapist wondered why she had thought he would be angry. Did it ever make her angry when she could not get what she wanted? Mrs. Woodruff thought perhaps a little, but she was grown up and could understand the reasons for things—Barry could not. The therapist reminded her that she had not always been so grown up. Could she remember any times when it had not been so easy for her? Actually, Mrs. Woodruff said, she did remember there were some unpleasant times when she was little—around 4 or 5 years old, she thought. She began to describe incidents with her brother, another sibling, and some other neighborhood children. They were older and if she was to play with them she had to do as they asked. She needed to accommodate herself to them. She was not quite sure how it had come to be like that but it was really awful. She described two different instances in which she was humiliated by the role she was forced to play but "knew" that if she did not obey she would lose her companions. Mrs. Woodruff, though distressed, expressed no anger about those events. Finally Mrs. Woodruff said, "Maybe I'm afraid that if I don't do what Barry wants he won't like me anymore and he won't want to be with me."

Mr. Woodruff was also involved in the sessions. He was out of work and eager to have a job, even a temporary one, but he could not find one. His discourses were similar to those following the collapse of his fantasy, but far less pain-filled and more distanced and intellectualized.

Mrs. Woodruff could now talk about her need for approval and her difficulty in setting limits, both in the joint sessions and with her husband. As the Woodruffs began to mention Barry's negativism in a number of areas, the therapist helped them understand how verbal communication might help prepare Barry for changes and transitions. The therapist also suggested that Barry could be expected to experience some difficulty as they raised their demands on him, because he was relatively unused to accommodating himself to his parents. The process would require tact, care, and thought, and could be explored in joint work.

At the next meeting, the Woodruffs focused on Barry. He was ill for the first time in the three and a half months since the start of treatment. He had been feverish and had severe cold symptoms. Nonetheless, it seemed to Mrs. Woodruff that his incessant demands were beyond what his sickness ought to produce. As the Woodruffs and the therapist began to examine the parents' complaints about Barry's "demandingness," it became clear that most of his "demands" were related to separation. Barry did not want anyone to go anywhere. He did not want anyone who came to the house to leave. He did not want their new cat or the dog to go out, and when they did he cried inconsolably. The additional stress on Mrs. Woodruff's feelings at the time of Barry's actual illness was discussed in the context of her long-standing fears regarding his well-being.

This was the first time Barry had been ill since the cat had taken sick and died. The therapist wondered to the Woodruffs if Barry might be worried about himself and what might happen to him. Their cat had been sick and had disappeared and never returned. Mr. Woodruff scoffed, "Nonsense, he doesn't even know he's sick." Mrs. Woodruff disagreed: "I tell him every five minutes all day. He even says 'sick.' " Then Mrs. Woodruff's face lit up and she added, "Remember that sewing case, the one he used to imitate me with when I was medicating kitty? Well, it just occurs to me that he fished it out of somewhere, and he's been doctoring everybody's ears. I think he is *scared*. I'm giving him medicine. He doesn't want the new kitty out, and he has started worrying about the dog going out, and he hasn't wanted us out of his sight. I think it all fits." The therapist asked what might be done if this were so. Mrs. Woodruff thought and offered, "I suppose, just know it. Reassure him that he is sick but that he will be fine, and know that he is especially scared." The therapist added, "Mommy and Daddy get sick sometimes, and then they are fine. Being sick isn't fun but it gets better."

Mr. Woodruff said very thoughtfully that he guessed being little like Barry was very complicated and you really had to try to respect what was going on in children's heads. But, he continued, "it's terrible to think he's afraid that something really bad is going to happen." The therapist asked if Mr. Woodruff remembered being scared when he was little. "No," Mr. Woodruff replied. "Well—maybe." Then he laughed and announced, "I've always been invincible." Mrs. Woodruff smiled but said, "Yeah sure, that's what we'd like to think. We don't like to think that Barry's scared but we don't like to remember that we were either." Mr. Woodruff did not respond directly to his wife's comment. He went on, however, to reflect, "Well, the good thing is that if that's what's wrong we can just hug him and tell him everything is fine and nobody's going anywhere and he's okay. That's one great thing about being a parent—you can do that for somebody." The therapist asked, "Only as a parent?" At this, Mr. Woodruff made a face and said, "Well—maybe a really good friend—like a wife." He laughed and Mrs. Woodruff smiled at him.

Later on in the session Mrs. Woodruff mentioned that

she was still limiting Barry's bottles and that this continued to be very hard for her. She said it made her feel very guilty and ungiving. With only a pause, she commented that Barry now had the words for bottle and blanket. She announced with pleasure, "All of those important things are named. I have a name, the bottle has a name, and as of yesterday the blanket has a name." Things were going so well, Mr. Woodruff suggested, that perhaps they might "begin to talk about thinking about termination." Mrs. Woodruff responded immediately but with good humor that the thought made her sick to her stomach. After discussion, everyone agreed, as Mr. Woodruff put it, "just to start to talk about thinking about it." Mrs. Woodruff made it clear that she was not ready and Mr. Woodruff was very willing that treatment continue, as it was proving helpful.

A few days later, the therapist had a phone call from Mrs. Woodruff. She was frantic. Barry was driving her crazy with the telephone and he wouldn't let her alone at all when she was talking on it. Also, he wouldn't eat any solid food and wanted only his bottle. After a lengthy discussion of the details, it became obvious that Mrs. Woodruff had essentially transferred the problem with the bottle to solid food. She had become unable to control what, when, or where Barry would eat, much as with the bottle, and she was leaving food out a great deal so that he could get it when he wanted it. Uncomfortable about "depriving" Barry of the bottle, Mrs. Woodruff seemed driven to accommodate him in other areas.

When the therapist pointed out this pattern in general terms, Mrs. Woodruff readily agreed and elaborated upon the idea. The therapist was able to offer some specific advice as to how to arrange set mealtimes, using smaller portions, and switching from "it is important to Mommy that you eat" to "Mommy doesn't like you to be hungry." These suggestions were embedded, however, in the discussion of why Mrs. Woodruff was handling the matter in the way she was, how Barry would experience her actions, and why the new method might work. The fact that Barry had effectively regressed from the usual stage of eating finger foods was also recognized, and the need to take this into account discussed.

This episode illustrated dramatically how monumentally difficult it was for Mrs. Woodruff to say no to Barry in any way. She was acutely aware of this by the end of the discussion. The possible relation of this sudden crisis to the earlier mention of termination, however tentative, was also explored.

Mrs. Woodruff followed the carefully worked out plan, and by the following appointment Barry's eating was no longer a serious problem. This continued to be true. From that point onward, Barry ate well at mealtimes, had only occasional snacks, and took two bottles a day. He was frequently disinterested in those and didn't finish them. At mealtimes he drank milk from a cup.

Mr. Woodruff began a new pattern at this time. He would deliver Barry to the friend's apartment and then arrive twenty minutes or so into the session. During these twenty minutes Mrs. Woodruff and the therapist would discuss Barry, and then Mr. Woodruff would arrive and speak about his own concerns. His failure to get a temporary job he had wanted precipitated a painful recital of both grandiose and demeaning aspects of himself. Mr. Woodruff was applying for many jobs of all kinds, and his lack of success made him feel denigrated and depressed. In these meetings with Mr. Woodruff, the therapist attempted to strike a tone that responded more to the pain he expressed than to the anger. Mr. Woodruff reacted by being constantly able to voice his feelings less defensively. He became much softer and more vulnerable and seemed to accept warmly the therapist's understanding, her genuine concern for him, and the value she placed on him as a person.

Meanwhile, the Woodruffs' house began to perk up. Mrs. Woodruff removed some boxes which had littered the rooms for as long as the therapist had been coming, and Mr. Woodruff put in some handsome beams and built shelves. Shortly thereafter, the couple began to discuss selling the house, taking a profit, and finding a place with less overhead. Mr. Woodruff was justifiably alarmed at his chances in the job market.

Christmas brought both joy and sadness. Although both parents missed their own families very acutely, they were able to give Barry a glorious holiday. The season led them to speak of their parents. Mr. Woodruff described his father: a clever man who had no patience with his son. Mr. Woodruff wished that Barry could have the close relationship with his father that he himself had never had, but he could not imagine how this could happen, given his mother's likely interference. Both parents felt that children needed grandparents and that Barry was being cheated since his relatives lived so far away.

Mrs. Woodruff brought up the "telephone problem" again. She recognized it as part of a general problem for her and also realized that Barry was making some independent strides that were difficult for her. The therapist responded by making a suggestion that built on Mrs. Woodruff's own attempts to give Barry a turn to speak on the phone. Barry would not respond to his mother's reasoning with him, however, and was unable to accept her plea for fairness. The therapist advised that Barry simply not get his turn if he was not quiet while Mrs. Woodruff was speaking.

With considerable difficulty, Mrs. Woodruff was able to try this approach. She was fair and considerate. She gave Barry something to do while she was phoning and limited the duration of her calls. Only on the first occasion did Barry not get "his turn." After that he said "Quiet" whenever the phone rang, waited happily, and then joyfully spoke when his turn came. Mrs. Woodruff was impressed with how well this approach worked and was simultaneously more puzzled by her own reluctance to institute such measures.

About this time, Mr. Woodruff failed to get two more jobs. He got angry and depressed but less so than in the past, and he responded quickly and openly to the support of both his wife and the therapist.

Despite the Woodruffs' difficult financial situation, their

home was newly carpeted, clean, and truly attractive. Mr. Woodruff had built more bookshelves. Many plants had been hung and placed around the house, which now looked like a home which someone loved, with people in it who cared about one another. Although redecoration had begun ostensibly to make the house attractive to potential buyers, the Woodruffs now were enjoying their home and were reluctant to sell. They genuinely felt that the house reflected their coming to life and loving again.

In one session Mrs. Woodruff reported that Barry, now 21 months of age, was beginning to have terrible temper tantrums, often lasting thirty or forty minutes nonstop. These usually occurred when Mrs. Woodruff had to bring him home from a visit or interrupt some other ongoing activity of his. She had tried reasoning with him and offering him extra time to finish the project, but nothing seemed to work. The therapist and Mrs. Woodruff established this as another "no" situation and recognized again Mrs. Woodruff's familiar difficulty in "depriving" Barry. This time the discussion expanded to include setting limits of all kinds. As Mrs. Woodruff and the therapist spoke about possible techniques, Mrs. Woodruff said that the therapist's suggestions sounded to her like threats. She could not effectively experience a difference between assuming control of her child and abusing him. Again it was necessary to examine the various sources of Mrs. Woodruff's sense of herself as bad and ungiving and of the need for approval which led to her compliant stance and self-exploitation.

Barry's temper tantrums led Mrs. Woodruff to experience both increased helplessness and greater irritation. She felt very exploited. "Even giving in to him," as she put it, resulted in only a brief respite, for he soon became enraged by some new frustration. Still, Mrs. Woodruff felt the therapist's "developmental" explanations of Barry's possible needs for limits suggested controls from her that would be "unfair" to Barry and "mean." At this point, the therapist suggested that Mrs. Woodruff might be experiencing some irritation at the therapist. After some initial hesitation, Mrs. Woodruff was able to say she felt the therapist was trying to control her on the issue of limit setting. The therapist inquired about how that made her feel. With great difficulty Mrs. Woodruff said she was afraid to express her anger toward the therapist out of fear that the therapist would no longer like her or wish to see her. She felt this although she "knew" that it was not true. Her resistance to experiencing and to expressing this anger impressed and disturbed Mrs. Woodruff. When the therapist suggested that it was just such powerful feelings and fears that might have made her so agreeable and compliant with her own mother, Mrs. Woodruff agreed. An angry child was a bad child and a bad child would be left. The "cardboard figure" to which Mrs. Woodruff had referred in the first of the five individual sessions was the compliant, nice, agreeable child who feared that she would be abandoned if anyone knew how angry she was. The therapist and Mrs. Woodruff recalled how Mrs. Woodruff had felt that if the therapist knew how she "really was" the therapist would "get up and go."

This connection freed Mrs. Woodruff sufficiently for her to be able to explore at some length her quick-shifting sense of Barry as alternately upset and helpless or angry and retaliating. In addition, she felt that at times she imagined Barry's experience in terms of her own different states and reacted accordingly, while at other times she reacted to Barry as if he were her mother. With considerable outrage she insisted, "It's not right that I treat Barry as if he were me or my mother. He is Barry, and I have to know that."

Mrs. Woodruff then began to empathize with how Barry felt to have so much control at 20 months. Finally, Mrs. Woodruff said that she could not imagine that it would be anything but terrifying for a child to have such power. She said simply, "I cannot do that to him. He needs me to love him in the right way."

Very gingerly, but with great courage, Mrs. Woodruff began to follow out the strategies that she and the therapist

devised together, and Barry's tantrums became shorter, sub-
sided, and then effectively ceased. This occurred within a
matter of days once Mrs. Woodruff was convinced that her
control was necessary and she became comfortable enough to
exert it. Barry became mostly happy, sunny, and reasonably
cooperative, and seemed enormously relieved. Mrs. Woodruff
clearly realized this when she said, "You know, that really
cannot have been fun for him either. He must really have
been miserable too."

When Mr. Woodruff's response to his wife's realization
was to say, "You know—I thought we should have been putting the screws to him for a long time," the therapist took him
seriously. Mr. Woodruff was abashed at this and said that the
therapist should know that this was simply "the way he talks."
The therapist answered that she understood this, but that the
remark was still unsettling. The therapist wondered if Mr.
Woodruff knew why he had said it. He reflected that he wasn't
sure, but he knew that he sometimes had trouble himself
being an authority figure. Recently, when there was a storm
and they feared that they might have to waken Barry and take
him to the basement, he and Mrs. Woodruff had decided,
giggling together, that they just might choose to blow away
or get in Barry's bed rather than risk taking him into theirs
again. Really, it was not easy for him either, Mr. Woodruff
said. He recalled that once he had put Barry in bed and then
said to his wife, "Don't move! He's not asleep." This story
reminded both of them, however, that although Barry was
usually quite shy when potential buyers came to look at the
house, he had recently made an announcement to one couple
when they got upstairs. He had run into his room and called,
"Own bed! Own bed! Own bed!" very proudly and very happily. The Woodruffs realized that the lines which they were
trying to draw were absolutely necessary to Barry's well-
being, and they seemed determined to continue their efforts.

During a subsequent session, Mrs. Woodruff told of a
frightful upset which Barry had experienced and which she

did not understand at all. She described it to the therapist, who could not make sense of it either. When Mr. Woodruff arrived after leaving Barry, the situation was mentioned to him, and he explained in a very scrambled way what the source of Barry's extreme unhappiness had been. The story emerged only gradually, and the therapist had to push much harder than usual for details from Mr. Woodruff.

Mr. Woodruff and Barry had been at a neighbor's house. Three-year-old Sally had uncharacteristically offered a sucker to Barry as he was leaving. On their way down the street, Mr. Woodruff suggested to Barry that he save it and had said, "You can have it in the morning after breakfast." Mr. Woodruff had then pocketed the candy, whereupon Barry had begun to protest. Mr. Woodruff said no again and that was the end of it. It was a lovely story. Barry certainly couldn't have done that a month before; none of them could.

The story did not stop there, however. Barry and his father arrived home and Mr. Woodruff put the candy on a high shelf, clearly visible to his son. He repeated that he could have it in the morning. When after a while Barry went over and said, "Reach it, up, reach it, up, reach it, canny, canny," Mr. Woodruff moved the candy and placed it on a lower shelf which Barry could reach. He said, "There, you can reach it in the morning." Mr. Woodruff then settled back to watch and said no more. Barry took the candy. He wandered around with it for five minutes, watching his father. Mr. Woodruff said nothing. Barry unwrapped it and watched his father. Mr. Woodruff remained silent. Barry began to whimper and smell the candy. Mr. Woodruff observed. Barry licked the candy and whined and started to cry. Mr. Woodruff looked at him.

Mrs. Woodruff, who had been reading, became aware of something happening and said, "What is it Barry? Do you want it? What's going on? You can eat it!" Mr. Woodruff was enraged at Mrs. Woodruff's interruption, although he had not told her anything about the incident. He then decided that the situation simply had no more to do with him. It was as if, he recounted, he had been building a sculpture with Barry or painting a picture and she came along with her brush and daubed it all up. Mrs. Woodruff took the already crying Barry upstairs. When she took off his shirt the candy fell to the floor and Barry became hysterical—crying for almost an hour. Mrs. Woodruff did not understand, and only later, after Barry was asleep, did Mr. Woodruff tell her of his anger at her interruption.

The entire session was spent on the incident. To Mrs. Woodruff, her husband's behavior was like putting a bone in front of a dog and telling him not to eat it. Mr. Woodruff responded that he was only at fault in not following through. After Barry ate the candy, he should have told him that it was all right. Everyone agreed that this would certainly have helped, and Mrs. Woodruff reminded him that Barry had awakened calling for his father in the morning. This was something he had never done. They fruitfully discussed better communication between them so that they would not trap Barry in the middle of their misunderstandings or be played off against one another.

The therapist then confessed some confusion. She wonderd what Mr. Woodruff was doing; was it a test? Mr. Woodruff replied by delivering a lecture on stretching, growing, and becoming strong. It was his duty, in a way, he said. The therapist asked why he had stopped telling Barry not to eat the candy but had left the situation entirely to Barry to manage. Mr. Woodruff looked confused and upset and finally, rather angrily, sputtered, "Christ, how do I know?" The therapist said that it seemed to her terribly hard—a great deal to expect of Barry, but that apparently it really didn't seem so to Mr. Woodruff. Mr. Woodruff reddened and became very uncomfortable. The therapist asked how he felt when he was dealing with Barry. He became more upset and said he didn't really know. He was just kind of observing and disinterested. In answer to a question, he maintained he had no idea how Barry felt.

Mrs. Woodruff then began describing how she imagined Barry must have felt: confused and overwhelmed. Her husband replied, "Well, you've got to learn; I do it to myself all the time." The therapist continued, "Yes, I know you do—the superman who doesn't need anybody." The therapist said that she knew that Mr. Woodruff often treated himself that way. Mr. Woodruff was quiet for some time. Then he said, "Yeah, I guess it was wrong—maybe—I guess I don't quite understand it but that *is* the way I treat myself." The therapist responded that she could only imagine that he would do that to himself if someone had done it to him. Mr. Woodruff said it was true that he had certainly had to learn to manage for himself when he was little. Nobody made it easy for him. He was expected to perform and do things right, and he did, and that was all there was to it.

It was Mrs. Woodruff who asked, "Did you like that?" There was a very long pause before Mr. Woodruff said, "It was the way it was. What does that have to do with the liking? That's life." At this, the therapist wondered, "Is it? Clearly someone was very hard on you." After a very long pause Mr. Woodruff said, looking very sad and with tears in his eyes, "I should not do that to Barry. Nobody should have to be all alone in the world that way." It seemed clear that Mr. Woodruff had been compelled to do to Barry what had been done to him. He did not plan it, but he could not stop himself once he had begun.

At the following appointment only Mrs. Woodruff was present since, most happily, Mr. Woodruff was beginning a new job. Mrs. Woodruff had much to say. Shortly after the last session Mr. Woodruff had had an interview for another job. Two positions were open, with three applicants. Mr. Woodruff was the one who was not hired. He was told that his work history was too erratic. The astonishing thing, however, was that Mr. Woodruff had come home and cried. He had cried and he had cried openly, and Mrs. Woodruff had held him. She said to the therapist, "I have never seen Dan cry. I have seen him maybe get tears in his eyes or something but I have never seen him really break down and cry in all the time I have known him, no matter how upset he was—never."

Mrs. Woodruff reflected that her husband's open display of tears seemed a good thing to her. It felt to her, she said, as though he had changed. Afterward he wasn't depressed or angry; he didn't lie around for days. He just went out job hunting. He got busy, and he went out looking, and he had this job now. She added that she didn't quite understand it, but during these months they had grown closer and closer, and it was really very different and very, very nice. The therapist responded that she was glad that Mrs. Woodruff felt good about that and glad that things were better between her and her husband. Mrs. Woodruff started to describe the changes in more detail. It was hard for Dan to cry, she said, adding, "for me too." She stopped and then began, "Oh, but you . . .," and said nothing further. The therapist answered that yes, she knew how that was for her. Quite thoughtfully, Mrs. Woodruff said, "I think I could cry with him now if I needed to, and I know that he would comfort me." She then focused on a complaint regarding Barry which she quickly recognized as really being a decision Mrs. Woodruff had to make regarding her own needs and wishes and how she might arrange things to accommodate them.

In the next session Mr. Woodruff was expansive. He had been fired by a small print shop for trying to form a union of white-collar employees on his second day of work. He explained that it was a choice he made. He knew he would get fired, but it was safe because he was going to start the job he really wanted within the week, and, besides, he had other part-time work. "Still," he said, "it's really not like me to take it so well. Usually I'd be in a rage or despairing." He was extremely pleased with the new job he was about to begin, which he described to the therapist in detail. He mentioned in passing that he had even called his mother to tell her. "At last," he said, "something she can be proud of and tell the neighbors." Mrs. Woodruff added, "Not only that, you remembered her birthday. You never have since I have known you." "Oh, what the hell," said Mr. Woodruff generously and laughed. The couple elaborated on how much the job meant. It felt good, as if it had some purpose and meaning beyond being just a livelihood. They also talked about what a lot of changes the new job would involve; at this, the focus shifted to Mrs. Woodruff and Barry.

The report on Barry was glowing. Mrs. Woodruff spoke of how good things felt. She realized that she had allowed Barry to tyrannize her and that it had been horrible for both of them. She told the therapist that they had put up an easel for her and that she had arranged to get some free time by sharing baby-sitting with a friend. Both parents spoke of how they had a long-range plan such that even moving would be a real transition rather than an impulsive, abrupt change, as their previous moves had been. Mr. Woodruff said, "It's like we're really becoming a family at last and we were a very long time aborning." Mrs. Woodruff agreed: "Yes, there were lots of bones to heal and mend." The metaphors were stunningly apt to their experience with Barry, but the Woodruffs both seemed utterly oblivious to these meanings.

During the following meeting, Mrs. Woodruff spent a great deal of time telling the therapist how good she was feeling about herself and Barry. She spoke of how much fun they had and of how delightful her child was. She proudly, and with great pleasure, described a situation which she had handled with ease and contrasted this with earlier times. She said it all felt so natural that she could not imagine doing it any other way now. Throughout most of this discussion, Barry was happily playing and entertaining himself in another room.

Suddenly Barry scooted into the living room saying, "Running, running." He stopped in front of the therapist and announced in a tumble of words within which the therapist could discern, "Mama—asleep—upstairs. Jimmy—quiet." It was an incident which his mother had described, and the therapist said, "Did you take your nap and sleep upstairs with Jimmy, and were you quiet?" "Quiet," Barry agreed, grinning and leaning forward with his hands on his little bent knees and his brown eyes shining. He looked irresistible, and apparently he was. Mrs. Woodruff, sitting directly across from the therapist, laughed and reached out for her son, saying, "Oh Barry, I love you. I love you more every day." He clambered onto her lap, facing her, and wrapped his arms and legs around her. As they hugged, he buried his head in her neck, and said, "Mommy, Mommy." She pushed him gently backward along her thighs, stretched out so that his head hung down from her knees. "Upside-down boy," she said. "See him?" The upside-down boy and the therapist exchanged greetings. Mrs. Woodruff leaned over and kissed his neck, and he giggled, and then she drew him up—hugging him close again—and said, "Right-side-up boy." Then she said softly, "He is such a lovely boy—so gentle—there is no meanness in him." The therapist smiled and asked her, "How did you happen to call him Barry?" Mrs. Woodruff said that partly it was because of an artist that Dan admired. She added, "I just liked the name. It's a handsome, strong name. A good name. He looks like a Barry, don't you think?" As Barry got down to run off and play, the therapist agreed that he did.

The moment was a touching one. There was the distinct feeling that Mrs. Woodruff was expressing her sense of Barry having been born again—this time the right way. The family had worked hard for many months to make a new start and to create relationships which would nurture all of them.

The following four months saw the consolidation of this work. At termination, after nine months of treatment, the Woodruff family was functioning well within normal expectations. It was striking that at the last session, Barry, then 26 months old, kissed the therapist goodbye and, without prompting and not in imitation of anyone, said to her, "Thank you." It was hard to resist imagining that he had really known all along that everyone had been doing all of this for him.

Conclusion

This presentation has attempted to describe in some detail the process of intervention with a family in which the parents' relationship with their child and with each other was developing in a variety of destructive ways. Problems were becoming more intense despite both parents' basic concern and love for the child and their deep commitment to each other.

In this family, an extremely difficult birth in a context of financial and social strain had interacted with the parents' own early histories to create extreme stress and disorganization. The mother was locked into a pattern of interaction with her toddler which guaranteed mounting obstacles to the development of his autonomy, her personal satisfaction, and a satisfying relationship with her husband. She was feeling abandoned by her husband, depressed and exploited.

The father, in turn, was experiencing significant anger toward both his wife and his son over his exclusion from their intense relationship. In addition, he was depressed and seriously hampered by internal difficulties as he tried to manage a recent work disappointment and adjust to the demands of the world. He was becoming increasingly alienated from his wife and his son.

Despite a basically positive relationship between them and despite basic abilities to provide a nurturing and very positive environment for their son, the parents were seriously considering divorce.

The 16-month-old boy in this family was excessively dependent upon extremely frequent bottle feeding and his mother's constant attention. He showed rather muted affect, his range of affect was restricted, and his language skills were lagging. At the same time, he was a basically intact youngster who was well loved, who experienced that love, and who had been provided an environment which was in many ways adequately nurturant and protective. Without intervention, however, the child would certainly have escalated his demands and become more tyrannical, and he would doubtless have remained locked into a destructive relationship with his mother.

Treatment for this family took a variety of forms both in content and structure. It was necessary to meet with all members of the family together but also to exclude the child at times so that discussion of certain material would not be inhibited by his presence. The child's periodic attendance at sessions was necessary, however, for purposes of careful observation of him and of his parents' interaction with him. In addition, the boy's presence provided a valuable affective, in-the-moment impetus to the parents' expression of the feelings he evoked in them. Along with these conjoint and family sessions, a brief series of individual sessions with the mother allowed exploration of important issues.

This treatment accomplished several tasks. The therapist had first of all to understand with the parents the pain and fear which had surrounded their baby's birth. In addition, it was necessary to explore the anger and anguish the father experienced at the disruption of his relationship with his wife as the traumatic delivery and the child's continuing presence interfered with the couple's sexual and temperamental adjustment. The father needed help in refraining from visiting upon his son certain conflicts stemming from his own history. Similarly, the mother in this family needed to disentangle from the present a number of concerns from her childhood which were driving her to respond to her son's every need and whim. Her own pain, anger, and overidentification with her child had to be sufficiently worked through to free her of their paralyzing influence. Finally, throughout the work both parents were guided to an understanding of their son's behavior and, particularly, the meaning of his expressions of concern or anxiety. This approach served not only to clarify for them what responses were appropriate on their part, but simultaneously to set a model for empathic understanding. The child himself responded quickly and positively to the shifts in his parents' ability to interact with him more appropriately. Basically, he was a rather easygoing, accommodating child whose contribution to the dilemma had been minimal.

This intervention occurred in a context of very high motivation on the part of both parents to resolve a painful impasse and to move forward. Within nine months of the beginning of treatment, they and the therapist agreed that neither the marriage nor the parents' relationships with their son was any longer in jeopardy. There was every reason to assume that barring severe external difficulties in the future the family would continue to progress. All later reports confirmed this prediction. The birth of a second child was met with pleasure by both parents and caused no unusual adjustment difficulties in the family.

Reference

Fraiberg, S., ed. (1980), *Clinical Studies in Infant Mental Health: The First Year of Life*. New York: Basic Books.

3

Infant-Parent Psychotherapy During Pregnancy

Alicia F. Lieberman, Ph.D.

This case illustrates the application of infant-parent psychotherapy in a family situation where the baby is as yet unborn but already at risk for affective disturbances due to parental distortions and projective identifications.

Infant-parent psychotherapy is a method of intervention developed by Selma Fraiberg and her colleagues to treat families in which there is severe conflict between the parents and their baby (Fraiberg, 1980). In this approach, the baby is seen as a representative either of important figures from the parental past or of an aspect of the parental self that is repudiated or negated. Treatment consists of an integration of nondidactic developmental guidance, emotional support, and psychoanalytically oriented psychotherapy in which the links between the parents' past and their present experience with the baby are explored and interpreted in ways that lead to insight. Throughout this process the baby remains the focus of the treatment through the provision of developmental information, discussion of parental concerns about the baby, and un-

Selma Fraiberg was the consultant in this case. I am deeply indebted to her insights.

derstanding of the parents' conflicts with the baby in light of their past experiences.

Infant-parent psychotherapy has been effective in bringing babies suffering from disorders of attachment to developmental adequacy in affective and socioemotional functioning (Fraiberg, Lieberman, Pekarsky, and Pawl, 1981). An important extension of the technique involves situations where pregnancy is experienced as conflictual by one or both parents. In such cases, the unborn baby has already been drawn into unresolved parental conflicts, with the distortions in parental perception that this entails. Treatment then properly focuses on the parents' fantasies of the unborn baby, on their fears and wishes regarding the baby's impact on their lives, and on any disturbing early memories awakened by the pregnancy.

Lieberman and Blos (1980) have documented the usefulness of preventive infant-parent psychotherapy during pregnancy with a woman whose early experiences with her own mother had led to neurotic conflicts regarding her ability to love her unborn child. The present case illustrates the importance of preventive intervention with a couple suffering from severe character disorders manifested in a long history of violence and alcohol addiction. Although both parents were now free from their addiction, the pregnancy triggered in the mother intense fears that her past would return, while the father struggled with fears that he would fail at being a father just as he had failed at everything else in his past. Both parents were afraid that the baby would become the target of their rage should they feel overwhelmed by parental responsibilities.

Eva was referred to our program from the Midwifery Clinic at our hospital. She was 42 years old and thirty weeks pregnant with her first child. The reason for the referral was Eva's combativeness toward her physician, who was concerned about the mother's severe hypothyroidism and its possible effects on the unborn baby. Eva had refused medication and wanted to remedy her condition through herbal infusions, which the physician considered ineffective. A stalemate between mother and physician had been reached, with angry confrontations between them. The staff at the Midwifery Clinic believed that Eva's attitude reflected an underlying ambivalence regarding her pregnancy, and hoped that we could help her accept the physician's advice. Eva welcomed the referral.

As it often happens, this crisis over medication had been resolved by the time Eva met the therapist. In the first session, she explained that she had agreed to follow the physician's advice and take the medication prescribed, but went on to complain bitterly that an altercation with the physician had been needed before she could get a referral to a mental health program. For months, she said, she had been talking to the midwives about her ambivalence toward this pregnancy, about her fear of not being able to love her baby, and about her sense of being trapped into being a mother only because, at 42, she no longer had the choice of waiting a few years until she felt ready to have a child. None of these feelings, she complained, had been taken seriously enough by the medical professionals to prompt the offer of referral to a psychotherapist. It was only when the baby's welfare was at stake that she was offered help. This statement was the first manifestation of a theme that would recur during treatment: the feeling that she was secondary to the baby, that, in Eva's words, she "counted only as the baby's carrier." The fact that this intelligent woman had not herself sought the help of a psychotherapist but chose to feel let down by the physicians is, of course, also telling. As Eva's history unfolded, this feeling could be understood as the expression of a pervasive pattern of feeling displaced and superseded by her younger siblings.

The Assessment Period

At the Infant-Parent Program, intervention always begins with an extended assessment. This period comprises between

five and seven weekly sessions, which ordinarily take place
in the home, although at least one office visit is scheduled for
a videotaped developmental assessment of the infant and a
free play sequence between infant and parents. (In Eva's case,
the visits took place in the office, since there was no separate
baby as yet whose everyday home routine it was important
to assess.)

The assessment process is designed to evaluate not only
the infant's affective, social, and cognitive functioning and the
quality of the parents' caregiving practices but also, and more
important, the parents' willingness to accept intervention and
their ability to use it on behalf of their baby. In this sense,
the assessment process has a built-in and very deliberate element of intervention. By carefully timed clarifications and
interpretations, and by close monitoring of the parents' responses, we gather information about their ability to use introspection and to establish links between their difficulties
with their baby and their own conflicts as individuals. In this
way we can arrive at important conclusions as to the potential
usefulness of treatment for this family.

During the assessment period some of Eva's remarks
raised concern regarding the possibility of a thought disorder.
On one hand, she spoke poignantly about her ambivalence
toward the pregnancy. She said, for example, "I feel nothing
toward the baby, no excitement, no love, no nothing. There
is a block inside me that does not let me love my baby. And
I want to love it." On the other hand, Eva said that she was
not concerned about having a mongoloid child (her physician's
dire warning if she did not take medication for her hypothyroidism) because she believed that "God sends defective children to people who are strong and can cope with them. Having
a defective child is a gift, not a punishment. Only special
people can give a mongoloid child the love he needs." The
implication was that having a mongoloid child would mean
that she was special. This was also why Eva refused amni-
ocentesis, which had been recommended because of her age.

When the therapist asked about her reasons for finally agreeing to take medication for her hypothyroidism, Eva replied, "I had a vision of the baby. It was beautiful and perfect, and made me feel that I did not need to take medicine, that the baby would be all right. But my husband said that in the vision I could not know whether that was the way the baby looked because I took medicine or in spite of my not taking it. That made me realize I had responsibility both toward my husband and toward the baby. So I agreed to the treatment."

Adding to our concern regarding a possible thought disorder was Eva's ready analogy between the task of caring for her several beloved pets and the obligations posed by a new baby. She expressed some fears that the baby might be allergic to animals, a situation that would force her to give the baby away because she "had the animals first." She described in elaborate detail her pets' ability to plot practical jokes on her, to show surprise if she returned home earlier than she had told them she would, to defy her by doing the opposite of what she advised them to do, and to laugh about her among themselves. All this was described in a jovial tone, as if Eva were speaking of pesky but lovable creatures. As we soon learned, the jovial tone was tinged with anger whenever she spoke of the unborn baby as an equally pesky but much less lovable being.

As the therapist explored with Eva the reasons for her ambivalence toward the unborn baby, she readily said: "I am afraid that the baby will make my past return." She then spoke of her adolescence and young adulthood as a time of turmoil and self-destructiveness. Her description of this period made it clear to us that there had to be earlier difficult experiences as well.

Eva described herself as the "momma" of a notorious motorcycle gang, hooked on alcohol and amphetamines, involved in interstate drug trafficking, always fleeing the police and the FBI. She had been married to one of the gang's leaders, whom she described as a "drug fiend." Nick had abused Eva physically and mentally. He inflicted deep wounds in her leg with a knife, and severe scars still remained from this attack. He had also been involved in two automobile accidents so severe that both he and Eva had almost bled to death on both occasions. Moreover, Nick threatened to kill Eva if she tried to leave him. For years Eva had fantasized that he would die in a shoot-out with the police, and wished him such a death, both as revenge and as a means of liberation. Instead, however, Nick drowned in a swimming pool while stoned on Angel dust. This peaceful death was a great disappointment to Eva, who had nurtured in vivid detail her fantasy of Nick's death. The discrepancy between this fantasy and the reality was so strong, she said, that for a few days she could not reconcile herself to the fact that he had died in a different way from what she had envisioned.

Soon after Nick's death, Eva became convinced that she would also die unless she could break the cycle of using amphetamines during the day and alcohol at night. She joined several organizations to fight addiction and had succeeded in breaking the habit seven years before becoming pregnant. Two years before the assessment, she had married a man several years younger than herself; he too had a turbulent past and had recovered from an addiction to alcohol and drugs. Eva described her present marriage as idyllic, but feared the baby would shatter her relationship with her husband and plunge her back into her former addiction. Since becoming pregnant, she had dreamed repeatedly that her first husband was not dead but had returned to claim her as his legitimate wife. Eva feared that these dreams were a portent of the danger she was facing: that becoming a mother would be so stressful that she would be tempted to drink once again. She also reported that she was waking up at night crying, "I don't want the baby."

As we traced the origin of Eva's use of drugs, she said that her mother used to give her whiskey, codeine, and paregoric when she was very little. Eva remembered liking the feeling. When she was a young child, she learned to sneak into the liquor cabinet; by the time she was 13 she was regularly drinking until she passed out. Her parents, she said, never noticed the steadily decreasing level of liquor in the bottles because they seldom drank. The therapist expressed amazement that her parents did not notice her passing out. Eva said that her father was an extremely withdrawn and occasionally violent man, and that her mother was "strange," "out in a world of her own." When a few years back Eva told her that she had just celebrated her fourth "sobriety anniversary," the mother expressed mild surprise at her daughter's alcoholism, of which this was the first hint she had. She showed no shock and, more important, no interest in pursuing the topic. For Eva this was a sadly familiar response. Talking to her mother, she said, was like "talking to a wall." What Eva said "never made any impact on her."

Eva's mother soon became a regular topic in the sessions. Eva recalled her mother telling her that she had never wanted to have children. The oldest of five children, she had lost her own mother at 14. The father subsequently abandoned the children, and the four youngest ones were sent to foster homes by the state. Eva's mother was sent to live with a maternal aunt, dropped out of school, and worked very hard to support her siblings and bring them out of foster homes. Her life's dream of becoming an engineer could never be realized. Instead she married an engineer and went on to have five children, just as her own mother had done. Eva was the oldest, precisely her mother's position among her own siblings. Eva remembered being made to take care of the others at a very young age. Her most fervent wish as a child was to be left alone, but she found herself constantly interrupted in whatever she did. If she read, her mother would call on her to feed one of the babies. If she played, the play had to be interrupted because another sibling needed changing. Not surprisingly, Eva described herself as a child whose happiest moments were when she was alone. Although her mother did not work, Eva did not remember spending time alone with her, except for occasional outings to the park.

Eva wanted to grow up in a hurry in order to be autonomous, and proudly recalled her mother's saying that as a baby she learned to run before she walked. Yet growing up also became a trap. An example: as a young child, Eva had for some reason conceived of washing dishes as the ultimate symbol of being a grown-up. She confided this fantasy to her mother, who told her that when she reached a certain height, she would be allowed to wash dishes. Eva eagerly awaited that day, measuring herself often and making marks on the wall. When she was finally tall enough, she was allowed to wash dishes as promised. But from that day on, washing dishes became her daily obligation. When she protested, her mother replied: "You said you wanted to do it, now you do it."

As Eva remembered her past, the therapist made occasional sympathetic comments and observed her response in order to assess Eva's ability to use the therapist for the exploration and understanding of affective experiences. Although somewhat guarded in the overt expression of emotion, Eva seemed able to acknowledge some of the pain she had experienced as a young child and was receptive to the possibility of a link between those experiences and her present difficulties. One example stands out. As Eva enumerated her many chores as a substitute mother to her siblings, the therapist commented on the burden of having to take care of children when she herself was a child. Eva nodded her agreement and remained silent for a while. She then made the connection the therapist was implicitly pointing to. She asked: "Do you think that is why I now have mixed feelings toward my baby?"

The answer to this question, of course, was given by Eva herself as she continued to talk about her past. She tearfully remembered her parents' lack of involvement in her life and the complete absence of rules that might help her decide what was right and what was wrong. Her mother told her that if she attempted to set rules, the children would disobey them anyway, so she did not bother to do it. Eva remembered her longing to have firm answers to her questions about issues such as when she should be home from a date. But her parents' answer was invariably, "Whenever you think it's right," and Eva looked at her friends' parents for guidance in these matters. At one point she bitterly said, "I guess that kind of child-rearing is all right if you can survive it."

During the third session, Eva announced that she had been able for the first time to buy some clothes for the baby. She was elated because until then, although well advanced in her pregnancy, she had been unable to prepare in concrete ways for the baby's birth. Shyly, she said, "So you are curing me." The therapist asked how Eva thought the cure was happening. Eva answered that she was not sure, but that she thought that talking about things that had bothered her for a long time was helping. Again, this was an indication of Eva's intuitive understanding that the root of her present problems lay somewhere in the past. While we remained concerned about the possibility of a thought disorder, Eva's capacity for introspection led us to the working hypothesis that such a disorder might be either circumscribed or linked to Eva's intense anxiety about her pregnancy. Treatment was certainly indicated, and Eva seemed ready for it. The therapist extended an invitation for treatment with the explanation that this process would entail a continued exploration of how Eva's past was reappearing in her present feeling toward her pregnancy.

Eva agreed readily to this invitation. She then said thoughtfully: "I am ready to be counseled, now that I got used to the idea." Addressing the underlying ambivalence, the therapist asked her how it felt to be a counselor being counseled (Eva had worked as a detoxification counselor with drug addicts until the sixth month of her pregnancy). There was an instant flash of acknowledgment in Eva's eyes as she replied: "Tough!" She went on to explain that she had been a

detoxification counselor for five years, and had recently re-
signed her position to become a housewife and a mother (a
situation that in the therapist's eyes paralleled that of Eva's
mother). There were few counselors as experienced in the
field as she was, Eva said, since most counselors had only a
brief work experience, and she missed her work and the feeling of being worthwhile that it gave her.

While sensing Eva's envy, the therapist chose to address
the incipient negative transference from a different angle. She
said: "It must be hard, being such an experienced counselor,
to come see another counselor about whom you don't know
very much." Eva immediately agreed, with visible relief. She
went on to say that counselors are the worst patients, that
they play games and that they "beat their counselors at their
own game. That way they stop you from getting close to them
and hurting them." The therapist replied that sometimes people put up barriers when they feel the counselor says too
much too soon and when they need some protection until
they feel ready to listen. Eva nodded in agreement, seeming
very much in tune. The therapist then said: "If you ever feel
that you are playing games with me, or that you have to put
up barriers because I am saying things that bother you, will
you please tell me? Then we can look at what is happening
and try to understand it together." Eva promised to be a most
forthright critic, and went on to talk enthusiastically about a
dear friend of hers who had the same surname as the therapist.
The first barrier to treatment had been successfully negotiated
by giving Eva a feeling of control over the treatment process
and a sense of partnership instead of competition with the
therapist.

The assessment period yielded a beginning understanding of Eva's situation that was important in formulating guidelines for treatment. Eva's almost poetic reference to the return
of the past in the future reflected an accurate perception of
her predicament. What she could not know was that what she
feared had already occurred: the past was being reenacted in

the present, but in ways that were unrecognizable for Eva. The past she was consciously afraid of was her tumultuous immediate past, which was itself shaped by long-suppressed early experiences. It was the feelings attached to these early experiences that were now making a forceful return, shattering the balance that Eva had painstakingly achieved over the last few years.

From the information gathered during the assessment, it seemed plausible that Eva had been subjected to both psychological and physical abuse by her distant, self-absorbed mother and a withdrawn father who had outbursts of violence. Eva's much-resented obligation to be her siblings' caretaker seemed superimposed on an inner depletion and unfulfilled longings to be taken care of. Eva's response seemed to be an identification with the aggressor that had many layers of meaning. By becoming an addict involved with a violent motorcycle gang, Eva was simultaneously defying the parents who had not given her the guidelines she yearned for; living a lifestyle which was consistent with her low self-esteem and which perpetuated the physical and psychological abuse she had experienced in childhood; inflicting this abuse on others; and trying to fulfill her unsatisfied needs through drug and alcohol abuse.

It was unclear to us how Eva had rescued herself from the addiction, violence, and lawlessness that filled her past, but it was clear that the unborn baby had rekindled the impulses that had led her to that earlier lifestyle in the first place. The unborn baby had become the representative of those earlier babies that, in Eva's childhood perception, were guilty of harassing her, depleting her, and robbing her of her childhood to convert her into a precocious, unwilling, and angry mother. The therapist's task would be to understand the mechanism that linked the present unborn baby to the earlier ones, and to help Eva reexperience the earlier feelings in connection with their legitimate, original recipients: her parents and siblings.

Treatment Begins: The Initial Sessions

In the sessions that followed, the predominant theme was Eva's fear that the baby would destroy her relationship with her husband, Sean, and make her lose all the gains that she had made in overcoming her addiction and starting a new life. As the therapist probed these fears, Eva spoke of her conviction that she would feel "left out" whenever her husband spent time with the baby. Her husband, she said, was ecstatic over her pregnancy, and in fact she had only agreed to having a baby because of her deep love for him. She now feared that he might not be able to love both her and the baby at the same time: that he, in fact, would be so enthralled with his baby that he would have little time left for his wife.

Exploring the feeling of being left out led to increasingly intense memories, first of the recent past, later of her childhood. She spoke of how her first husband, Nick, had taken a young lover whom he brought into the marital bedroom, and how the three of them had slept together in the same bed. Eva remembered feeling very much left out. She then remembered vividly her suspicion that this girl was a police informant. "I hated her so much that I told her I would kill her if Nick was not around." The girl believed the threat and disappeared forever, much to Nick's annoyance. When the therapist asked Eva if she really intended to kill this girl, she replied: "You bet."

The therapist commented on Eva's anger that somebody had come between herself and her husband, an anger so intense that it had made her want to kill. The therapist then asked whether Eva had experienced those feelings before. After thinking for a long time, Eva spoke of how angry she had been at her mother when she was pregnant with her fifth child. She said, "It was terrible. When my little sister was born, I was thirteen. I wanted to kill my mother and I wanted to kill my baby sister by cutting into my mother's stomach. When the baby was born, I could not look at her for two weeks, I refused to be in the same room with her for two weeks. Later on, when I was fifteen and my little sister was two, I was supposed to take her to the beach. I remember all these cute guys, and I was walking trying to look good and my little sister used to call me mama. I yelled at her to shut up, that I wasn't her mama."

Again, as before, the therapist sympathized with the burden of having to take care of a child when herself a child, and went on to restate the connection between Eva's early experience and the present prospect of taking care of another baby as yet unborn. Eva replied thoughtfully that she really did not feel as if she were 42, that psychologically she felt quite young, certainly not at the stage where she would like to have a child. The therapist commented that Eva was only now beginning to enjoy the freedom she had not had before. As a child, she had to do things that were beyond her age, and then she had spent many years locked in a marriage and a lifestyle that were painful for her. The therapist added that she could well understand Eva's fears that her baby's birth could put her back in a situation where she was not in control of her actions. Eva agreed with tears in her eyes.

This theme was continued in the following session, which Eva began by complaining about her inability to fix up the baby's room. She could not even walk into the room, she said, let alone buy furniture or make drapes. The therapist asked what Eva felt when she thought of fixing up the room. She thought for a while and said, "It feels just like moving." She then went on to talk about what moving meant for her: rootlessness, constant pursuit by the FBI, being forever suspicious of friends and acquaintances who might denounce her, the danger of drug traffic across state lines. As she spoke, she again went on to talk about the violence, about guns and shooting and people being killed, both by the police and by other drug dealers. And she again remembered her husband's lover, whom she had wished to kill. The therapist said that when Eva had first talked about wanting to kill this woman, she had also remembered that she had wanted to kill her baby

sister even before she was born. Eva seemed receptive to this
parallel, and the therapist enlarged the analogy by pointing
out that this baby sister was somebody else who had come to
change things for Eva in painful ways, just as her first husband's lover had changed things for her by coming between
her and her husband. Eva thought for a while and said, "You
know, I always had this fear that I would squish a little puppy
or a little kitten, or a baby, squish them real hard and kill
them. I have always been scared of that impulse, for as long
as I can remember. I think that what terrifies me is that I
might feel like doing that to my baby." The therapist said,
"And you really want to protect your baby from that impulse
that you are so afraid of." Eva said yes. She then remembered
that once her girlfriend had asked her to hold her baby. Eva
had agreed, but as she held the baby, she became increasingly
scared of harming him. She ended up panicking, and screamed
to her girlfriend, "Take this thing, take this thing." The therapist commented that Eva was trying very hard to protect the
baby from the impulse that she feared so much. Eva said,
"Yes. I knew that the baby was innocent, that he hadn't done
anything to me. Like maybe there was this baby three weeks
ago that did something wrong to me and I felt like killing him,
but I didn't want to transfer that feeling to this baby here
right now, who didn't do anything to me." The therapist said
that perhaps there was a baby that, in her view, had "done
something wrong to her," not three weeks ago, but perhaps
a long time ago, when she was a little girl. Eva looked very
thoughtful. The therapist added: "Perhaps you don't want to
transfer those feelings to the baby that you are carrying right
now, the baby who is innocent of the things that happened
to you then."

Eva looked very sad, and said that she had been trying
to remember what happened when her mother was pregnant
with her first brother, and her parents had promised her that
this baby would be a gift to her. Eva believed this promise.
But when the baby was born, the parents took the baby into

their bedroom, and left Eva all alone in her room. The therapist said, "It must have been awfully lonely to be in that room at night, knowing that your baby brother was with your parents in the grown-ups' room." Eva said yes. The therapist then made the connection with the present by adding: "No wonder it is so hard to go into the baby's room right now." Eva answered, with tears in her eyes, "I never thought of that. Maybe you are right." She then went on to talk about how little attention she had received after her baby brother was born.

When the therapist inquired about Eva's feelings for her little brother, Eva said that whenever she thought of him, she could only remember her fear of smothering a little chick or a puppy or a kitten. She added: "Maybe when I was little, I accidentally smothered some animal, and that's how the fear started." The therapist said that young children confuse wanting to do something with actually doing it, and are afraid that feeling something is equal to doing it. She added that maybe Eva had been so upset at her baby brother that at times she felt like smothering him, even though she never did it. Eva's eyes filled with tears. She sobbed for a few minutes, and then spoke again about the loneliness and the disappointment of her brother staying in her parents' bedroom and getting all the attention she once had. She then said, in a choked voice, that maybe she had been so angry that she had wanted to kill her brother. The therapist said, "Maybe the feeling, when it comes, is so very scary because it almost feels like it is going to become an action." Sobbing, Eva blew her nose and said, "Maybe that's what makes me so panicky about having this baby."

The therapist asked what Eva meant. Eva said, "I think I'm afraid that this baby will be so much trouble that I'll feel like smothering it too." The therapist said, "Yes, maybe the feelings that you had toward your brother are now coming back and are making you afraid of hurting this baby. And you want to protect this baby, you do not want to hurt it." Eva cried for several minutes. She then said, "It is such a relief to know that I am afraid of hurting this baby because I really want to protect it. That means that I really love it." In later sessions, Eva and the therapist were able to link Eva's fear that the baby would come between herself and her husband with the early experience of feeling displaced by her brother in her parents' affection.

Until the emergence of this material, which was pivotal in the treatment, Eva's husband Sean had not participated in the sessions despite repeated invitations extended to him through Eva. The therapist had understood his absence as a sign that Eva needed to work through her conflicts about being left out before she could bring her husband into the treatment. Each of Eva's siblings had left her feeling empty and displaced in her mother's affection. We believed that Eva could safely invite Sean in only after these feelings had emerged and become conscious. And indeed, as predicted, Sean came in for the first time after this session.

How can we understand what happened? In the supportive context of treatment, Eva had been able to remember and examine her murderous impulses toward her first sibling, who had displaced her from her parents' affection. The therapist then made explicit Eva's unconscious equation of that first sibling with the baby she was now carrying. Most crucially, the therapist helped Eva to understand her fear of her murderous impulses as an effort to protect her unborn baby and, hence, as an indication of her love for it. In siding with Eva's embattled and perhaps impoverished ego, the therapist was providing her the kind of supportive, ego-building experience she had lacked in her childhood and adolescence, when the absence of clear and caring parental guidelines had left her unable to counterbalance her aggressive impulses with loving, nurturant ones. The therapist's intervention reassured Eva that she was capable of experiencing love and that she had the desire to protect and nurture her baby. The relief clearly experienced by Eva was eloquent proof of her agony in thinking of herself as capable only of rage.

As is apparent in the process notes excerpted above, there were many alternative approaches to interpretation. The therapist could have used Eva's anxiety about her murderous impulses to explore further into her past—for example, to delve into the possible oedipal implications of her parents' promise that the sibling would be Eva's own baby, or into Eva's perception of the parents' breach of that promise. Such an approach would no doubt have been fruitful in the context of individual treatment for Eva. But the thrust of our therapeutic task was not to understand the intricacies of the maternal psychodynamics; it was to enable her to surmount the emotional conflicts that stood in the way of her becoming a mother with a positive emotional investment in her baby. This therapeutic goal informed clinical decisions about what material to seek and what interpretations to make. As the mother's history and psychodynamics became better understood, the therapist chose to focus on and to pursue the material that seemed promising for helping to resolve the conflicts Eva experienced around her baby and her role as a mother. This goal underlined the technique of linking the emerging experiences and feelings from the past with the feelings that Eva reported toward her pregnancy, her unborn baby, and her role as a mother.

Eva's Husband Joins in the Treatment

Sean's presence changed drastically the affective atmosphere of the treatment. A tall, bearded, profusely tattooed, and tough-talking man, he filled the initial session with a mixture of bravado expressed in four-letter words, a recital of his many virtues and grandiose plans for the future, and finally a touchingly timid confession of his fears and of his physical disabilities (he had recently had a disk problem and was still experiencing some pain). Eva seemed half embarrassed and half amused as he monopolized the session by talking about himself, explaining in painstaking detail the financial difficulties and interpersonal complexities of his job as a delivery truck driver.

After the first hour of a very long first joint session, Sean finally broached a topic that was clearly of great concern to him: Eva's labor and delivery. At first he presented his own role as an auxiliary one: he would be there simply to assist Eva, and his feelings were of no importance since the delivery was not "his trip." As both Eva and the therapist reassured him that this was a "joint trip" and that his feelings were important, he started talking about his guilt for putting Eva in a situation that she wanted only partially and where she would have to endure physical pain. He explained that Eva had agreed to have a child because he wanted one, and he now felt guilty because Eva was having so many mixed feelings and he did not know what would happen. Eva hastened to remind him that she had also been actively involved in the decision to have a child, and assured him that although she had not wanted children in principle, she did want a child with him. "I would not have a baby only for you, not even for you, dear," she said, playfully but tenderly.

Sean then went on to speak of his fears of being present in the delivery room. He spoke of his discomfort in situations where he was not in control and had to defer to authority figures. He wanted the delivery to go smoothly, but when he was uncomfortable, he said, he became angry, and when he was angry, he often resorted to physical attack. The therapist asked whether he was afraid this would happen during the delivery. He said yes. He was afraid that if the nurses or doctors were bothering Eva or "ordering her around," he would first ask them nicely to leave her alone, but if they did not obey he might "punch their noses or crack their heads." The therapist commented lightly that this would certainly have the opposite effect of what he wanted—to help make the delivery go as smoothly as possible for Eva. Both Eva and Sean agreed.

As Sean spoke of his fear that he would attack the doctors or nurses, Eva also began to express her own fear that she would react violently if she felt out of control. For both Eva and Sean, who had lived for years outside the law, violence had long been the customary way of responding to frustration, anger, and fear. They had worked hard to find alternative modes of expression, but feared that under the pressure of the delivery they would fall back on their most familiar response.

The therapist then said that they had two tasks ahead. One was to plan the practical aspects of the delivery so that the doctors, midwives, and nurses were aware of Eva's and Sean's wishes and had an opportunity to negotiate alternatives should the parents' wishes run contrary to the usual practices at the hospital. This procedure would ensure that the parents and the medical personnel knew each other's positions and agreed on a delivery plan, thus minimizing the chance of unpleasant surprises for the parents and the possibility of angry outbursts at the staff. The second task was to work with Eva's and Sean's feelings, so that once they were in the delivery room they would find it easier to remember that a bossy nurse was nothing more than that, not an awesome authority figure in control of their lives. Eva and Sean laughed and found this plan quite congenial.

At the end of the session, with his hand on the doorknob, Sean revealed the very concrete reasons for his fear of his own violence. Noting that the entrance door was kept locked, he asked, "Did you have any break-ins?" When the therapist answered that there had been a few, Sean remarked in an offhand manner: "That's what I went to jail for the last time, in 1978."

Still with his hand on the knob, Sean spoke for fifteen minutes about his various experiences in jail. "One night in jail my buddy and I got loaded and I went crazy. I tried to kill him with a chain saw. I got transferred to San Quentin for that. Six months. That was really awful. Lousy food. The guards steal your food and beat the shit out of you to keep you in line. Just like on the outside. When I was outside, I was working for this drug king. I had to take care of the guys that were giving trouble. Knocking heads, if you know what I mean. I'm glad I got out of that. Eva and I are in another space now."

While it might be true that they were in "another space," it was also very clear that both parents were struggling very hard with the encroachment in the present of a violence-laden past.

Joint Work with the Parents

In the next few sessions, Sean continued to talk a great deal about his life. He spoke about the years of being a "dope fiend," constantly on the run. He would decide one day that he had had enough, take a suitcase, and leave everything and everybody behind to start the same lifestyle again somewhere else. "I could leave everything because I did not care about anything or anybody, I only cared about myself." He talked about betraying people, about being betrayed, about not trusting anybody and not being trusted in return. He talked about making a lot of money and using it all in his arm, "shooting up"; he also talked about being so abjectly poor that he made detailed plans to kill the drug dealer he was working for and make off with his money. Eventually Sean gave up on this idea because he was convinced he would be discovered and sent to jail "for good." He decided instead to go straight, and asked his landlord, who took a special interest in rehabilitating people, for help. This man lent Sean some money, got him a job, and helped him get in touch with Alcoholics Anonymous and other similar organizations. It took a long time, Sean said, and added: "Now I find that the straight life is much easier. Even when things are difficult, it is much easier. For one thing, people trust you." Eva agreed, saying, "If you are sleazy, nobody trusts you, and that is hard."

The therapist commented that the past seemed to be coming back with great force, and added that having a baby often did that, it forced people to remember their past because they needed to prepare for the future. Sean agreed, and said thoughtfully that he had been thinking a lot about becoming a father. And, he added, there was some news that made him think even harder. The day before, in her medical checkup, Eva had been told that the baby was in a breech position, and that a Caesarean section might be needed unless the baby turned around. "I keep telling that little asshole to get his ass in gear or I'll kick the shit out of him." The therapist said lightly that, with that kind of warning, it would not be surprising if the kid was too scared to even move. They laughed and Eva said, "I tell him it's either the Caesarean or his bicycle, that we don't have money for both."

It was clear that in spite of the laughter this was a most serious topic and that these parents might easily resort to violence as a way of disciplining their own child. Although this was not yet an immediate reality, it was an important topic to pursue, partly because it reflected the parents' perception of the unborn baby as willfully inflicting pain on them, and partly because their comments opened the door for preventive intervention before violence actually occurred.

As the therapist inquired about their thinking about physical punishment, both parents said it was the natural way of teaching a child not to do things he was not supposed to do. The therapist disagreed, and asked them whether they themselves had been physically punished. Both parents said yes. The therapist asked them to remember how they felt at the time. Both said they could not remember. The therapist said that this was quite understandable, that when children were hit they felt so much resentment and fear that they tried very hard to forget those feelings when they grew up. After a long silence, Sean turned to Eva and said, "Maybe that is why I feel the way I feel toward my parents, honey."

Slowly, Sean started talking about his parents. They were both "lightweight" and he did not respect them. His mother was a "sniveling bitch"; his father was an alcoholic who was "Mr. Niceguy" to everybody but Sean, whom he beat often and for a long time. Sean then remembered an episode that had occurred when he was 5 or 6 years old. He and his friend were throwing dirt clods from a hill onto the highway below. At one point, a car was passing by and Sean did not see it because he was further back, but his friend enticed him to throw a dirt clod right then. The clod fell on the car's windshield and shattered it. The driver got out of the car and caught Sean's friend, who readily told on Sean, who had run away. The man went to Sean's house and spoke to Sean's father, who went out with a tree branch in his hand to find his son. When they met, the father held Sean by the arm and dragged him home while hitting him in the leg with the branch until Sean's leg was bloody. Describing the scene, Sean said, "At first I cried, but then the pain turned into hatred and I stopped crying. I did not want to show any feeling. My father started yelling at me, saying, 'Cry, for God's sake.' But I refused to cry. That is the last time I remember crying in front of anybody. From then on, I only felt rage. He didn't even let me explain."

Sean remained silent for a while, his eyes reddened, trying to compose himself. He then said, "I don't understand why I was so scared at first and then I could only feel anger." The therapist said it was easier to be angry than to be scared. "You were so frightened, and there was nobody there to help you feel less scared. So you had to help yourself, and used your rage to protect yourself from that fright." Sean's eyes filled with tears, and he sobbed for a few minutes. He then said, "And I've been carrying that rage inside me ever since. I could never do anything else with it."

After he regained some composure, Sean looked at Eva and asked her how he had started talking about his childhood. Eva said that they had been talking about spanking their baby so he would get in the right position and Eva would not need a Caesarean. There was a silence. The therapist then said to Sean, "I can understand better how you feel about Eva having a Caesarean. You have suffered so much, and now it's hard to think that the woman you love can be hurt like that and you can't protect her. Eva's pain makes you so scared that once again it's easier to feel the anger." Sean's eyes filled with tears again, and he again sobbed for a few minutes. He then put his foot on Eva's chair, and Eva rubbed his foot gently. Eva then said, "We will not let it happen, honey. That baby is still going to turn around." They talked quietly with each other for a while, lightly trying to reassure each other. The therapist then said, "I think that you are trying very hard to find new ways of raising your child, to overcome your own childhoods and the way you were raised. You are trying very hard to raise a child that will not have the memories that you have and that you are still struggling with." Sean sighed and said, "That's exactly true. And, man, is it hard." The therapist said she knew it was hard and added that the important thing was that they had the courage to look at those feelings now, before the baby came, and to come to grips with them. The therapist added that the feelings would probably still be there after the baby came, and the baby would reawaken other feelings, but they were already finding ways of handling them. The therapist also cautioned the parents that the intensity of the feelings they spoke about might make them want to stop talking about them for a while; they might even find that they did not feel like coming for the next few sessions. They might also find themselves upset at the therapist because the feelings were so strong that they could spill over. Both Sean and Eva denied firmly that this would happen, and said they felt ready to continue working on their feelings.

Preparation for Labor and Delivery: Work with the Parents

Sean was present in two of the four remaining sessions preceding the delivery. His absence was explained to the therapist in terms of his work schedule; however, it is also likely that he both needed to maintain some distance from the highly charged affective material that was emerging, and that there was an unspoken understanding between Eva and him-

self that Eva would continue to have individual treatment
sessions. No effort was made to explore these possibilities,
since both parents seemed to be using the sessions quite
effectively to get a grip on the issues that were tormenting
them.

The material that emerged in these sessions revolved
around two main issues. The first issue was Eva's fantasies
about the fetus and her fear of how she would react to seeing
the baby immediately after birth. The second issue, described
in its essentials in the previous section but reworked again in
the course of the two sessions in which he was present, was
Sean's fear that seeing his wife in pain would trigger in him
an irresistible impulse to attack the medical staff. These two
themes were linked by a concrete concern: the possibility of
a Caesarean should the baby continue in the breech position.

Both parents perceived the baby as willfully refusing to
turn around. Eva, in particular, believed that the baby knew
what it was expected to do and was too stubborn to do it.
When asked to elaborate on this perception, she said airily,
"My pets know what they are expected to do. Sometimes they
do it and sometimes they do precisely the opposite just to
show us that we can't order them around. Why should a kid
be any different?" (Not since the first session had there been
such worrisome evidence of the possibility of a thought disorder.) This comment was followed by many others reflecting
Eva's perception of the baby as stubborn, willful, and determined to have its way. This perception triggered in turn Eva's
wish to retaliate. "If the kid cries at night, I will feel like
sticking it in a closet so it will learn that I won't be manipu-
lated." The therapist speculated that the possibility of a C-
section was mobilizing in Eva a profound fear of body damage,
which in turn elicited rage and the wish to punish the perceived cause of this damage—the baby.

The therapist's effort to explore Eva's possible fear of
body damage led in some fruitful directions. Eva revealed
that for many years she had been unable to experience pain.

For example, she had burned herself while ironing, but did not know it until hours later, when she happened to glance at the burn. "I guess I learned to turn off my dopamines when I was little." Eva went on to talk about being beaten by her father with the buckle of a belt whenever she did something wrong, and recalled trying to "live through that by pretending it did not hurt." These memories led to her recalling many violent scenes with her siblings while she was growing up. Eva remembered that on one occasion she had raised a knife over her brother during a fight. She said the scene was still in her mind "as a dream," devoid of emotion. Yet she knew herself capable of experiencing deep rage. The therapist asked whether she also knew herself capable of acting on that rage. Eva said yes. Bringing the theme of anger back to the imminent delivery, the therapist said, "No wonder you are so worried about the delivery. You experienced violence all your life, and you learned to defend yourself through violence. And now you are facing a situation where violence will not protect you, a situation where you have to submit your body to somebody else and hope that they will not hurt you."

This interpretation, repeated many times with slight variations, had far-reaching effects: it led Eva to talk about her lifelong fear of dependence, a theme that she had alluded to in earlier sessions when she spoke of her wish to "grow up in a hurry." Now she described episodes in her past in which she had gone to great lengths to avoid asking for help even in tasks that she clearly could not complete unaided. She remembered crying with frustration because she could only reach to within a quarter-inch of the ceiling where she wanted to hang a planter, and straining for hours to bridge the gap so that she would not need to resort to a taller person for help. She also recalled spending half a morning moving a huge rug from one end of her room to another, a little at a time, again in order not to ask for help.

The therapist asked how Eva explained to herself her reluctance to depend on others. Eva talked at first at a rather intellectualized level about her mother's unavailability and her loneliness as a child. She then said, almost casually: "As a matter of fact, I used to confuse my mother with my aunt who lived with us. I used to call that aunt Mom. And sometimes when one of them came into the room I did not know who it was, whether my mom or my aunt." As one memory brought another, Eva spoke poignantly about this aunt, who took her everywhere, read her stories, and allowed her to help in the kitchen. Then, when Eva was 4, this aunt decided to move to another city. She left and never came back, leaving only a box of books behind. Years later, Eva still liked to look at the books while thinking about her aunt. Remembering, she said sadly, "Maybe that is why I learned to read at four."

The therapist sympathized with the feelings of loving and losing somebody, and added that such an experience could well have made Eva feel that she did not want to rely on anybody anymore, for fear of losing them again. It was easier to be an independent grown-up; this way, she could hope to avoid the sadness of being disappointed in her love.

Eva agreed thoughtfully. She then began to speak of her dog, Clarissa, who according to Sean was restless whenever Eva was gone, and waited for her, moaning softly next to the door. Eva wished Clarissa could be content with Sean's presence and not miss her so much. The therapist said, "It's hard to need somebody and it's also hard to be needed." Eva replied, "She doesn't really need me. She's just laying a trip on me so I will feel guilty and not leave her. I bet she's not next to the door all the time. I bet she's doing her thing and as soon as she hears me she rushes to the door and pretends that she has been there all along."

The therapist commented that it was easier to think that Clarissa was playing a game because Eva loved Clarissa so much that it would be painful to think of her as really suffering while Eva was gone. Eva replied, with much feeling, "Well, I would not want to leave her if I knew she suffered. And I don't want to be trapped, never going out by myself even for an hour just because I don't want her to suffer." The therapist said, "Does it have to be either that Clarissa is only laying a trip on you, or that she suffers so much that you can never leave her?" Eva considered this for a while. Then she said, "No. I tell Clarissa when I'll be back by tapping on the table, once for every hour I'll be gone. Then she knows what to expect. And she stays with the cats, or with Sean, so she knows she'll be well cared for until I come back." The therapist said this was a very thoughtful way of handling separation. Eva then spontaneously made her implicit worries quite clear: "But will it work for the baby?" The therapist responded with some developmental guidance, speaking to the issue by linking Eva's easy intuition regarding her care of the pets with the needs of a baby: making separations gradual, helping the baby understand what would happen through clear greetings and departures, providing familiar and trusted substitutes. When coached in the language of what her pets needed, this information became less frightening to Eva. She was clearly relieved that babies were not mysterious organisms, that they were not all that different from her pets.

Using the pets' feelings as a launching point to explain a baby's needs proved fruitful in releasing Eva's empathy for her unborn child. In the following session, Eva said, "You know, I thought that I would just leave the baby in its room and let it cry at night if I felt too tired to get up, but now I feel differently. The whole family sleeps in the master bedroom: Sean, me, Clarissa, the cats. Why should the baby be any different? I'll put the crib in our bedroom for the first few months so the baby doesn't feel left out."

From identification with the aggressor, casting the baby off to a lonely room the way she had been cast off by her parents when her brother was born, Eva had progressed to an empathic identification with her unborn baby. The infant had joined the family.

Further Preparations for Labor and Delivery: Liaison with the Medical Staff

At the same time that the infant-oriented psychotherapy with the parents was taking place, the therapist also took concrete steps to minimize the chances of violent parental behavior during the delivery. The therapist spoke to Eva and Sean about their wishes, fears, and fantasies about the medical procedures and about the midwives' delivery practices. Unlike some mothers, Eva had no objection to intrusive medical procedures should these prove necessary. But she had very strong feelings about some of the practices used by the midwives to enhance early parent-infant interaction. She particularly disliked the idea of having the baby placed on her stomach: "All that artsy-craftsy bonding stuff gives me the creeps." She also disliked the use of dim lights: "Please ask them not to have dim lights. Dim lights drive me nuts. I know that's supposed to be good for the baby to come in with violins in this wonderful semidarkness resembling the womb, but *I* need bright lights to keep my sanity." And, most emphatically, she did not want painkillers even in the event of a Caesarean because she was afraid they might trigger her addiction again. When the therapist suggested that she could consult with the doctors about a painkiller that contained no addictive substances, Eva's face took on a pained expression as she said, "You don't understand. When I worked as a counselor, these addicts would come in with prescriptions given to them by their doctors. I would look at the chemical components in the PDR and invariably there were potentially addictive substances. Most doctors don't understand how vulnerable ex-addicts are to most substances." Eva also wanted to have only local anesthesia in the case of a C-section. "Total anesthesia freaks me out. I am afraid of breaking down if I have it."

Sean concurred with his wife's concerns, and added his own. He wanted the staff to consult with them before "taking over"; he wanted to be told what would be happening before people began "handling Eva and doing things to her." Serious consideration was given in these sessions to the question of whether Sean would be present or not in the delivery room should a C-section be needed. Both parents preferred to defer a decision, and to see how they were feeling at the time.

With the parents' permission, the therapist met with the medical staff to discuss her own concerns about the possibility of parental violence and to apprise them of the parents' wishes and their reasons for them. The staff was sobered by the therapist's account, and they had no objections to changing their management procedures to meet the parental requests, which seemed to them reasonable. A delivery plan was written up, reviewed by the parents, approved by the medical staff, and put in Eva's chart so that everybody present during the delivery would have ready access to the guidelines. Eva and Sean relaxed considerably after this task was completed, and anticipated the delivery with less tension. Their mood (and the therapist's) lightened considerably when in the weekly checkup before Eva's due date the physician announced that the baby had turned around and was now in position for a vaginal delivery. A C-section would be most unlikely. Eva and Sean greeted their offspring's move with a relief reminiscent of parents whose toddler agrees to end a tantrum. The therapist was grateful that an aggravating element was likely to be absent from the delivery situation, as parent-infant interaction was already at high risk.

Reesa Is Born

Reesa was born one week after Eva's due date. She was a beautiful, placid baby of average weight and length and in excellent health. As the physician had predicted, the C-section had not been necessary, although the baby was in a transverse position and labor and delivery had been long and, by Eva's account, painful. One complication was that the placenta had not been delivered spontaneously and Eva had screamed in pain and refused when the midwives attempted to remove it manually. "I had reached my limit—I could not stand one more second of pain." The midwives agreed to remove the placenta surgically, but this presented the problem of giving Eva total anesthesia, which she feared because she thought the experience might trigger her addiction again. The problem was solved to Eva's satisfaction by the anesthesiologist, whom she praised warmly and who induced a "gentle sleep" before giving her the substance that would make her experience a "high."

Eva sounded happy and relaxed on the phone when she notified the therapist of Reesa's birth, although she spoke for twenty minutes about the delivery without mentioning the baby. She was particularly relieved that Sean had been "wonderful" during the entire process, remaining very attentive to Eva's welfare during the full day of the labor and delivery and negotiating nicely with doctors, nurses, and midwives. "Things between us were fantastic. It was a wonderful experience between us, although I would like to forget all about the delivery."

When she finally began to speak about the baby, Eva said, "She's long, but she doesn't weigh very much. And she's actually pretty." To the therapist's question of what the baby was like, Eva replied, "Pretty good, but greedy. It is hard to pry her off the breast."

In a hospital visit a day later, the therapist observed parents and baby together for the first time. The scene when the therapist entered the room was a lovely one: mother, father, and baby were cuddled together in the mother's bed. The parents were speaking softly and looking at the baby. Reesa was an unusually beautiful newborn who nursed well, cried seldom, and was readily soothed. She turned readily to the human voice and established eye contact with her mother when Eva spoke to her. She seemed like a rewarding baby who would not pose extraordinary demands on a mother's resources of patience and nurturance.

During the hospital visit, both parents seemed enchanted with the baby. They praised her looks and her temperament and expressed a quiet confidence that things would go smoothly for themselves and their baby. But even more impressive than their investment in the baby was their pride in themselves. Eva said, "Even when I yelled at the midwife to stop trying to get the placenta out, I knew I was not going to lose my temper and kick her in the stomach." Sean admitted having had fantasies of "kicking everybody out." He then said, "I remembered what you said, that a bossy nurse was not a prison guard even if she reminded me of one. That made me feel calmer." Both parents praised the medical staff for their patience, understanding, and willingness to explain to them what was happening. The medical staff on their part praised the parents for their self-control. One of the midwives commented to the therapist: "One could sense the potential for anger, but we all tried our best, and the parents really co-operated. And I tell you, it was a hard delivery."

In light of the real hardships of this delivery, the parents' ability to use their growing understanding of themselves to control their impulses was a very encouraging sign for their emerging relationship with their daughter. Yet Eva's initial comment about the baby's "greediness" sounded dangerously similar to the earlier perceptions of the unborn baby as willful and stubborn. Both before and after birth, Reesa was perceived as someone with murky motives and inclinations that Eva would have to grapple with.

The First Six Months: Maternal Distortions Emerge

After Reesa's birth, most of the weekly sessions took place in the home. Sean continued to be present periodically, but it was clear that he wanted the freedom to come or not to come, as he wished. His presence was always a sign that a joint issue between parents and baby needed to be worked on: his absence allowed Eva to continue exploring her own difficulties with her baby, something that she was clearly reluctant to do freely when Sean was present. This arrangement seemed satisfactory for both parents, and the therapist decided not to interfere with it.

During Reesa's first month of life, the therapist observed that Eva's and Sean's interactions with their baby were unfailingly appropriate. But Eva's descriptions of Reesa soon began to reflect increasing distortions in her perception of the baby. These distortions were both positive and negative in their affective tone. Eva believed, for example, that Reesa's motor skills, linguistic abilities, and capacity to make sense of the world around her far exceeded the capacity of other babies of the same age. She credited the baby with being able to turn over in her crib and crawl, to laugh at conversations between Eva and Sean, to reach for and grab appealing objects such as a little doll, and to throw away objects she did not like, such as the pacifier Eva sometimes used as a replacement for the breast. Eva was radiant with pride as she described these abilities.

Eva was particularly struck by what she called Reesa's sense of humor (something that she also delighted in when it came to her pets). She described in detail the "jokes" that Reesa played on her during feeding. In one of these instances, Reesa had stopped sucking and had her eyes closed. Thinking that the baby was asleep, Eva very gently tried to get her nipple out of the baby's mouth. Suddenly, Eva reported, Reesa opened her eyes with a "big smile." Eva interpreted this response as an "I-fooled-you joke" in which the baby was pretending to be asleep in order to catch the mother un- awares. When the therapist asked Eva how she felt about this joke, she answered, "Oh, I loved it. It is really funny to see what she considers to be a joke. It's like the fifth-grade joke about what is green and furry and had a hundred feet. Reesa and I laugh about that one a lot."

There were other distortions that were negative in affect and hence more immediately worrisome. Several of these involved feeding. Eva often conceived of Reesa as a greedy and uninvited guest at her breast. She believed that the baby pulled up the mother's nightgown at night, nursed, and then pulled the nightgown down again so Eva would not notice that the baby had had a clandestine sip at the mother's breast. (Reesa was brought into the parents' bed for the 2:00 A.M. feeding and was often not returned to her own crib in the parents' room.) Once Eva even suggested that the baby had jumped from her crib to the parents' bed and had helped herself to the breast. The mother found no other way of accounting for the unusual lightness of her breasts on that particular morning.

Other negative distortions involved, not surprisingly, the baby's aggression. Once, when the baby's hand lightly touched Eva's cheek, the mother said, "Are you hitting me? I am not hitting you . . . yet." On other occasions, Eva commented that the baby "pulls hair real good" and "gets big handfuls of hair off my head." She also complained that the baby had the "temperament of a speed addict," with a few days of intense activity interspersed with a day or so of sustained quietness and prolonged sleep.

Eva's tone in making these comments was initially either amused or flippant, but as the first month progressed she became increasingly less tolerant with what she perceived as the baby's constant demands. Gradually, Eva's anger at her baby became focused on one particular area: feeding. Eva's initial description of the baby as greedy had been an early sign that this might become an area where Eva's conflicts would be played out. Yet she at first denied any difficulty in feeding her baby, and spoke proudly of her abundant milk and sturdy nipples. She acknowledged finding nursing more a routine than a source of pleasure, but her affect remained neutral whenever she spoke about this topic and she seemed competent and self-assured when she fed Reesa in the therapist's presence.

Indications of trouble were given indirectly. In a session when Reesa was 3 weeks old, Eva persistently ignored the baby's fussing. She finally offered a pacifier, which the baby refused. Eva asked the baby whether she was hungry, but she did not offer the breast. The therapist asked when Reesa had eaten last, but Eva said only that she did not remember and did not elaborate. This sequence contrasted sharply with Eva's sensitive responsiveness to her baby in previous visits. It was clear that something was amiss.

Looking for a tactful way of addressing Eva's failure to remember the baby's feeding schedule, the therapist commented that maybe she had had a hectic morning and could not remember what had happened when. Eva replied that she had not had breakfast herself that morning, things had been so hectic. The therapist commented that perhaps when Eva did not eat herself it was hard to remember about Reesa's eating. Eva laughed and said that in the rush she could not remember anything. She then began to feed Reesa and changed the topic.

The therapist waited for an opportune moment and returned to the topic of feeding. She commented that Eva's failure to eat breakfast made her worry that Eva was not taking good care of herself. Eva responded in a sullen, angry voice that she did not have time to take care of herself. "Meals are always being postponed. I never eat on time anymore. When I am getting ready to eat and Reesa starts crying, I feel that she's interfering with my well-being and threatening my health."

The therapist listened with sympathy and elicited some information about the daily routine of baby care and household chores. It emerged that Eva's own eating habits involved many snacks throughout the day instead of three main meals. Sleeping also involved many "catnaps" instead of one long stretch of sleep. Eva resented the baby's intrusion in this routine. She said that she could no longer eat in peace because whenever she cooked the baby smelled the food and woke up crying for it. "And when I am hungry, I have to eat right away, I can't wait because I get ravenous and get a headache and stomachaches. And there is that baby screaming and not letting me eat."

The therapist asked whether Eva had ever tried putting the baby to the breast while she was having a meal. Eva said that she could not do that because eating was something that she had to do alone and with intense concentration. She disliked to eat and talk, or even to eat and read. Anything that detracted from her complete absorption in eating was an un-welcome interference. Eva went on to explain that Sean felt the same way. It had taken them one year of strained polite-ness over shared meals, but they had finally confessed to each other that they preferred to eat alone. Now Sean ate in the bedroom watching TV, while Eva ate in the dining room thinking her own thoughts.

As Eva continued to speak about eating, it became in-creasingly clear that this activity was closely linked with her sense of self and that she was fiercely protective of her privacy whenever she felt someone might interfere. She spoke of how her first husband had once attempted to snatch a morsel from her plate, and Eva put her fork on his hand and threatened to drive it through the flesh if he stole her food. He never did it again. She also remembered mealtimes at her parents' home, which were marked by angry yelling among siblings. "Sometimes I doubled up in pain at the end of the meal, I was so tense. And I was always afraid I would not get what I wanted because somebody might have taken it before the platter came around to where I sat."

The therapist commented on the many kinds of hunger that Eva had experienced as a child, hungers that she had struggled with and that nobody had helped her satisfy. It was no wonder, the therapist added, that when those hungers came up now Eva had to satisfy them right away and could not tolerate delay. Eva answered sadly: "There are all kinds of hungers I tried to satisfy in whatever way I could. That's why I used speed and alcohol and I don't know what else. And I always was a compulsive eater, although I was always very skinny. I have always been ashamed of how skinny I was, but I could never gain weight."

In the following session Sean was present and gave a new slant to the unfolding theme of Eva's hungers. Turning to his wife, he said, "There are lots of hungers that you never talk about. Like when you told me yesterday that you had been horny the whole week and were waiting for me to start. How could I know?"

The theme of sexuality thus made its appearance in the sessions. It emerged that both Sean and Eva had used drugs in their respective pasts to make sex "more kinky" and their interest in sex had waned since they had stopped using drugs. Sean complained about Eva's lack of interest, but it was apparent that for both of them it was easier to attribute their sparse sexual activity to Eva's lack of interest than to Sean's or to the relationship between them. As they spoke about their relationship, it was clear that this couple, both of whom had enormous difficulties controlling aggression, had resorted to elaborate rituals to protect each other from their anger. In the process of suppressing aggression, they had also suppressed sexuality, but this was an acceptable price to pay for the preservation of their relationship.

The therapist knew that addressing the dynamics involved in this situation was beyond the therapeutic agreement with the parents and beyond the therapeutic goal that had been set. Accordingly, the therapist limited herself to supportive intervention in this area, encouraging increased communication between Sean and Eva about their desire to have sex and about their likes and dislikes in lovemaking. Interestingly, three weeks later Eva commented that they no longer enjoyed eating separately: they were taking their meals together and conversing about the events of the day while they ate. Eva could not understand what had happened but welcomed it as "a new way of feeling close to Sean." In a later session, she referred obliquely and with much shyness to an improvement in the sexual arena as well.

This work represented a temporary diversion from a direct focus on the baby, but the urgency of Eva's conflicts regarding her child made itself felt very soon again. In a sequence of sessions in which Sean was absent she complained of an intense desire to give Reesa away. She did not quite know how to do it, and went over and over different alternatives, only to find that every plan had a drawback. If she yielded to fantasies of leaving home, she knew that she would leave not only Reesa but also Sean and the pets, and she felt unable to live without them. If she left Reesa on the doorsteps of a church or a hospital, as she often wished to, she feared that Sean would kill her for giving his baby away. (This fear had some basis in reality: Sean had threatened to kill her when Eva presented the plan to him in a moment of despair.) Eva found herself worrying also that nobody would understand the baby and care for her as well as Eva herself did. Hence every plan to leave the baby ended in a paradox: Eva found it unbearable to relinquish the baby's care to somebody else, but also found it unbearable to carry on with it.

Searching for an understanding of these feelings, the therapist asked when the wish to leave the baby had begun. Eva said that the baby had lately become very fussy, and that she had episodes of screaming, getting purple, and thrashing about with her arms and legs. Eva complained that she had no patience for this behavior. The therapist said that she would like to understand more about Reesa's behavior. Could Eva talk about the sequence of events that led Reesa to scream so intensely?

After much exploration, it finally became clear that, by Eva's own account, she was waiting "anywhere from one second to half an hour" before responding to Reesa's cries. The therapist suggested that Reesa's most intense crying might be occurring when Eva waited half an hour before responding. Eva readily agreed, and asked with some reluctance whether she should respond sooner. The therapist answered that half an hour was too long to wait for a young baby, and went on to offer some developmental guidance by saying that babies depend on the people around them for help with their needs, and crying is a way of signaling those needs. If they get no help, they get increasingly more desperate and cry more and more as the needs become more intense. The therapist added that unmet needs can lead to experiences of panic and disorganization in the baby, and that Reesa could well be having such experiences when she had to wait a long time before her crying was answered. With this comment, the therapist hoped to address Eva's own firsthand experience with the feelings generated by unmet needs.

Eva was silent for a few minutes, and then said that it scared her to think of her daughter as experiencing panic. In a more plaintive tone, she then objected that she had things to do—take a shower, dry her hair, make dinner, fold the laundry. She could not always be interrupted, and the baby needed to learn to wait. The resonance from the past was clear in her words. As a young girl, Eva's mother had forced her to stop what she was doing and attend to her sibling. As an adult, Eva was now doing what she could not do then: make the baby wait until her own needs were met. Eva's desire to give the baby away could be understood as the wish to flee from a situation in which she was either victim or aggressor; victim if she postponed her own pleasures to respond to her baby, aggressor if she did not. Either way, the memory of unmet needs was inescapably reawakened, her baby's unattended cries and her own rage as she reluctantly responded serving equally well in this regard.

In attempting to pursue these links with the past, however, the therapist met with unexpected resistance on Eva's part. With her eyes full of tears, she said, "I know there is a painful childhood behind me, I know that I was never happy as a child and that I always wanted to grow up. But I don't know if I care about the connections and I don't know what I'm going to get out of it. All I know is that every once in a while I have this feeling that I am living a life that I don't want to lead, that I want to run away. I think that it's almost like the three faces of Eve, that there is an Eve inside me that is not Reesa's mother and that is dead, and I'm mourning because I don't want her to die."

The therapist heard this statement as a poignant protest against the treatment focus on Reesa's welfare and on Eva's feelings as a mother. Once again, as many times in her past, Eva felt left out. This time the feeling was triggered by a therapist who was listening not to Eva but only to Reesa's mother.

The therapist spoke to this feeling, and Eva acknowledged with deep embarrassment her wish to have more of the therapist's attention. Quickly resorting to the flippant humor that served her so well as a defense against pain, she then said, "You are not giving me what I want, Mommy." But she could not pursue directly the genuine feeling behind the satire. Instead she began to speak about a previous therapeutic experience many years before. Eva was desperately seeking help for feelings of anxiety and worthlessness, but found herself unable to talk to her counselor. After a few initial sessions, this counselor told Eva that he had a salary and did not need Eva's money, and that he was wasting his time because Eva was unwilling to face her problems and work on them. He then announced that he would stop treatment with Eva because there were too many other people who could make better use of his help. Recalling the scene, Eva said, "I was so incredibly hurt. I could not believe that he was throwing me out just like that."

The present therapist expressed sorrow and horror about this experience. She then said, "Could it be that when you get angry at me for trying to find the links with the past, you are afraid that unless you are willing and ready to look for them I will also throw you out?" Eva laughed and cried at the same time, and said, "Yes. I was so happy when after the first few sessions you asked me if I wanted to continue. I was so grateful to you. I was afraid you would say to me that I was not ready for therapy, that you had your salary and did not need me and that you were going to use your time on somebody else."

This confession led to an exploration of transference feelings which led back to Eva's intense fear of dependency and her determination to fend for herself. As the transference feelings were explored and clarified, Eva was able to empathize with her daughter's experience when she waited to be fed. "I hate to wait to eat; why should she like it?" But she still believed that if somebody had to wait, it should be Reesa.

The themes of waiting and of unsatisfied needs led to Eva's own dissatisfaction with Sean. She complained that she was forced by her present circumstances to depend on him, yet she was unsure about his reliability. He had been fired for cursing over the truck's shortwave radio, and the financial situation was tight. But even more difficult for Eva was Sean's attitude toward the baby. He liked playing with Reesa but took for granted that Eva should take over whenever the baby cried or needed to be fed or changed. This made Eva particularly bitter, because throughout the pregnancy Sean had promised her that he would step in whenever she felt overwhelmed by the baby's demands. This information gave additional meaning to Eva's fantasies of giving the baby away: it was a way of retaliating against Sean's failure to live up to his promise.

It was very difficult for Eva to talk about her anger toward Sean, even when he was not present in the sessions. For this woman, for whom feeling was so closely tied to action, discussing feelings of anger and disappointment presented the serious risk of her taking impulsive action. Once again, as she had done during the pregnancy, the therapist stressed that feeling and talking need not be translated into action. She also stressed that feeling angry did not negate her deep love for Sean. This permission for ambivalence was an important revelation for Eva, similar in its importance to her early discovery, during pregnancy, that fearing her impulses to hurt the baby showed the love underlying the anger.

Once again, as during the prenatal part of the treatment, Sean started attending the sessions after Eva had come to grips with an important issue in her own individual treatment. And once again, Sean became the center of the ensuing sessions by talking about his problems with violence. Much work was done helping Sean understand the difference between feeling like cursing and actually doing it (the reason for his dismissal from his job), talking with him about the different expectations he encountered in the white-collar world he was now seeking to enter and the world of "dope fiends" he had once frequented, and encouraging him to find new ways of expressing his anger. Here, too, as in the work with Eva, feelings toward the therapist had to be carefully watched and sometimes explicitly elicited. The therapist's role as an auxiliary ego helping Sean with his reality testing implied that she often had to say unpalatable things. While these things were phrased in respectful ways, the impact of her remarks had to be carefully gauged to ensure that they did not elicit violence. To his credit, Sean was remarkably candid. Once, for example, he referred obliquely to fantasies of breaking the therapist's jaw. The therapist responded that this would cause many troubles for both Sean and the therapist, and added that the whole point of the sessions was to find ways of avoiding such trouble by finding words to replace the actions. Sean replied: "I'm so relieved that you are not scared of me. If you were scared, I would really feel like hitting you."

This comment opened the way for an exploration of the link between feeling rejected and reacting with violence. This link was vividly illustrated in Sean's response when Reesa cried and he could not console her immediately. Reesa's cry then felt like a rejection, and Sean had an intense impulse to hit her. It was then that Sean gave Reesa back to Eva.

Understanding each other's feelings of being overwhelmed helped this couple find solutions for helping each other. Eva became more tolerant of Sean's occasional withdrawal from the baby. Sean, in turn, became better able to offer concrete assistance to Eva. This was particularly evident in the stalemates that occurred between Eva and her baby when both were hungry at the same time. Sean said that he could not eat anyway when Reesa screamed, and suggested that in such a situation he would give Reesa a bottle until Eva finished dinner and felt ready to offer the breast. Eva was at first afraid that Sean's offer to feed the baby would contain an implicit criticism of her mothering, but she finally agreed with relief to the plan.

In ensuing sessions, the parents reported that this system was working smoothly. Reesa's screaming declined, and Eva no longer mentioned any desire to leave the baby. Sean commented: "It helped me when Eva told me about your comment that Reesa could be disorganizing. We know all about that, and we don't want Reesa to find out about it." He added a comment that showed there was still reason to be worried about the parental perceptions: "Reesa has the temperament of a speed addict." Eva readily agreed and said, "We want her first words to be 'beer' and 'Valium.' That way, if someone asks her what she wants, she won't answer that she wants speed, like we did." Even this comment, worrisome as it was in its implications, was said in a light and accepting tone very different from the earlier complaints of the baby as malevolent and willful.

Reesa was present throughout these sessions. Her presence enabled the therapist to assess both the accuracy of the parents' perceptions and the adequacy of the child's development. The observations yielded no evidence that Reesa had an unusually "intense" temperament, as the parents believed. She was a baby with unusual sending power, whose signals of pleasure and distress were clear and who was readily satisfied once her needs were attended to. She remained a beautiful baby, with sparkling eyes and a ready, contagious smile. During the period when Eva complained of the baby's fussiness, the therapist did note an increase in the baby's irritability and some frantic tone in her search for the mother's breast, which she often used for comfort. This could be readily understood as a response to Eva's unpredictability. Since by her own account Eva would either respond immediately or wait as long as half an hour, one can surmise that the baby had difficulty developing reliable expectations about her mother's availability. However, the baby's frantic search for the breast as a means of comfort proved short-lived. This behavior declined as Eva became better able to respond promptly to the baby.

The technique of treatment was modified substantially after Reesa's birth. During Eva's pregnancy, her fears that the past would return could be readily linked to childhood memories, which flowed with remarkable ease. After Reesa's birth, Eva spoke less directly about her childhood, and the transference to the therapist and her feelings toward Sean became much more relevant in understanding her difficulties with Reesa. It is possible that this shift was due to the powerful oral needs evoked by the baby sucking at her breast. Her fears during pregnancy that she would harm her baby could be linked to the rage she experienced as a child for having to become the mother of her mother's children. The feelings experienced after Reesa's birth were more diffuse and much more primitive. To protect the baby, Eva had to supplement her understanding of her feelings with her husband's concrete assistance because she needed to satisfy her own needs before she could become available for her baby. As Eva was reassured again and again of both her husband's and her therapist's availability, negative attributions to the baby occurred more and more rarely. When they did arise, their appearance usually signaled the presence of negative feelings toward either Sean or the therapist, which when explored and understood could be readily detached from the baby.

The importance of the transference during this period illustrates a delicate technical problem in infant-parent psychotherapy: the need to balance the treatment focus on the baby with an awareness of the potential for maternal feelings of envy and rejection. In mothers with a relatively sound character structure who suffer from neurotic conflicts in mothering, the commitment to the baby usually supersedes the conflicting feelings of envy and resentment, and the therapeutic focus on the baby can be sustained with relatively few disruptions. In mothers with severe character disorders, however, feelings of depletion, rage, and deprivation may become so overwhelming that treatment might paradoxically have to temporarily depart from the focus on the baby's well-being in order ultimately to serve it best.

The Second Six Months: Positive Distortions and Their Treatment

The decline in negative attributions to the baby led to a shift in the focus of treatment to Eva's claims that the baby was capable of reasoning and judgments that, in our present state of knowledge, are deemed to be beyond the capabilities of an infant. In themselves these distortions seemed harmless. They involved, for example, Eva's conviction that Reesa could recognize letters, thought TV commercials for sugar-frosted cereals reprehensible, and got excited when she overheard her parents talking about a possible trip to the zoo. But the distortions were worrisome nonetheless, as they involved a faulty interpretation of Reesa's behaviors, the attribution to her of thought processes and motivations she did not have. As Reesa began to acquire the capacity for symbolic representation, it was possible that she might incorporate these maternal misinterpretations into her own thinking, leading to distortions in symbolic representation in the child herself.

Before deciding on a course of action, the therapist tried to gain an understanding of the psychological function that these distortions served for Eva. Through careful listening and observation, the therapist hoped to understand the areas of Reesa's behavior most commonly involved in maternal distortions and the effect that these distortions had on Eva's interaction with her.

The process of watching and listening led to an important discovery. Eva registered the baby's behavior accurately and responded to it appropriately, but assigned to it a communicative intention it could not possibly have. Thus, the distortions, although numerous, could be understood in terms of a basic underlying process: they negated the baby's helplessness and attributed to her communicative skills that, if

real, would in effect give Reesa the power to tell Eva how to
take care of her. For example, Eva described an episode
where Reesa had started to cry without apparent reason.
When Eva looked at her, she noticed that the baby kept
stretching her head in the direction of the crib, which was
next to them. Eva concluded that the baby was sleepy and
was telling her that she wanted to be put to bed. Eva did this,
and Reesa, satisfied, fell promptly asleep. There were many
similar examples. At 8 months, Reesa was credited with purs-
ing her lips for "yes" and rolling her eyes for "no" when asked
if she was hungry. She was also thought to complain about a
tummyache by fussing while tapping her stomach with her
hands.

In some ways, Eva's attributions were similar to the working hypotheses that ordinary mothers use to guide their ministrations to their preverbal babies. The difference was that
ordinary mothers rely on their empathy and on their knowledge of their babies to make educated guesses that they acknowledge as guesses. Eva's own educated guesses could not
be perceived as her own: she relinquished responsibility for
her own decision making to her baby. One can speculate that
she feared the blurring of boundaries that is inherent in the
empathic response, and that she needed to affirm her separateness from her baby by clear role assignments in the communicative process between them. The intriguing feature in
this situation was that Eva could respond with empathy, but
could not acknowledge this to herself.

This formulation laid the foundation for the ensuing
course of treatment. One important decision was not to address distortions that seemed to facilitate Eva's empathic response, such as the examples noted above. Instead the
therapist decided to focus only on those that might lead Eva
to expect a premature self-reliance on the baby's part. Such
distortions were, of course, based on Eva's own conflicts over
neediness and dependence. Just as she wanted to grow up
"in a hurry" when she was a child, she now wanted her baby

to grow up in a hurry and relieve her from the conflicts she experienced over her child's dependency on her.

Eva provided many opportunities to work with these distortions. She reported, for example, that Reesa's face had a disgusted expression whenever somebody affectionately called her "baby," while she beamed with joy when she was called a "big girl." Eva also believed that Reesa looked bored whenever she was told that other babies would come to visit, but was positively ecstatic when told she would play with a 4-year-old. Other reports involved Reesa's perceived frustration when her mother attempted to feed her solid foods because being fed made her feel "like a baby" and she wanted to eat by herself "like a big girl." Eva often preceded anecdotes about Reesa by talking about the times "when Reesa was a baby."

The therapist worked with these maternal distortions in a variety of ways. When Eva's claims about her baby's self-reliance were particularly preposterous, the therapist showed surprise and mild skepticism, which she explained in terms of the departure of the mother's descriptions from "what we currently know about children's development." The therapist also asked Eva to show her the baby's behaviors the next time they occurred so that the therapist could understand better what the mother was describing. This approach often took the form of good-natured banter between mother and therapist, in which the mother teased the therapist for working with children yet not believing in their hidden powers, and the therapist replied lightly that she needed empirical data to be convinced. This teasing enabled Eva to save face by preserving her self-protective view of herself as a counselor speaking to another counselor. At the same time, the mild and respectful skepticism expressed by the therapist enhanced Eva's reality testing, and many times she acknowledged that she was reading too much into her child's behavior.

At a different level of intervention, the therapist responded to Eva's description of Reesa's adultlike responses by sympathizing with her desire that the baby grow up and by cautiously offering links with Eva's own early wishes to become an adult. Eva readily acknowledged her wishes that the baby become more self-reliant, and saw similarities between her baby and herself in this regard. But she was not able to examine these perceived similarities in terms of their subjective component as projective identifications. Neither could she explore how her perception of the baby as a quasi-adult was rooted in her wish that Reesa outgrow infancy. Reesa's adultlike qualities remained for Eva an uncontestable reality. Yet these distortions remained isolated from Eva's actual behavior. She encouraged the baby to achieve locomotion but was not inappropriate or intrusive in doing so. She remained attuned to the baby's signals. And, most interestingly, she continued to breast-feed until Reesa lost interest in the breast at 15 months.

During this period, Sean's participation in the treatment continued to be sporadic. He usually came to the sessions when he was concerned about his performance at work or when there were marital tensions triggered by his tendency to let Eva do all the household work and take care of Reesa. He was playful with his daughter and liked to roughhouse with her, but did not mind avoiding the caregiving routines. This gave rise to periodic tensions with Eva which were usually discussed in joint sessions. Once the tensions decreased, Sean stopped coming again. His was a task-oriented approach to treatment, and Eva seemed to accept this well.

Reesa at 14 Months: Developmental Assessment

The therapist's ongoing observations of Reesa showed that she was developing adequately in all areas. She was an ebullient baby with a radiant smile and laughing, mischievous eyes. She showed clear preference for her mother, whom she sought out both for social exchange and for soothing with a readiness that denoted her confidence in Eva's availability. She was also clearly attached to her father, approached him often, liked to play with his beard, and responded with bellyfuls of laughter when he played "horsie" with her on his shoulders.

Reesa had taken her first step at 11 months, and cheerfully marched throughout the small apartment seeking out the pets, finding minuscule wonders on the floor, and delighting herself with discoveries such as the possibility of playing with the toilet water. She ate well and liked to feed herself; she was also very interested in breast-feeding throughout the first year, although her interest declined progressively thereafter. Breast-feeding was uneventfully stopped at 15 months. She expressed anger and frustration unambiguously but responded well to her mother's firm limits.

The only area of temporary concern was Reesa's sleeping. Throughout the first year, she slept in her crib in the parents' small bedroom, very near their bed. Both Sean and Eva went to sleep well past midnight, and talked, watched TV, and played with the pets on their bed until then. Reesa was expected to join in the fun, and as a result her sleeping schedule was very erratic. This did not worry Eva, who saw no particular virtue in a predictable cycle of sleep and wakefulness. However, this casualness had to end when Sean decided to attend a community college during the day and then work until ten at night to support the family. Nights were then for sleeping, but Reesa had not had an early chance to learn it. For several nights, she woke up crying and seeking to play. Finally, Eva and Sean decided to move the baby's crib out of their bedroom and into the baby's own lovingly decorated room. Reesa's problems with sleeping stopped two days later.

At 14 months, Reesa's performance in the Bayley Scales showed an alert, friendly, and expressive baby whose language and fine and gross motor skills were entirely age-appropriate. Her developmental quotient showed that she was performing one month above the expectations for her chronological age.

The Last Six Months of Treatment

As Reesa achieved locomotion, Eva's perception of the baby became increasingly more accurate. She showed remarkable skill in the process of helping Reesa move away, yet welcoming her return for solace and refueling. She read Reesa's communications accurately and responded to them appropriately. There was a noticeable decline in Eva's need to explain Reesa's behavior in terms of the child's desire to become an adult. As these changes occurred, there was a concomitant decline in Eva's anxiety about her competence as a mother. Eva often consulted with the therapist about aspects of Reesa's behavior that puzzled her but did so with a tone of relaxed curiosity rather than with anxious self-doubt. The sessions took on a relaxed, chatty tone. Everybody had fun watching Reesa. The therapist began to consider terminating treatment.

This mood was interrupted by Sean's dramatic return to the center of the sessions. He had begun college after dropping out of high school fifteen years earlier, and was combining studying with nighttime work to support his family. He was under stress, unsure of himself, feeling he might not be "smart enough to make it." And he expressed this insecurity in an outburst of violence in the classroom: he threatened a female teacher, who criticized him, by hitting her with a chair and raping her. He then fled the classroom, vowing to drop out of school.

The ensuing three months focused on working with Sean on this crisis while continuing the format of home visits with Eva and Reesa present. The result for Sean was successful: he returned to school and ended the year with high grades and with renewed insight into the mechanisms that triggered his aggression.

After the crisis was over, the therapist spoke about Eva's and Sean's self-confidence as parents and about the fine job they were doing raising Reesa. Eva replied, "You know, I've been thinking the same thing. I enjoy seeing you and will be sorry to stop, but I think we can now do it on our own." The old need for self-reliance was reasserting itself, but now it had a solid base supporting it.

Conclusion

The therapeutic process in this case can be divided into four fairly distinct phases, each characterized by a different focus in the pathology of the mother-child relationship and each requiring a different technical approach to treatment.

The prenatal period, which lasted eleven weeks, was marked by intense maternal anxiety over a pregnancy that, although planned, was now perceived as unwanted. Eva sensed that there were profound psychological reasons involved in her fear of becoming a mother, and expressed this unconscious awareness in a beautifully succinct formulation: her fear that the pregnancy would bring back the past. Articulated in this way, the conflict offered the clue to its own resolution: the exploration of the past, the dread of whose return could only be understood by bringing to awareness forgotten but still actively painful secrets.

The process of uncovering early experiences was guided by the therapist's specific goal of bringing insight into the unconscious conflicts underlying Eva's ambivalence toward her pregnancy and her unborn baby. This goal imparted a particular direction to the therapist's interventions. By linking the emerging experiences and feelings from the past with present feelings toward the pregnancy and the unborn baby, the therapist sought to bring understanding to a particular aspect of Eva's neurosis: her unresolved conflicts over becoming a mother. Other neurotic symptoms and conflicts, although perceived by the therapist, were not pursued in treatment unless there was a compelling link with the conflict over mothering. To do otherwise would have run counter to (and hence diluted) Eva's explicitly stated therapeutic goal of coming to love her child.

Indeed, it is quite likely that Eva's remarkable ease in

recalling and affectively reexperiencing early events was due to the developmental crisis brought about by the pregnancy (Benedek, 1970). This possibility is supported by the fact that it was only during this period of enormous psychological turmoil that Eva was able to seek insight through the exploration of intrapsychic conflict. It was a remarkable coincidence that the baby's birth followed soon after a pivotal session in which Eva recalled and reexperienced her early murderous impulses toward the brother that, in her view, deprived her of her parents' undivided affection. After this session the urgency of Eva's self-exploration diminished noticeably, and it never regained its former momentum. It is possible that Eva unconsciously strove to solve this fundamental conflict before her baby's birth in order to protect her daughter from murderous impulses rooted in the past. This task achieved, Eva's previous borderline personality functioning regained stability. The treatment might well have enabled Eva to fend off psychological collapse by relieving her of displaced murderous impulses toward her daughter, relegating those feelings safely to the past, and reassuring her of her present ability to love.

The baby's birth marked the beginning of the second phase of treatment. This phase was characterized by a decline in Eva's motivation for self-exploration and an increase in negatively charged and ego-syntonic distortions of the baby's motives. Eva was clearly resistant to recognizing these distortions as expressions of her ambivalence toward the baby. All attempts, however tentative, at suggesting that this might be so were met by flat and persistent denials. Even when planning dramatic moves such as giving the baby away, Eva refused to look inside herself for clues about the meaning of these fantasized actions. The presenting neurotic conflict over mothering, alleviated through treatment, was superimposed on an underlying character disorder manifested in her marked distortions and the danger of explosive acting-out behavior reminiscent of her past lifestyle.

The only avenue for broaching the feelings of ambivalence proved to be a supportive exploration of Eva's negative transference toward the therapist and her feelings of being betrayed by Sean, who had not kept his promise of rescuing her when she felt overwhelmed by the baby. A focus on these relationships allowed Eva to speak plaintively of her own needs. She was able to express her feelings of being ignored as a result of the therapist's focus on Reesa and of her husband's prevailing interest in his own pursuits. As powerful oral longings emerged, the dilemma that Eva faced became clear. In responding to her baby, this mother had only two roles available: victim or aggressor. Responding to her baby meant postponing her own needs, hence she became a victim. Alternatively, choosing to ignore her baby to attend to herself instantly converted her into the aggressor she both feared and longed to be. Her child's helplessness triggered in Eva unbearable feelings of panic and disorganization. This psychological dilemma made any viable reciprocity with her baby quite impossible.

The technique of treatment in this phase consisted, in essence, in utilizing the transference to reassure Eva of the therapist's interest and availability and in developing concrete safety mechanisms to ensure Sean's psychological availability in periods of stress. Again and again, the emergence of negative distortions of the baby's behavior was met with an exploration of Eva's disappointment or anger with regard to the therapist or Sean. The distortions invariably declined as these feelings were experienced, but the link between these two phenomena could never be explicitly addressed. Intrapsychic exploration had been replaced, in this phase of treatment, by emotional support, sympathetic acknowledgment of Eva's negative feelings toward the therapist and Sean, and the reassurance that anger need not destroy love.

The third phase of treatment coincided approximately with the second half of Reesa's first year. During this phase, the negative distortions were gradually superseded by the predominance of positive distortions centered on what Eva perceived as Reesa's unusually precocious attributes. These distortions served to relieve Eva of any awareness of the empathy needed in order to understand her child. For this mother, empathy was equated with a sense of merger and loss of identity. As a result, her remarkable accuracy in reading her child's signals had to be disguised as stemming not from her own sensitivity but from Reesa's precocious communication skills. An overdetermining factor was Eva's need to negate her child's neediness and to perceive her as autonomous and self-reliant. The treatment technique in this context consisted primarily of nondidactic developmental guidance, imparted in a light, collegial manner that alone could enable Eva to listen without losing face.

The fourth phase coincided with the onset of Reesa's locomotion. In this phase, there was a dramatic decline in the number and intensity of positive distortions, and almost complete disappearance of negative ones. This welcome development was probably a combination of two factors: the beneficial results of treatment and, quite crucially, Reesa's ability to alleviate her mother's fear of merger and helplessness through her own self-reliant mobility.

Sean's participation in the treatment was sporadic but crucial. By coming to grips with his own violence as a response to rejection, he was able to become a more available father and a more supportive husband to a mother much in need of support.

The versatility of intervention techniques was a key feature in this treatment. The insight-oriented technique used during the pregnancy had to be adapted to the new stresses experienced by the parents after Reesa's birth. Even for parents with a sound personality structure, the concrete demands of a real baby have a different psychological impact than the fantasized changes anticipated during the pregnancy. For Sean and Eva, who had painstakingly reached a tenuous psychological balance, the baby's presence and her demands constituted a constant reminder of their vulnerability to violent acting out. As a result, intervention during the postnatal period had to be responsive both to the realistic possibility of violence and to the rigid psychological mechanisms employed by the parents to protect themselves and their baby. Nondidactic developmental guidance, emotional support, and judicious use of the transference predominated over insight-oriented psychotherapy during this period.

Despite the varying thrust of the interventions, the baby and her welfare remained at the center of treatment both before and after her birth. This unwavering focus represents the unifying link in the variety of methods employed in the course of infant-parent psychotherapy.

Epilogue: Follow-up Ten Months After Treatment

Ten months after termination, Eva called to say that Reesa's second birthday was approaching and that she wanted to thank the therapist for having helped her to enjoy her daughter so much. Interestingly, the phone call took place in the same month that treatment had been initiated two years earlier. Reesa's second birthday was still two months away.

The therapist had the distinct impression that this was an anniversary call, and surmised that Eva might want a brief reencounter with the therapist. This impression was reinforced when Eva lingered on the phone, asking questions about the normal development of 2-year-olds in an idle, easygoing manner, as if the contact with the therapist was more important to her than the answers to her questions. The therapist responded by inviting her in for a visit, and suggested that a videotaped assessment of Reesa might be a good way of talking about 2-year-olds. Eva accepted with delight.

A two-session encounter was set up. The first session involved chatting with Eva about herself, her daughter, and her marriage and doing a videotaped developmental assessment of Reesa. The second session, with Sean present, involved viewing the videotape, discussing Reesa's performance and her overall development, talking about Sean's accomplishments since the termination of treatment, and discussing plans for the future.

The family was doing remarkably well. Sean had received governmental loans to finish college, and the financial worries of the past were at least temporarily relieved. He was succeeding at school and planned to pursue a career in acupuncture after finishing college. He spent much time away from home because he studied, worked, and had a strenuous schedule of physical exercise. This was a source of tension between Eva and Sean, but they managed the conflict in ways that protected the stability of their marriage. Eva was planning to return to work on a part-time basis. She believed that Reesa could now stand a few hours away from her without undue stress, and felt the need for more contact with adults after two years as a mother and housewife.

It was quite clear to the therapist that Eva had continued to think about herself and her past since the termination of treatment. Eva reported that she had become very close to one of her brothers, and they often talked with each other about childhood memories. Eva was surprised at the similarity between her brother's perception of her parents and her own. "They were never there for us. We really needed to make it on our own. No wonder all of us had trouble of one sort or another while we were growing up." She spoke with a gentle sadness, as if regretting the past yet coming to grips with it. She seemed to have the same attitude toward her present. She was aware of the limitations in her relationship with Sean: his self-absorption in his pursuits and his tendency to panic when she spoke of her dissatisfactions, so that she needed to keep many of her thoughts to herself. She expressed acceptance of this situation as one that reflected both his and her personalities, and felt relatively at ease with the present balance in their relationship.

Most impressively, Eva had become a mother comfortable with herself and with her child. She was able to negotiate mutually acceptable solutions in conflictual situations and to use humor as an adaptive way of coping with stalemates when she and Reesa could not reach a compromise. She was firm yet matter-of-fact in enforcing rules. She seemed like a veteran mother, largely unruffled by the trials and tribulations of her role. She did get very angry at times, and occasionally slapped Reesa when she was at her wits' end. But she always explained to Reesa afterward that she regretted doing so and that hitting was not a good way of dealing with anger. (Reesa herself seldom used hitting when angry or frustrated.) Eva expected Reesa to understand and follow rules, and was proud of what she called "grown up behavior"—Reesa's ease in interacting with other children and adults, her firmness in defending her toys, her lack of clinginess. Eva often described Reesa as more "grown up" than older children with whom she played. It is difficult to know how true this was. However, Eva's earlier massive distortions in her perception of Reesa's behavior had largely disappeared. The only trace of distortion the therapist could detect was a tendency to overestimate the sophistication of Reesa's speech, particularly sentence length and complexity of grammatical structure. Eva had no difficulty in interpreting accurately and responding appropriately to the *content* of Reesa's communications. Here again, as in the past, it seemed that Eva needed to attribute the success of their exchanges to her daughter's skills, and could not acknowledge that her own empathy played an important role in helping her understand Reesa's competent but toddlerlike communications.

Reesa herself was blossoming. She was a gentle, smiling little 2-year-old who showed delight in her parents and friendly interest in the therapist, and who had a wonderful ability to engage in rich representational play. She cooked for the adults and ceremoniously served dinner, complete with after-dinner coffee; she took good care of a doll, cuddling her, feeding her, and putting her to sleep; she made pies and cooked them in the oven. Her parents reported that she had an imaginary friend named Reggie who lived in the attic and who was responsible for strange noises and misplaced toys.

Reesa had a full range of affect and could be quite forceful in making her wishes known. She had tantrums, which were not long-lasting or frequent and which the parents tended to manage by "timing out," reasoning with her, or sometimes by teasing her for being "a baby." Reesa's performace on the Bayley Scales was approximately three months above her chronological age. She was cooperative and enthusiastic throughout the testing, but tended to give difficult items back to the therapist, with the implicit message: "You do it for me." This may have been related to Eva's emphasis on promoting grown-up behavior. Although Reesa was largely able to comply with the maternal demands, it seemed that sometimes she coped with the pressure by declining to even try. Interestingly, Eva tended to accept Reesa's requests for help and responded to them in a good-natured way.

In summary, the picture emerging from this follow-up was that of a well-functioning family unit, with a thriving child and growth-promoting relationships between Reesa and her parents. The strains and stresses they experienced were well within the range of expectable difficulties in living, and did not pose a danger to the child's development. The changes facilitated by treatment had endured many months after its termination. Further follow-ups are planned for continued evaluation of the enduring results of treatment.

References

Benedek, T. (1970), The psychobiology of pregnancy. In: *Parenthood: Its Psychology and Psychopathology*, ed. E.J. Anthony & T. Benedek. Boston: Little, Brown.

Fraiberg, S. ed. (1980), *Clinical Studies in Infant Mental Health: The First Year of Life*. New York: Basic Books.

———, Lieberman, A.F., Pekarsky, J.H., & Pawl, J.H. (1981), Treatment and outcome in an infant psychiatry program: Parts I and II. *Journal of Preventive Psychiatry*, 1 (1 & 2).

Lieberman, A.F., & Blos, P. (1980), Make way for Abby. In: *Clinical Studies in Infant Mental Health: The First Year of Life*, ed. S. Fraiberg. New York: Basic Books.

4

A Family in a Mental Health Day Care Center: Clinical Assessment Procedures and Services

Peter B. Neubauer, M.D.
Virginia Flynn, M.S.
Christina Sekaer, M.D.

Since 1969 the Infant Care Center of the Jewish Board of Family and Children's Services' Child Development Center has provided mental health services to children in the first three years of life and their families. Some thirty years ago the Child Development Center became one of the first community mental health clinics to address itself to the needs of preschool children; the infant unit represents part of its ongoing effort to reach out more effectively to the population of Manhattan's Upper West Side.

Housed in several apartments on the ground floor of a high-rise New York City Housing Authority building, the Infant Care Center (ICC) serves predominantly black and Hispanic families, many of whom live in the building itself or within a ten-block radius. The ICC staff includes two psychiatrists, two social workers (an administrator and a clinician), a caseworker, a day care supervisor, eight day care teachers (three with graduate degrees), a child psychologist, a public health nurse, a cook, a receptionist, a custodian, a psychology intern, and several social work students.

The ICC program offers a variety of services to parents and children, including full- and part-time day care, mother-infant interaction groups, and individual and family therapy. Relying on community ties built up over the years, staff are also able to help parents use resources outside the ICC to obtain medical care, education, housing, financial assistance, job counseling, and other services. The flexibility of planning made possible by this wide range of services seems to ICC staff to be essential in meeting the multiple, changing needs of the families served.

The ICC's formal day care program aims both to improve the mother-infant relationship and to further the child's development. With two teachers for five to six infants in each of four day care groups, the center provides intensive, individualized care for the infants, who may enter the program soon after birth and stay for up to three years. A social worker sees each day care mother in weekly individual therapy sessions; group therapy for all mothers also takes place weekly. (Fathers and extended family members may also be included.)

Staff are also available to mothers on an informal basis throughout the day. This intense involvement with families provides ICC staff with an abundance of data on families' problems, progress, and interaction. And this very abundance makes our assessment, integrative, and treatment planning procedures crucial to the ICC's operation: we have found that the various staff members working with a family need planned time to share information and concerns and that getting a periodic perspective on a child's development and a family's situation greatly enhances the effectiveness of daily work.

In presenting our work with Mathilda and her daughter Claudia, we will focus on the assessment, evaluation, and treatment planning procedures that guided our intervention. The selected records which we have presented illustrate the data we gather, its recording, and our use of it to increase our understanding of the essential issues. A limited description of the modes of intervention with the child has been included, along with a discussion of long- and short-term aims for Claudia and her family. It should be noted that Mathilda, like many of the mothers involved with the Infant Care Center, had many dependency needs and limited emotional and intellectual resources with which to express, let alone fulfill these needs. Providing mental health services to Mathilda and her family through the vehicle of a long-term involvement with a concrete service—the Infant Care Center—may be one of the few effective ways to learn, albeit slowly, about the capacities and needs of young women like Mathilda and to devise ways of helping them promote their children's development and increase their own abilities to cope, adapt, and grow.

Intake

Intake is a highly individualized procedure at the Infant Care Center. Many of our referrals come from families using the center or their friends and neighbors, as well as from local schools, clinics, hospitals, and drug rehabilitation programs. This intake summary was prepared by the Center's social worker.

INTAKE SUMMARY

Reason for application. We have known about Mathilda since the Infant Care Center started, because her two sisters each had a child at the Center. As a young adolescent, Mathilda made frequent trips to New York from Santo Domingo, where she lived with her father and stepmother. On these visits, Mathilda stayed for periods of time with her adolescent sisters. When Mathilda, then age 16, came to New York in 1978, one of her sisters asked us to see her. The sister felt responsible for Mathilda, who was not going to school with any degree of regularity and who frequently stayed out late at night with her boyfriend. Both sisters complained that

Mathilda would fight with their husbands and at times with them. Most of the fights were over Mathilda's truancy.

Interview. As the Center social worker, I saw Mathilda informally before her first appointment. She impressed me as being withdrawn and shy. I suggested going out for ice cream on our first appointment, thinking Mathilda would be more comfortable doing this rather than staying in my office. Mathilda eagerly accepted my suggestion to have lunch when we were out. Even though she said she wasn't hungry, she ate a complete meal, with ice cream for dessert. Since Mathilda had mentioned to me that she was seeing Frankie, her boyfriend, I asked her to bring him along. She did not bring him until the third interview.

Significant information. Mathilda asked why I wanted to see her. I told her that her sister was worried about her since she was not going to school and frequently stayed away from the sister's house all night. Mathilda was very surprised and responded, "I thought no one cared about me." I told her that both sisters had called me to tell how worried they were about her. I asked what was going on in her life—whereupon she told me she wanted to stay with her boyfriend.

Mathilda appeared depressed and sad, but when she mentioned Frankie, her eyes and face brightened. When I asked about Frankie or school, she did not respond. Mathilda had a blank look on her face, devoid of feeling. She did respond when I asked about her past. She talked about her home town, after hearing I came from there too. She spoke freely about her father and his family, saying that he had remarried after her mother had died when Mathilda was 10 years old. Her father now has two sons, ages 5 and 2. Mathilda said she did not get along with her stepmother. They fought often, but she was very vague about the nature of the arguments. She exhibited more positive feeling when she talked about her half-brothers. She liked them and baby-sat for them. She said she was sick most of the time when living with her father and stepmother, and gave the impression that being sick was im-

portant to her. She described in great detail a bout with sal-
monella, when she was 14 years old, which had resulted in
a two-month hospitalization and in missing a year of school.
Mathilda said that she couldn't remember much about her
mother except that she was very beautiful and that Mathilda
used to sleep with her frequently and grab her breast. She
mentioned that her maternal grandmother used to take care
of her mother.

When Mathilda had come to New York at age 16, she
had lived for a while with her maternal grandmother, then
about 90 years old, but because of boredom did not stay with
her long. She moved to one sister's house and then to the
other's, had fights in both homes, and decided she wanted to
stay with Frankie. When I asked Mathilda whether she was
using any birth control, she told me she wasn't, because she
wanted to have a baby. When I questioned her about the
reality of taking care of a baby, she could only say, "I don't
know."

The second time we met we continued to speak about
the baby. Mathilda was convinced that she wanted a baby.
I called the Manhattanville Prenatal Center, where she had
gone, and spoke to the social worker, who said that Mathilda's
case had been closed since she had told the staff that she
wanted to have a baby. When I asked the worker why no
additional counseling had been offered to help Mathilda with
her decision, she agreed that this should have been done.

Frankie seemed more realistic than Mathilda in assessing
the role a baby might play in their lives. He did not object
to Mathilda's using birth control. He was concerned about
not being able to take care of a baby financially. He was
supporting himself and Mathilda on the thirty dollars a week
he received as a superintendent's helper. In addition, he was
given the use of a very small one-room basement apartment.
Frankie seemed very protective of Mathilda.

Evaluation. In summary, Mathilda is a 16-year-old girl
whose intelligence appears very limited. She is sad, helpless,

and vague about many things. Her mother died when she was 10 years old, after a long illness. Mathilda had always been taken care of by many people—her mother, grandmother, father, stepmother, and sisters. She had moved back and forth many times between Santo Domingo and New York City and did not seem rooted in any one place. Her schoolwork had always been poor, and her illnesses and long absences from school made matters worse. The few things Mathilda responded to in a positive way were her recollection of sleeping with her mother, her father's two young children, Frankie, and the idea of having her own baby.

Disposition. We should continue seeing Mathilda as an outpatient. We need to understand more about the meaning of a baby for her and to help her recognize some of the realities involved in having a child. In order to evaluate whether Mathilda should continue in school, I called her high school guidance counselor. He said that she should look for a job, since she was so limited educationally. He felt Mathilda would never finish school and made no recommendation for a remedial program. He had tried to talk to her several times, but this contact was not productive. Mathilda was also unresponsive to tutoring class in the bilingual program.

DISCUSSION

In this case, a referral was made to the Infant Care Center on behalf of an adolescent girl who was not yet pregnant, but whose psychological condition and background alerted us that she might need help. Her expressed wish to have a baby coincided with our desire at the ICC to understand the intense need to have babies found among certain adolescent girls whose developmental stage, economic and educational resources, and family backgrounds suggest extremely poor preparation for parenthood. (After years of work with Mathilda and other teenage mothers we still lack a satisfactory explanation of this phenomenon.)

Mathilda's reaction to her sisters' referral impressed us.

Instead of being resentful, she was surprised and pleased, stating, "I thought no one cared about me." Not only did Mathilda experience a feeling new to her—that of being taken care of—but she gave us a clue about her expectations surrounding our role in her life.

The intake process emphasized to us Mathilda's closeness to her mother and father and her fondness for her father's new sons, which we kept in mind in trying to understand her need and wish to have a child. Still, we were unable to determine from the data gathered during the intake process whether the pleasure of taking care of children was based on Mathilda's wish to please the adult, due to an identification with the adult parental role, or an externalization of her need for care, her doing for others expressing what she wished to have done for her.

During the three-quarters of a year following the initial referral, Mathilda was seen one to three times a month by the ICC social worker. In accordance with Mathilda's need for service and the goals of our study, these meetings focused on Mathilda's wish to have a baby, her relationship with her boyfriend, and the many daily survival issues of work, welfare, and health care with which both Mathilda and Frankie had to cope. During this period Mathilda announced that she was pregnant and that despite all of her difficulties, including a number of asthmatic attacks severe enough to require hospitalization, she was insistent on continuing the pregnancy to term. Discussion about the reality of the demands which Mathilda would have to face when the baby was born exposed her confusion and elicited the same reply: "I don't know." She expected that her child would be able to enter day care at the Infant Care Center, and made an explicit request to this effect.

When Mathilda arrived at the Center with her baby girl, who was then a week old, an assessment was undertaken to see whether day care would be appropriate as a service to Mathilda and her infant. At the time of the assessment there were no day care openings at the Center and a substitute plan for Claudia had to be worked out. Finally a place was found for the baby at age 3 months. A report of the intake conference follows:

INTAKE CONFERENCE

The child was born in April 1979, and the conference took place July 16 of the same year. Present were the director of day care, a case worker, a social worker, and a staff psychiatrist.

Presenting problem and relevant history. Claudia weighed 8 pounds, 3 ounces at birth. The pregnancy was marked by the mother's repeated asthma attacks, for which she was hospitalized several times, and for which she was treated with Isuprel on a self-administered basis as needed. The child has been in apparent good health since birth.

The mother came to the Infant Care Unit primarily because she wanted day care. Due to the multiple problems in her family, an intake screening was carried out.

A number of interviews and observations revealed that Mathilda was having difficulty as a parent. She is a poor housekeeper and poor planner. She knows very little about child care. For example, she does not know how to hold her baby properly, and she sometimes feeds the child in an infant seat instead of holding her. On a home visit Mathilda was seen to make very little physical contact with the baby, preferring to relate to her from a distance. The child has been receiving solid foods in her bottle, and she appears to be overfed. She is a difficult-to-soothe baby, who does not seem to like close physical contact and cuddling. It is difficult to determine whether the child's reactions are innate or whether they are a response to her mother's style of handling.

Mathilda relies heavily on her boyfriend for help in all areas of managing the household. Frankie is aware of Mathilda's problems, but because he works he can do little about the situation.

Assessment. Claudia would appear to be an at-risk infant who is receiving inadequate maternal handling. Her mother is generally ignorant of child care techniques and is very dependent on others for managing her general life situation. Mathilda appears to be immature and of somewhat limited intelligence. She is also asthmatic and overweight.

The mother-child interaction, characterized by the baby's irritability and a lack of comforting physical contact between the pair, compromises the chances for development of an optimal attachment which would serve as a substrate for Claudia's development. Constitutional factors may also make Claudia more vulnerable than usual to stress. Possible lingering effects of Mathilda's asthma and the effects of medication on the baby *in utero* are speculative, but these may have exerted an adverse influence.

Preliminary diagnostic impression (DSM II). Child: (308.9) Other reaction of childhood—irritability and poor soothability associated with poor maternal handling. Mother: (308.9) Other reaction of adolescence—inadequate and immature response to parenthood; (305.2) Psychophysiological respiratory disorder.

Recommendation and Treatment Plan. Day care is recommended on the basis of the very poor adjustment which Mathilda has made to motherhood. There are no substantial family or other outside supports which could make the situation significantly better. Mathilda should receive extensive counseling, parent education, and concrete service supports until she seems ready for more independent functioning.

Mathilda's longing for a baby needs further assessment. Is this a fantasy fulfillment based on her wish to be recognized as an adult, or at least an equal to her sisters and mother, or does she have a strong maternal disposition which asserts itself so early? Is the confusion, lack of planning, inability to appropriately care for her baby an expression of a disorganization, or is it the absence of a true interest in being a parent?

DISCUSSION

When Claudia was placed in day care at age 3 months, her mother's mood had changed for the better, although she continued to be unable to plan and organize the care of the baby and her housework. Mathilda was still unable to stimulate the baby appropriately, to hold her close, or to provide continuity and consistency. Following is a review after one week in day care taken from the day care records:

> Claudia, age 3 months, has just been out one of these first eight days, due to an asthma attack her mother had. Mathilda has stayed in the room with Claudia most of the time. (She has been staying here 1–3 hours.) She watches the caregivers intently, asks questions, and seems to need their support when Claudia cries in order to be able to try and comfort her. Mathilda has accepted instruction in how to prepare the bottle and hold the baby for feeding, although she still prefers to feed her in the infant seat. She reportedly feels that Claudia will get "spoiled" if she holds her too much.
>
> Baby sucks vigorously on fingers when sleepy, although if she gets upset she seems unable to "find" her finger for comfort. Mother's slowness in caregiving activities such as dressing, diapering, and taking the baby out of her stroller often makes Claudia cranky. Not a very "cuddly" baby. Very active in arms, wriggles. Baby can turn over.
>
> Mathilda is shy but friendly with the teachers and seems to have made a good start. She clearly needs much help in becoming comfortable in her mothering.

The first summary of the clinical assessment after Claudia's entry into day care was carried out by the social worker and discussed in a conference with staff and consultants. Its purpose was to provide material both for study and for developing therapeutic plans for Mathilda and Claudia.

SOCIAL WORKER'S ASSESSMENT

Claudia has been in good health since birth. My observations of Claudia have been of her sucking her finger to sleep. She is not a cuddly baby and does not elicit or respond to being picked up. She is not smiling or cooing at the age of four months.

This mother is of limited intelligence. She has been giving Claudia solid foods in the bottle and we have been working with her to change this. Although she speaks of Claudia lovingly, Mathilda has not been able to cuddle or hold her baby. She seems afraid to do so. Mathilda experienced many losses in her childhood. She lost her mother at an early age, then lost her father to another woman, her position of youngest in the family was lost when her father had two additional children with his new wife. Her paternal grandmother is old and has been unable to care for Mathilda. Mathilda's older sisters have been busy with their own lives and their own children, and they too were unable to care for Mathilda.

Even though Mathilda has not been able to get much love, attention, or education, within her own limited capability she is trying hard to learn to care for her child. When she started Infant Care Unit for the first time on July 20, she was awkward with the baby. She did not know how to hold the baby, could not give her what she herself had never experienced. Even though Claudia is what she wanted—a baby of her own—she doesn't know how to play with her. Since Mathilda's start at the Infant Care Unit for day care, the staff has been aware of Mathilda's needs. Each teacher or staff member has made herself available to Mathilda. The child care worker has taken special time with Mathilda in showing her how to cuddle Claudia, how to hold her tenderly, how to play with her, how to give her the milk, how to feed her, and even how to cook the cereal.

Mathilda has responded to all of the attention given to her. She has become more attentive. We also have noticed that Mathilda improved with Claudia, has given her a sense of security. Mathilda seems stronger than when I met her a year ago. Since Claudia's birth there has been an improvement in Mathilda's awareness of what is going on around her. She seems to be more alert. By the middle of the month we noticed her strength increasing even with Claudia's father, who at first seemed to be stronger and more intelligent than Mathilda. The roles seem to be changing. Mathilda now seems to remember more of the things that have to be done. For example, she remembers the dates of their Welfare appointments and who to see. In my presence Frankie seems to be depending on Mathilda more than before.

Frankie seems to be acting more as an adolescent than Mathilda. He shows more tenderness to Claudia when alone with me in the office, but he seems self-conscious with the baby in the playroom. Frankie is having a hard time keeping his temporary job. When I met Mathilda, I questioned her ability to care for a child because of her age and her limitations. She seems to be blossoming into a concerned mother. Our intervention at the Infant Care Unit seems to have bolstered her self-esteem tremendously, and this reflects in her handling of her child.

Defined at this stage of the therapeutic program are the following goals:

Child. Long-term: Continue toward a more appropriate mother-child relationship; provide stimulation in motor activities. Short-term: Help achieve a satisfactory phasing into the day care center.

Parents. Long-term: Help them fulfill their parenting roles and, simultaneously, their own developmental needs. Short-term: Give Mathilda support and help her in child rearing; help her with the essentials she needs to know in her mothering role. We need to continue to give her a feeling of being wanted in Infant Care Unit, a feeling of belonging and of helping her in dealing with day-to-day concerns.

Plan. I will be seeing Mathilda on an individual basis and Frankie and Mathilda together. Focus will be on job counseling and helping them to know themselves as individuals, as a couple, and as parents.

Prognosis. Guarded, for all three. Depends on coordination, at least for baby.

Integration Conference

In this conference, which occurred August 20, 1979, when Claudia was 4 months old, the data from all sources were discussed and integrated. Present were the director of daycare, the caseworker, the childcare worker, and a staff psychiatrist. The psychiatrist's summary, formulations, and explanatory statements follow.

PSYCHIATRIC SUMMARY

Physical condition and health. Child was a full-term infant weighing 8 pounds, 3 ounces at birth. Her mother's pregnancy was marked by the onset of asthma with recurrent episodes requiring hospitalization and medication with Isuprel mist. Child was born in apparent good health, and she has been a well baby during her first four months. She is moderately overweight, apparently as a result of overfeeding.

Motor development and activity level. Child is a moderately active infant with good motor development. She is able to turn over as well as to pivot her body when in a prone position. Head control is within the average range for a 4-month-old.

Sensorimotor patterns. Child attempts to and is beginning to reach for objects. She shows beginning capacity to direct her fingers to her mouth in order to suck on them. She grasps objects offered to her but as yet she does not actively shake or bang them.

Sensory reactivity. Child gives her attention most rapidly to sounds. The sound of a rattle is very effective in distracting her. She does not seem to have any oversensitivity to specific forms of stimulation, although her tendency to react negatively to cuddling may indicate a tactile or kinesthetic sensitivity. Child prefers being held in an upright position.

Physiological regulation. Patterns for eating and sleeping appear to be fairly regular. Changes in physiological state seem to be difficult for Claudia, who becomes very irritable when tired or hungry. She is not easily comforted at these times.

Affective range and intensity. Shows a broad range of affect. Negative affects of displeasure seem very intense, though of short duration. She cries very hard, especially when tired. Although she shows fairly intense pleasurable responses of laughing and/or excited interest in objects, she lacks spontaneity and sometimes requires a lot of stimulation to be "brought out."

Vocalization. Engages in cooing and gurgling, which apparently started to be a regular behavior for her just as she began day care.

Relation to human objects. Appears somewhat deficient in her responsiveness to people. Although she shows social smiling behavior, it is not very frequent or spontaneous as compared to the "average" 4-month-old. None of her social behavior suggests an "autistic" condition. There does not appear to be any real differentiation of responses shown to her mother as opposed to the child care workers or to strangers. As previously noted, Claudia is not a "cuddly" baby, and she hasn't been since birth, according to her mother.

Relation to inanimate objects. Relation to inanimate objects appears to be age-appropriate.

Relation to body and self. Shows the capacity for self-soothing by sucking on her fingers, usually when she is tired. She also shows an interest in looking at parts of her body. An observation made today indicates that the child now smiles in response to seeing her mirror image.

Parenting experience. The child care skills of the parents must be considered quite inadequate at this time. This appears to be the result of a poor fund of knowledge coupled with a reaction to the emotional stresses of parenting. The child's mother and primary caregiver is an intellectually limited person who has significant difficulty interpreting her infant's needs. The mother overfeeds the child, and does not respond to her signals that she is full. During feedings Mathilda either holds Claudia very awkwardly or else feeds her in an infant seat. Several observations have indicated that there is little eye contact or other mutual exchange during feedings. Mathilda herself complains of an inability to react to Claudia's crying, due to the anxiety it creates for her. Sometimes Mathilda uses successful techniques at the wrong time, such as when she shakes a rattle to try to calm her sleepy child. It is difficult to determine whether Mathilda doesn't hold Claudia very much because the baby does not like to be held, or because Mathilda avoids holding her. Mathilda does not attempt to play with her daughter very much, so that it would seem that Claudia does not receive much stimulation at home. Despite her extensive shortcomings, Mathilda seems to want to be a parent, and she has shown interest in learning how to care for her child. She often looks for information and guidance from the day care staff. Her tendency to linger at the Infant Care Unit in the afternoons indicates her own need for attention as well as for the support offered. The child's father has only been seen with her once or twice. He seemed awkward and nervous when handling his daughter, possibly because of anxiety about being watched. Frankie is reported to be quite affectionate with Claudia, however, and he may provide more intense social stimulation than is offered by Mathilda.

Significant parental history. Mathilda has had a disrupted life history marked by chronic family problems and by the death of her mother when she was only 8 years old. Following her own mother's death, Mathilda lived with her father, but she moved back and forth between his home and New York, so that her upbringing was inconsistent and her schooling was interrupted frequently. She has lived in New York steadily for the past two years, but for much of that time she was moving from one household to another among family and friends. She has lived with her child's father for the past year. Mathilda became pregnant because she wanted to have a baby. She became pregnant at age 16 despite strong efforts to dissuade her from having a child at such a young age, and at a time when she had no source of income or permanent home. Mathilda is an obese, somewhat pathetic-looking girl with a shy manner. At times she appears apathetic and depressed, with a constricted affect. She gives the impression of being intellectually dull, and it is possible that she would test at a retarded level on intelligence tests. Her limited intellect would seem to be the result of environmental deprivation. She does not appear to be psychotic in any way. Her reality testing is adequate, but her overall judgmental capacities are limited.

PSYCHOLOGICAL TESTING

To be performed when Claudia is 6 months of age.

SPECIAL EVALUATIONS

None indicated.

DIAGNOSTIC STATEMENT

Claudia is a 4-month-old girl showing mild deviation in social development, as seen in her limited responsiveness to people. She is a difficult-to-soothe infant who does not like to be cuddled. The child's mother is an intellectually limited young woman who is unable to meet the demands of providing good child care. Mother is a very passive person who appears depressed. In addition, her health is compromised by her obesity and recently developed asthma. There is clearly a problem in the style of interaction between mother and child which could lead to significant developmental disturbance for the child.

IDENTIFIED PROBLEMS

Child's limited social responsiveness; difficulty in soothability; apparent understimulation by mother; mother's lack of knowledge of child care; mother's chronic personality features of passivity and apparent depression; parents' lack of goal-directedness and ability to plan.

TREATMENT GOALS

Short-term. Support of mother and infant adjustment to day care; education of Mathilda in child care techniques; support of greater social interaction between mother and infant; general increase in Claudia's responsiveness to human interaction; assessment of effective means for *minimizing* Claudia's intense distress responses.

Long-term. Development of an optimal mother-child relationship; support of Claudia's general development; support of development of higher levels of adaptive functioning for Mathilda; exploration and implementation of educational and/or vocational possibilities for Mathilda.

PROGNOSIS

Prognosis must be considered as somewhat guarded at this time due to the significant deficits in the mother's ability to care for and relate to her child. Claudia's own temperament seems to contribute to some of the difficulty experienced by her mother, and this complicates the problem of improving their relationship and patterns of interaction.

TREATMENT PLAN

Child will be attending day care five days a week. Mathilda will be seen for individual counseling by the social worker. In addition, she will participate in child care workshops given by child care workers at the Infant Care Unit. Mathilda's participation in the weekly mothers' group will also be encouraged.

Day Care Supervisor's Report

The treatment plan was pursued essentially as outlined above. A report by the day care supervisor when Claudia was

9½ months of age summarized the interval between July 20, 1979, and January 31, 1980.

Attendance. Irregular, with frequent absences during the months covered by this report.

General description. Child is long for her age. She has large eyes with long eyelashes. She was hospitalized at 5 months for diarrhea.

Relation to self. She is an active baby, often in motion. She achieved early motor milestones—pivoting and rolling over at 4 months, at 5 months rocking on her hands and knees, crawling at 5½ months, pulling to stand at 6 months, and cruising around in an upright position holding furniture and walls at 9 months. She has a wobbly gait, leaning forward and often standing on tiptoe. She is alert to sounds and prefers sweet tastes. She seems sensitive to physical discomfort, is wiggly and squirmy, and takes a long time to find a comfortable position when falling asleep. She uses thumb or finger-sucking to soothe herself. She is not a cuddly baby, nor is she easy to soothe with holding or rocking. She has poor eye contact, seeming to avoid it. She smiles and coos a little. She gets most upset when hungry or tired, and complains if not fed quickly.

Relation to adults. The child was very slow to respond to any social stimulation, almost seeming to actively avoid eye contact. She did not seek attention and seemed indifferent to the caregiver's interactions. Much work has been done by the teachers to get her involved in one-to-one social situations. At 6 months she was more relaxed being held; by 8 months, she was more focused, more relaxed. At 9 months, she enjoys social games. She seems in a better mood with caregivers than with her mother. No preferred caregiver.

Mother and father. Her mother is unorganized and does not plan well, taking a long time to dress the baby, forgetting to take her bottle, etc. The mother was initially very ill at ease with her baby, fed her in an infant seat, did not hold her much, and did not seem able to respond to her crying. The mother's usual response to her child's crying was to shake a noisy toy or rattle in her face, which sometimes briefly distracted her. Claudia did not distinguish between adults at 5 months. At 6 and 7 months she showed no distress or excitement at her parents' arrival or departure, and paid no specific attention to her parents. At 8 months, on return from a visit with her mother to their relatives in Santo Domingo, she seemed more specifically related to her parents and was excited when she saw her father. At 9 months she still does not protest when they leave her.

Relation to children. Very little response, positive or negative, to peers.

Play. At 4 months Claudia played with her hands, was able to grasp toys and bang them. She seemed object- rather than people-oriented. At 9 months she enjoys the Busy Box and is responsive to social games.

Language. She cooed a little at 4 months. She "chatters" a lot, mostly when falling asleep. Has a deep voice.

Relation of parents to center. The parents observe the baby, compare her with other children, like to share anecdotes about her. Both parents are open about sometimes feeling at a loss with the baby. However, their accessibility to teaching is limited. The mother's intellectual capacity is limited. She is lethargic and passive. The father is constantly on edge, in motion, talking, restless. In addition, they use the baby as a tool in acting out their own conflicts. We often see the father competing with the child for Mathilda's attention, culminating in his complaints, while the child was hospitalized, that he needed Mathilda with him. She maintained that the sick baby needed her more. The father is unable to function well in Mathilda's absence, was very agitated when she was in school. He alternates between wanting mothering for himself from Mathilda, and feeling the need to be fatherly to her ("I'll be her father as well as Claudia's"). They argue about the child constantly.

Integration Conference

One month later, in an integration conference, the case was again reviewed for evaluation and planning. Present were the administrative supervisor of day care; the administrative supervisor of social work; a psychologist; a psychiatrist; a psychometrician; the case worker; and the child care worker. The psychiatrist's report follows.

Summary of recent months. In September the child was to leave the United States. Instead she was hospitalized with diarrhea for a week. She then left the country for two weeks in November-December. The mother had educational testing here, scoring at third-grade level in math and reading, though her school said seventh and fifth, respectively. Mathilda did not get started in school. Concern was expressed over the child's social development. She was felt to be "ahead of herself" motorically, crawling and moving before developing a sense of control. She would not make eye contact. Attendance was poor, about ten absences per month.

Development. Claudia bumps into things and seems to feel motorically driven. She has not made much eye contact since birth, but now she smiles at others and makes contact. (She had been tied down in the hospital.) She was not a cuddly baby; she would writhe and squirm. Now she comes to you to be picked up and cuddles to fall asleep. In the Infant Care Unit work was done alone with her, without distracting visual stimuli, to encourage relatedness. The child seemed more relaxed after she and her mother returned from Santo Domingo.

Psychological testing. On psychological testing conducted February 5, 1980, it was noted that the child made little eye contact and seemed more interested in auditory and visual stimuli—e.g., a motion visible in "the corner of her eye," or screaming in the hallway. She did show more relatedness to the psychometrician than in prior testing. Claudia tested way above average on motor scales, but otherwise her scores were uneven and not well integrated. However, on average she scored at age level or above, though not as high as the "way-above" motor levels.

Medical. Incisor teeth developed before side teeth. In September she was again in St. Luke's for diarrhea. She had had a low Hematocrit in October 1979, and a changed diet was recommended. In January she had conjunctivitis. The staff worked hard to clarify instructions and to get Mathilda to follow through on medical treatment. For example, she believed the doctor told her "no meat, she's anemic," whereas in fact the doctor's written statement said *more* meat. Mathilda believed feeding with a spoon led to diarrhea. She had also given Claudia medications with opium for diarrhea when they were out of the country. The father can accept suggestions and sit more calmly, even feeding the child with staff help. Both father and mother are more at ease when alone with child than when together. Both appear calmer. Welfare checks are regular. The mother refuses to stay in the welfare hotel where they are living since she saw a rat and learned that a man had been shot and murdered there. They are looking for an apartment but have trouble following through in making and keeping appointments, even with help. The father had a job for four days but was laid off. The coded diagnoses (DSM II) at this time were as follows: Child: (308.9) Other reaction of childhood—deviation in social development. Mother: (300.89) Mixed personality disorder with depressive features. Goals for treatment were unchanged.

Plan. Continue day care for the child, and weekly individual and group sessions for the mother. Kathy will continue to work with the father in the playroom toward being and feeling like a more competent father.

Prognosis. Guarded, due to deficits in parenting abilities. Improvement in the child's relatedness has been noted and hopefully will continue.

Day Care Summary

Claudia's attendance in day care was irregular between ages 8 and 15 months. When she was 15½ months the day care supervisor summarized her development during this interval.

General Description. Claudia is an active toddler; she has a strong drive to motor achievement, and is very persistent and directed. Moving toward independence, beginning to have tantrums when frustrated.

Relation to self. Stood alone at 11 months and took a few steps. By 12½ months going up play stairs, and up the slide. A slightly strange gait, often looks down when walking. Affective range broader, takes more pleasure in play. A determined, persistent quality often leading to tantrums. Helped feed herself from 10 months, using neat pincer movement and helping with the spoon.

Relation to adults. Much more focused on adults. Demands to be picked up, is more cuddly. Gives good cues to what she wants. Occasionally does not respond when called and when absorbed in activity, reminiscent of her earlier lack of focus on people. She now initiates games. Seems to be starting to prefer Katy over other caregivers.

Mother and father. During this period has developed a more focused attachment to her mother, going to her when she comes to pick her up. Claudia has never cried when either parent leaves, occasionally crawls after them, and occasionally whines briefly. Has started to wave "bye-bye." Lately has been fussy with her father, who feels rejected by her.

Relation to peers. At 10 months Claudia started to show interest in peers, watching them, starting to kiss and pat them. By now she initiates play, hugs, is tender with other children. She often engages others in her play, or simply joins a group of children.

Play. Loves to dance, loves music, loves peekaboo. Is curious, more aware of her surroundings. Loves books and dolls and tends to have favorites.

Language. Laughs, chatters, tries to repeat words. Good receptive language. Has some single words in both English and Spanish. Parents are both bilingual English/Spanish.

Relation of parents to center. Parents continue to argue openly about their daughter. The focus seems to have shifted from Frankie's competing with the child for Mathilda's attention, to his competing with her for the child's attention. They fight about who will greet the baby first, whom she prefers. Frankie continues to be disturbingly careless about his conversation, censoring nothing, expressing disturbing fantasies: "Why don't we just sell this girl, she's too much trouble"; "We have to keep her locked up at home so she won't get hurt" (Claudia had begun to explore her environment more actively). He also can be verbally aggressive to the other children, even threatening. Mathilda was more attentive to Claudia on their return from Santo Domingo. Frankie is better with Claudia when Mathilda is not present, although he is impatient with her. For instance, he did not want her to crawl once she'd taken her first step.

Plans. Transition to Toddler Room this month. Get Mathilda to stay in the playroom to help Claudia with transition.

Caregivers' Weekly Notes

The following excerpts from the caregivers' logs offer vignettes of Claudia and her parents during the child's fifteenth through eighteenth month.

July 7–11. Parents really seem to be enjoying Claudia. Mother was trying to get her to say "papi" while father was there. She was very patient and seemed to enjoy Frankie and child then. All three were very pleased when Claudia said "papi." Claudia fell in the park Tuesday, and when the parents were told, Frankie said he would have to take the child out of the Center and keep her home locked up because he couldn't let her get hurt again. He wanted to know if we watched the children while outside; said he would have to hurt someone if anything happened to Claudia. He seemed to be trying to keep his anger under control. Mathilda seemed to accept Claudia's fall as something that happens to children, and helped the caregiver explain that Claudia is doing a lot of things by herself and is bound to get hurt; that she can't be stopped from doing everything she wants to do, but that we can stand by her and try and help her. Although Mathilda didn't say all this, she did agree and made Frankie and the caregiver aware of things the child has done at home where she has gotten hurt, and how she is getting into a lot of things and how hard it is to keep her from doing some of the things she does. Frankie calmed down after a while, and agreed with some of what she said. Mathilda reported Thursday that Claudia chipped her tooth when she fell and that Frankie was upset about it.

October 27. When Claudia smelled the bleach Katy poured into the washing machine, she made a face and waved her head in a "smell" motion and wrinkled up her nose. She often hands objects to an adult to get the adult to interact with her. She takes our hands so we will accompany her. She has been asking for a lot of adult attention since her mother went into the hospital.

October 29. When Claudia cries or pretends to, as in a temper tantrum, she covers her mouth. She throws tantrums when, for example, she takes play-dough or pegs away from the table and we tell her to come back. She says "no" loud and clear and watches us as she lies on the floor. At lunch she ate all her macaroni, then asked for more (leaving the string-beans and meatloaf in her bowl). She eats well with a spoon, managing her applesauce well.

November 17. Child was active outside in the park, climbing up on the park benches and walking along them. She was not too cautious. I had to stay beside her to make sure she did not fall off. She has a habit of running with her eyes closed—which could be dangerous for her.

November 18. I find Claudia asking for both affection and adult attention. Sometimes in the stroller she wants me to hold her hand. She responds to affection from various people who are here part time.

Claudia at 18 months

Process notes and assessments reveal that in many ways Claudia has made a good deal of progress in her maturation and socialization. Still, in both areas she is either slow or deviant relative to normal development. Low cognitive function is also apparent. In view of the child's environment and parental care, it is difficult at this time to make an assessment of the relative importance of limited or abnormal endowment as compared to social retardation in Claudia's level of development. If the child had spent most of her life at home, rather than in a day care setting which provides a great deal of individual and group stimulation in all areas of development, we would have given more credence to the influence of the environment.

It was of great interest to observe that Claudia made a stronger attachment to the mother than to any of our caregivers. The mother's inability to cuddle and to stimulate, her own need for parental care, and her immaturity and disorganization led us to predict that one of our caregivers would be selected by Claudia for attachment and bonding. We may have underestimated the mother's ability to improve her skills and to use our Center, which was offered to her as much as to her child. Mathilda's early wish to have a baby may have also corresponded to a capacity to transmit affection, however inconsistent or immature, which provided the basis for mutual attachment.

We assume that the work of the ICC staff in carrying out the short- and long-term goals formulated and periodically reevaluated at integration conferences contributed significantly to Claudia's capacity to attach herself to her mother. In its daily functioning, the staff provided individual stimulation appropriate to Claudia's developmental status, assisted her socialization with other children, and provided an atmosphere in which Claudia could expect continuity of care.

It is clear that Claudia needed more than the usual child, for her own deviations demanded much individualized attention. While we were becoming increasingly sure of her overall limitations, we were not certain of her potential, either in motor maturation or cognitive function.

When Claudia was 18 months old, psychological testing was repeated. Claudia's intent pursuit of her own interests did not allow her to accept the test situation easily; she often cried, "No, no, no," and would lie on the floor crying. That same persistence made it difficult to disengage her once she was involved with a test task. Claudia's MDI was below normal. Her performance fluctuated; her perceptual motor integration, in particular, was variable and below age level. Language skills also varied; she was unable to use words to make her wishes known or to identify body parts on a doll. Visual tests did not reveal any negative findings.

Claudia at 25 months

At 2 years, 1 month, Claudia was described by the day care staff as a tall, sturdy child whose negativistic behavior was particularly strong and intense and who was easily frustrated. Her motor skills were well developed, and she used them to feed and dress herself as well as to climb and run. Claudia was attached to her mother and affectionate toward her caregivers at the Center. With children she was alternately aggressive and gentle. Claudia was able to make known her wants and needs through gestures and single-word utterances in both Spanish and English.

Child care staff planned at this point to continue working toward more regular attendance for Claudia, who still averaged only two or three days per week at the Center. They also hoped to help Claudia develop greater tolerance for frustration and more positive interaction with peers, using words instead of hands. Knowing that Mathilda was pregnant, the staff planned to give Claudia more physical comfort and cuddling, assistance in dealing with the idea of a new sibling, and help with language development. They also agreed to work with Mathilda so that she could help Claudia in these areas.

Psychological Evaluation

When Claudia was 2 years, 11 months, she was given a psychological evaluation because of concern about language development and fine motor coordination. The Psychological Evaluation Report below is followed by the psychiatrist's report of the subsequent integration conference.

Claudia was tested in the presence of her father. After a brief period of introduction in her classroom, she readily accompanied the examiner to the testing room without directly interacting with her father. She appeared to be aware of the strangers in the room but disregarded them as she participated in the testing. She maintained a cooperative, task-oriented attitude to the materials and seemed interested in mastering each task that was presented. She remained seated throughout the testing and overcame the temptation to reach for the testing materials herself, gesturing toward them instead.

Throughout the testing Frankie maintained a steady stream of conversation. He narrated the testing session, commenting on her achievement with, "We've teached her that," and on her failures with, "We didn't teach her that yet." He carefully observed what she was doing and reminded her to "concentrate—look at what you're doing." Despite efforts to request that he not talk, he did not seem able to watch silently. It is interesting to note, however, that his talking did not seem to distract Claudia. She rarely looked at him and appeared to be "tuning out" his conversation entirely.

The Stanford Binet Intelligence Scale was administered, and the child achieved a mental age of 3.0 (one month above her chronological age). This gave her an IQ score within normal limits, 88. Her range fell between 2 years, 6 months, and 4 years, with most of her difficulty in the language area.

Claudia has a great deal of difficulty organizing her experience with age-appropriate verbalizations, and she has problems with both expressive and receptive language. Although she is able to provide labels for some objects, she cannot generate sentences and is only able to use two- or three-word utterances. Her first failure occurred in labeling a "box," for her vocabulary is severely limited. She was not able to distinguish between "larger" and "smaller" objects in a systematic fashion. In telling stories about pictures, her verbalizations were restricted to labeling a few objects ("chair," "door," "dog") without addressing the activity that was depicted.

Receptive language is also problematic, for the child seems to be lagging in her ability to process language. She was not able to obey even simple commands such as "Put the button in the box" that should be present at 2 years, 6 months. More difficult questions, such as "What must you do when you are thirsty?" were not answered, and it is not clear that the child can understand long sentences.

There is a question as to whether or not Claudia has difficulty with auditory sequencing. When asked to repeat even two numbers, she repeats only the last digit she hears. Similarly, when asked to repeat "I am a big girl" she replies with "girl." It is not clear whether she does not understand the directions or whether she cannot recall a series of words or numbers, but this difficulty in reciting what she hears interferes with her ability to effectively process language.

Claudia also demonstrates a significant problem with articulation. She said "fower" for "flower," "kissors" for "scissors," and she is often unintelligible in both English and Spanish. It may be that this speech problem is related to her general difficulty with language acquisition.

In other areas she exhibits many strengths. She has good fine motor coordination and is able to effectively mediate tasks of eye-hand coordination such as block building and puzzles. Similarly, her grasp of motor skills is adequate. She draws a line and a circle quite well.

Both visual discrimination and visual memory are quite strong, and she was able to recall forms that were visually presented at the 4-year-old age level. When objects were hidden, she could remember which ones were missing, demonstrating a strong capacity for visual recall. Her visual discrimination was also above age level, for she could locate a copy of a picture from a group of different pictures. This visual attention to detail, combined with high powers of concentration, enabled her to correctly identify eight of the ten pictures.

It is also noteworthy that Claudia was able to attend to the testing for the entire duration of the session. She approached each task as a novel challenge, attempting every task with interest and perseverance. She was able to modulate her impulses so that even when she was frustrated by a task she could dismiss it without becoming upset. When asked to identify a word that was too hard she would reply "that," as if to dismiss the subject. This enabled her to move on to other sub-tests with relative ease. Similarly, she relinquished objects in a give-and-take fashion, substituting new materials for old ones in a cooperative manner.

In summary, Claudia is an attentive, perceptive girl of 2 years, 11 months, who demonstrates an interest in learning. Her normal intelligence is based on a somewhat uneven level of functioning, for she exhibits a considerable lag in language development (both expressive and receptive) and auditory memory. Other areas, however, are proceeding smoothly and enable her to make useful cognitive strides. She has an excellent capacity for visual discrimination and visual memory, and her fine motor coordination is good. Her good attention span and ability to concentrate facilitate learning, and she is responsive in a one-to-one relationship. Claudia should be given intensive help in the language areas with encouragement for her verbal behavior. It is also recommended that she be given speech evaluation and, if necessary, speech therapy to improve her problem with articulation.

Integration Conference

This conference was held when Claudia was 2 years, 11 months old. Present were the administrative supervisor of day care, the administrative supervisor of social work, two child care workers, the case worker, and a staff psychiatrist.

Past. Mathilda has a second baby now who is doing well. She has consistently shown tenderness and maternal caring for the new baby. She has been responsible also about keeping appointments or calling. She and Frankie seem very happy together. They are managing money well without crises. Frankie cut himself off from Welfare for 5–6 months. Mathilda has had a couple of colds but no asthma, making this a long time for her to go without being in the hospital. (Her sister was hospitalized for a long time last year.)

Father. Spends time watching TV, playing handball, skating, etc. Doing better. He periodically goes to a friend's house and stays days. He has some insight that his personality is a problem in getting a job or planning. He would like a job as a security guard or apartment house super, though he doesn't qualify for the latter. He had tried a "business"—selling watches, on the street—but could not comprehend basic financial issues, e.g., that buying a watch for six dollars and selling it at the same price does not earn him six dollars.

Mother. Much improvement is evident with the new baby and with Claudia. Mathilda requested day care but understood that she is doing well with the baby and the baby may not need it. Claudia's language is delayed and Mathilda may be able to help her with this. Claudia's urinating or saying she has to—on walks, on the bus, etc.—causes concern, particularly to Frankie.

Child. Claudia is very jealous of her new sister now. She told the case worker, "You can keep her." Mathilda seems to deny this but has worked with the case worker on this. The baby is now doing well, and is standing up. Claudia had been sleeping with Frankie but now apparently is not. Limited use of language. Lots of hand-teasing anger. She gestures and struggles to talk and seems frustrated. She understands a lot but has few names for anything. Also, Frankie seems to tease her a lot. When Claudia comes with him she acts depressed and quiet. Frankie is easily turned off by this rejection.

Medical. Mathilda is healthier. She has been without asthma for some time.

Psychological tests. Done (see above).

Other tests. None.

Problems. Mother's request for day care for baby; father's lack of job skills, low self-esteem, lack of insight, and very low anxiety and frustration tolerance that limit realistic discussions re the future; child's toilet control; child's poor speech articulation (she points and says "uh").

Short-term goal for mother. Continue progress with mothering skills with two infants.

Long-term goals for mother. Plans for Claudia for next year; plans for baby day care.

Short-term goal for father. Attempt to help him tolerate small amounts of frustration and anxiety long enough to consider some realistic future plans.

Long-term goal for father. Some adaptation to limitations and to an appropriate job.

Short-term goals for child. Improved relationship with father, with less teasing; evaluation of speech, possible evaluation with consultant about lack of learning words.

Long-term goal for child. Progress toward normal development.

Plan. Continue day care. Discuss baby's progress and the fact that she doesn't need day care. Discuss Frankie's limits as a parent. Teachers to work with Mathilda to teach her to assist Claudia with language.

Prognosis. Good, with continued intervention. Frankie's teasing seems to have a negative influence.

Concluding Discussion

This report has not chronicled the day-by-day conferences of the staff involved with an individual family, encounters in which events and observations are shared, nor has it emphasized the role of the observations which parents are able to make as they watch their child and the staff in inter-

action. This record, therefore, remains a summary statement
rather than a complete reflection of the many significant factors that are part of the mental health milieu of the Infant
Care Center.

The record of the final Integration Conference reported
here reveals that Mathilda has had a second child. She continues to express the need for a baby in spite of her economic,
social, and psychological difficulties. It seems that with an
infant, the mother is able to satisfy an overriding need for
closeness, intimacy, and nurturing, which she reenacts in the
mother-child relationship. Mathilda's relationship to the
father has similar features—for her, he too is a child in need
of maternal care.

Accepted by the Center and nurtured, guided, and directed, Mathilda received sufficient gratification to be able to
establish a positive relationship with Frankie and with her
children. Her earlier state of disorganization has changed,
giving way to increased stability and better management of
daily affairs. Frankie too is warm and affectionate to his child
and was able to maintain a sense of function even during
Mathilda's hospitalization.

Claudia has become a very active child in need of much
space. It is not surprising either that she is competent in
feeding herself or that her emerging, age-appropriate negativism is a shade too intense. We find additional conflicts
stemming from the stage of development, such as fussiness
about food, demands to be cleaned immediately, and insistence upon correct personal appearance at all times. The intensity of this struggle may be based on Claudia's increasing
anger, which is an expression of her fight with Mathilda and
her own frustration at being unable to integrate and organize
the uneven areas of her development. The anger in Claudia
is particularly noteworthy, for her mother and father always
treat her with much patience, in a soft-spoken way, and with
no expression of anger.

We have observed in Claudia an increasingly strong tie

to her mother, in preference to the teachers and to her father. Her response to strangers is one of caution and reserve, and she does ·not allow a casual approach without responding to it with "No." Claudia's insistence on continuity is outstanding. In the test situation, she also showed an inability to absorb new situations and to change from one activity to another. In the group she shows aggression when she feels interfered with, but at other times she can be caring and affectionate. Claudia's favorite play is with dolls, feeding them, talking to them, and putting them to sleep. Here she mirrors the relationship of Mathilda to her and her own corresponding needs.

Claudia's history indicates that early and continued efforts to assist her development and equally intense attention to her parents' needs still leave the child struggling with many developmental conflicts and with maturation lags and unevenness. In spite of the progress in her development, and to a certain degree because of that progress, we find conflicts emerging in succeeding stages. Limitations in Claudia's endowment may not be modifiable. Nor do we assume that her parents, although they have improved, have as yet consolidated their development enough to carry out the appropriate parental role. Claudia's parents may fail her even more as she gets older, and we cannot yet assess the influence of the new sibling. As Claudia struggles against intrusion, Mathilda may turn more to the baby, adding new problems to the picture.

In this chapter we have chosen purposefully to present a family which does not document a "happy ending," for most of our work is based on a continuing struggle for further development and maturation. Here, as with so many of our families, we observe that in spite of our prompt interventions and our assumptions that we can prevent serious malfunction and interference with early development, Claudia and her family will need a mental health program for years to come.

5

Babies Everywhere: Assessing and Treating a Toddler's Pervasive Developmental Disorder

Kyle D. Pruett, M.D.

> I'm terrified of my son. He's like a little monster prowling through the house destroying things at night, and terrorizing all of us during the day. I never expected to have him in the first place, but now that I do, about all I feel towards him is hate and fear. Please help us before we destroy each other. I don't know who will go first.

Thus did Nancy Ames describe life with 20-month-old Gary at the beginning of our 2½ year involvement with the Ames family. In this case report we hope to illustrate the opportunities and complexities of psychotherapeutic intervention in the lives of pre-verbal children and their families and to examine the prescriptive capacities (and shortcomings) of the diagnostic process, as we engage in it with a very young child with severe developmental psychopathology. The record of our work with Gary reminds us that intervention with infants is rarely simple or easy and that professionals who attempt such assessment and treatment must be prepared to integrate information from a variety of often disparate sources.

The account first outlines the data and symptomatology

presented to us—a fairly typical, if one can use the word, mosaic of severe infant and family distress. We note the consultant's role as liaison with the local pediatric community and with a hospital pediatric ward. As naturalistic observations are integrated with data from standardized infant assessments, we follow certain diagnostic threads as they are spun out and finally woven into a prescriptive plan for intervention.

Our involvement with Gary began with a phone call from a respected pediatrician in a nearby suburb who called to say that he was "deeply concerned" about a 20-month-old twin boy in his practice who, according to his mother, had not slept more than three to four hours a night for the past six months. The physician reported that his patient's language development seemed significantly slower than that of his female twin. Finally, the child directed considerable random, unprovoked aggression toward his siblings and parents. The pediatrician asked me to see the family in consultation and to assist in the management of this complex and distressing problem.

In the first telephone contact with Gary's mother, she reported that Gary had not slept well since his third month and was now averaging only three to four hours of sleep a night. She said the family was "coming apart at the seams" because of him. I arranged diagnostic assessment as quickly as possible in order to respond to a rising sense of urgency and panic within the family. During the next month there took place an initial interview with the parents, an office visit with both parents and Gary, an extended home visit, several subsequent office visits in which the Yale Developmental Schedules were administered, and additional consultation with the pediatrician.

The First Interview

When I first met Gary, his parents, Mr. and Mrs. Ames, were sitting at opposite ends of the waiting room, while he was on the floor, intensely involved in assembling and taking apart a complex Russian doll. As I opened the waiting room door, Gary met my gaze with wide, watchful eyes in a flat, expressionless face. He appeared pale, cautious, and exhausted, with the prominent rings under both eyes partially hidden by long shocks of disheveled blond hair. As I made small talk with his parents, Gary stared at me with a somber visage; he maintained his rigid, expressionless appearance for the rest of the visit.

Although somewhat stocky, Gary appeared to be of average height and weight for his age and seemed to have adequate comprehension of his parents' language and my own. When invited into my office, he came quickly, but silently. As he walked into the office, he collided sharply with the arm of a chair but registered no response whatsoever. His mother, tall, blond, obese, and blue-eyed, seemed the source of much of Gary's physical character. Holding his hand as they walked into the office, she too appeared exhausted and anxious. She did most of the talking for the rest of the visit, while her husband deferred to her, as mute as his son. Mr. Ames was a tall, slightly overweight man with dark hair and mustache, and an unkempt and overworked appearance. When he did talk, he spoke a little too loudly, and commented frequently on how obvious his discomfort must be.

In this meeting, Mrs. Ames reported, with a slight giggle, that "Gary does not like anything, especially sleep." She indicated that her son would go to bed easily enough, but simply refused to lie down and fall asleep. After exhaustion finally carried him into sleep, he would awaken several times during the night, frequently with a panicky crying. Gary's mother reported that although at first she had wondered if he were having nightmares, this explanation no longer seemed persuasive to her. She felt Gary had become increasingly belligerent over the last several months, and noticed that he was eating ravenously. She said, "He seems to get stranger and stranger; he doesn't seem to be able to adjust to the rest of us."

Although I shall review Gary's developmental history in

greater length later, Mrs. Ames's first remarks, reported as
I first heard them, convey a vivid impression of the distress
and turbulence of the situation:

> Gary was very sick the first four or five months; he
> couldn't relax and neither could we . . . ever. His twin
> sister seemed to adjust so much better, but he had colic,
> milk allergies—the list could go on and on. We tried
> everything we could think of to help him get to sleep,
> but it really ruined life for the rest of the family. After
> around four months, we had to bring him into our bed-
> room because the rest of the family complained that he
> was keeping them all awake. This won't sound very good,
> but for a week we locked him in a room at night when
> he was trying to go to sleep, and all that happened was
> he got panicked. I wondered if he didn't think we were
> trying to kill him. My husband and I also thought he was
> getting up at night to try to have some time with us
> without Lucy, his twin sister, being around.

Throughout this first interview, Gary was actively involved with the toys provided him in the consultation room—a
ball, a few dolls, some toy trucks, and blocks. He and his
father were actively engaged in building and destroying various structures, and Gary made an attempt to play ball with
his mother while she was talking. Although he showed obvious
drive and curiosity toward the materials on the floor, neither
his facial expression nor his visible affect changed from the
moment he walked into the room.

The parental distress evident in this first visit, as the
Ameses talked about the destruction of the family at the hands
of this toddler, led me to arrange a home visit in order to
assess more accurately the depth of the crisis already evident
in the family. The family lived in the finished basement of a
moderate-sized home in a rural Connecticut suburb. In the
eight rooms of the upper two floors of the house lived Gary's

maternal grandmother and grandfather. Gary's family's basement quarters, consisting of a single common room, a kitchen,
and three tiny bedrooms, were cramped, damp, and chilly.
Children's toys in various states of disrepair were scattered
over the floor and throughout the yard.

Mr. Ames greeted me at the door, apologized for "the
mess," and hoped that I would understand that their life was
very busy and that housecleaning was "pretty low down" on
their list of priorities. The next person to venture forth was
4½-year-old John, followed by 3-year-old Mary, and then
Gary and his twin sister. John asked if I was the doctor who
was going to "make Gary go to sleep." Gary showed some
faint recognition, and took me by the hand to show me the
room, one of two fashioned from what had been a garage,
where he was now sleeping with his older brother. What Mrs.
Ames was to describe later as "a feeling of babies being everywhere, with no sleep, no help, and no rest," was almost palp-
able.

Family History

Gary's mother was the youngest of three children, reared
with three orphaned cousins who came to live with her family
when she was 8 months old. Hers was a Roman Catholic
family, and the children all attended parochial elementary and
secondary schools. She described her own mother as a kind
but strict disciplinarian. Although unable to do so at first,
Mrs. Ames eventually told of her distress about the conflict
she experienced with her mother, both as child and adult.
She was pained by her mother's intense, apparently irrational
disapproval of Mr. Ames. She was also distressed and irritated
by her mother's frequent complaints of exhaustion, which
seem to intensify whenever Mrs. Ames asked her to assist
with the children. Gary's mother described her own father
as a patient and loving man who had worked two jobs most
of his life to provide security for the family. Though he was
frequently unavailable because of his work schedule, Gary's

mother found it easy and comfortable to idealize him, and reported that her children felt closer to him than to her mother.

Mr. Ames, Gary's father, who was 36 years old at the time of the initial referral, was the last of five children. He reported that his father was an "abusive alcoholic bum" who was hated by all his children. When Mr. Ames was 2 years old, his mother had asked his father to leave. He was subsequently raised by his mother and older siblings, and felt that he was "spoiled to beat the band," especially by his older sisters. Mr. Ames said that intermittently through his life he saw his father "hanging around bars." One such confrontation during Mr. Ames's adolescence remained painfully vivid: his father in a "drunken stupor" had criticized Mr. Ames's mother, and the son had barely controlled an impulse to "beat him to death."

Mr. Ames described his mother as a "bossy, nosey lady" in her seventies, who "doesn't always remember what she says." A good deal of tension existed in the relationship between his mother and his wife, and Mr. Ames felt deeply hurt by his mother's disapproval of his wife. He described his adolescence as "fun most of the time," only occasionally miserable. After graduating from high school with average grades, Mr. Ames served as an Army MP, did odd jobs, and finally joined a public utility as a truck driver.

Mr. and Mrs. Ames met through a mutual friend at work and dated for two years, despite the intense disapproval of both mothers. After marriage they both worked for five years to "save money and enjoy life" before the arrival of their first son, a planned and wanted child. Shortly after the birth of John, Mr. Ames decided to "improve himself" and began night school to obtain a college degree. When Mary, also planned, was born a year and a half later, Mrs. Ames felt compelled to give up her cherished part-time job. The increased financial burden led the father to leave school and take a second job, while the family moved into the mother's childhood home with the maternal grandparents. They did not forsee the consequences of having two children so close in age.

Two months prior to the move, when Mary was five months old, a third pregnancy, both unplanned and un-wanted, began. Mrs. Ames had discontinued birth control pills due to protracted nausea, and had changed to the rhythm method when she conceived. Feeling intense guilt over this pregnancy, Mrs. Ames told no one but her husband about it until the last trimester, even though she gained over a hundred pounds during the pregnancy. Since a prepartum ultrasound study had revealed only a "normal pregnancy," the parents were stunned at delivery when a *second* seven-pound infant was born twenty minutes after Lucy.

The mother left the hospital with her twins after three days, and began to experience severe nausea immediately. She was placed on a liquid diet, and Valium was prescribed. Mrs. Ames described a vivid nightmarish feeling of "having babies everywhere." Two months after the babies were born, the father underwent a vasectomy to insure no further con-ceptions. Twenty months after the birth, Mrs. Ames still car-ried the hundred pounds she had gained during pregnancy.

As a newborn, Lucy cried frequently, but stopped at three months and slept well, averaging nine to ten hours of sleep a day after the third month. She sat up at 6 months, walked at a year, talked at 15 months and was toilet-trained at the time of the evaluation. Like Gary, Lucy had a somewhat somber face but seemed more vigorous and displayed a larger repertoire of affect and expressive language than her brother.

Gary was described as having been colicky *always*, and "needing" to be held constantly. Vomiting and "stomach cramps" during his first week home suggested constitutional vulnerabilities. By 3 months of age, Gary had developed eczema, rarely slept for more than an hour at a time, either day or night, and was usually "crying incessantly." From 6 to 9 months, relief from crying occurred only when he was moved into the parents' bedroom. Gary had recurrent ear and upper respiratory infections which could not be treated with penicillin because of an allergy. From the ninth through the thirteenth month, the twins' mother complained of severe backaches, and bed rest was prescribed by her physician. The maternal grandmother entered the children's lives as an ongoing caregiver during this period.

When Gary was a year old, the family's beleaguered pediatrician prescribed small doses of Benadryl for the child to induce sleep, but met with failure. By 18 months, Gary had learned to climb out of his crib in the middle of the night and was wandering about the house scattering and destroying things in his wake. The parents tried to place him in a "regular" bed to see if his poor sleep was related somehow to "fear of the bars" in his crib, but this effort failed as well. Gary would awaken, call for his father, and cry. He was usually inconsolable, and when Mr. Ames returned to bed after failing to quiet him, Gary would begin to wander about the house. On one occasion he turned over several of his mother's favorite plants, evoking in the mother what she described as a "wish to kill." Most of the damage, however, occurred in the kitchen. No matter how often he was put to bed, in his room or his parents', Gary would somehow repeat his rampages, climbing over barriers of plywood and half doors set up to block his path. During this period, his daytime life became more aggressive; he was described as throwing things without provocation at his siblings, and occasionally biting his parents for no apparent reason. In striking contrast to such aggressive, monsterlike behavior, Gary became extremely "clingy" and would ask to be held when his parents' friends visited the home.

When Gary was 20 months old, another tranquilizer for sleep was prescribed by the pediatrician, again without benefit. It was after this final pharmacological failure that a referral was made for developmental assessment and consultation.

Developmental Assessment

When we used the Yale Developmental Schedules to conduct the task-oriented portion of Gary's assessment, we saw the child once in the presence of his mother and, on a second visit, in the presence of his father. Seeing a child with the parents in this manner often provides useful diagnostic clues regarding child-parent interaction. Although two sessions proved sufficient in this instance, the number of appointments varies, depending on the child's work tempo, his physical state at the time of the testing, and the examiner's time, patience, and ingenuity in giving the child the opportunity to do his best on the standard test items.

The assessment tool we use is itself a composite protocol, consisting of items drawn from several standardized scales: Gesell, Hetzer-Wolf Test from the Viennese Scale, Binet, and Merrill Palmer. Originally organized by Sally Provence, the Yale Development Schedules have been used extensively in clinical and research work at the Yale Child Study Center for more than twenty-five years and provide a reliable matrix for assessing, recording, and following a child's performance in motor function, problem solving, language, and personal-social skills over time.

Gary evidenced an interesting if uneven profile on the developmental schedules. Though chronologically 23 months of age, Gary demonstrated the motor skills of a 30-month-old child. He was able to walk up and down stairs well and to jump from a low chair to the ground with considerable agility and confidence. He could imitate various vertical, horizontal, and circular printed forms with a crayon, holding the crayon in a mature grasp. Despite these signs of adequate body mastery, however, Gary frequently used his precocious motor skills to place himself in dangerous positions, climbing to teetering heights and hurling himself recklessly to the ground narrowly escaping injury on several occasions.

In the adaptive, or problem solving area, Gary showed an active, curious interest in the simple puzzles and cube structures more typical of the 30-month-old child's problem solving and manipulative skills than of a toddler not yet 2 years old. When we looked for signs of personal and social development, Gary seemed interested in domestic mimicry and portrayed several scenes of "helping around the house," showing some pleasure in imitating adult activities. He seemed to take pride in his accomplishments, albeit with muted affect.

The source of greatest concern developmentally was Gary's language delay, highlighted all the more by his competence in other areas. His expressive language consisted of only a few simple words, and he rarely combined two or three words spontaneously. He made his wants known by either pulling or shoving adults toward desired items.

Although Gary's play was vigorous in quality, it was narrow and repetitious in content. He was unable to play even briefly with other children and showed only the most rudimentary fantasy play. Though he had achieved only partial control of his bladder in his early toilet training attempts, he did place several life dolls on the dollhouse potty and said "poop." Throughout the testing, his somber, rigid facial expression persisted; he made occasional, but only fleeting, eye contact.

At this point in the assessment, it was clear that Gary and his family were suffering pervasive difficulties. The favorable mutual adaptation of mother and infant one hopes to see, with its indication of reciprocal, harmonious communications and signs of attachment was quite disturbed. Gary had achieved few if any steps in self-regulation and self-comfort. Motility was by far his preferred mode of interacting with others and with the material world, eclipsing language and social relationships. He had been a devastating surprise to his mother who, not knowing she would have twins, did not have an opportunity to prepare herself emotionally for him and could not effectively deal with the adaptational crisis of parenthood that ensued. The affective tie of Gary and his mother seemed

woven primarily of the warp and weft of aggression and retaliation.

In what was planned as the final parent conference of the
evaluation, Mrs. Ames entered the office saying she was at
the end of her rope. She found Gary now "impossible to relate
to." At night he asked only for his father, who usually did not
return from his second job until 11:30 P.M. Gary seemed more
interested in the parent he *couldn't* have than in her. She was
feeling "totally frustrated and overwhelmed." Mr. Ames confessed, meanwhile, that he was now more distant and less
supportive than ever, reporting that the night before he had
yelled, "Why in God's name did you have so many kids?"

Mrs. Ames reported that the behavior of Gary's siblings
now made her think that "the family was falling apart." Mary
wanted to be fed only from her bottle again. John was refusing
to go to bed at all. Lucy confided to her mother that she was
afraid Gary would eat her. Mrs. Ames also reported that Gary
was now "screaming like I was beating him" when he refused
to go to sleep. He would sob inconsolably for "daddy, my
daddy, daddy."

Since the family seemed to be in a rapidly deepening
crisis, we planned a second meeting two days hence. On this
occasion we heard clear but disturbing signals. The first occurred the night after the final evaluation conference. Mrs.
Ames had been up all night with Gary and, while holding
him, had accidentally spilled a cup of hot coffee, narrowly
avoiding scalding him seriously. The following night, in his
by now routine nighttime ravaging of the house, Gary had left
newspapers on the top of a gas range. Mother inadvertently
turned on the burner in the morning and ignited the newspapers, avoiding a fire only narrowly. At this point we became
seriously concerned about the family's ability to control Gary's
destructive impulses, as well as their own, in the face of their
rapidly mounting feelings of helplessness. In response to the
familywide deterioration, we arranged a hospitalization for
Gary on our Pediatric Research Unit.

Hospitalization

At the time of the admission, we lacked answers to several questions regarding the etiology of Gary's sleep disturbance. We had no clear, objective data regarding the quality of Gary's parenting, or even of his mood over a twenty-four-hour period. With Gary's admission to the Pediatric Research Unit, the pediatric and nursing staff and the child psychiatric consultant could make detailed naturalistic observations. Consultation would also be sought from other departments in the medical center to investigate thoroughly any organic contribution to Gary's inability to establish successfully a stable sleep and wake cycle. Could there be an endocrine or neurochemical disturbance disrupting the normal diurnal variations between sleep and wakefulness, or contributing to what was described as "Gary's voracious appetite"?

The earliest observations in the research unit reported that while Gary had few spontaneous vocalizations and that those he did have were whining and plaintive, the nurses were impressed by his high level of language comprehension. They found him to be active, but careless and reckless in the use of his body, repeatedly climbing on top of his bed and sliding off, narrowly avoiding serious injury.

At the end of his first hospital day, Gary looked distressed and sad following his mother's departure. To the amazement of the head nurse, he watched his mother walk out the door, looked at the nurse, and put his index finger down his throat as far as he could, seemingly to induce vomiting. This dramatic event allowed the nurses to quickly appreciate the intensity of Gary's distress, and several nurturing attachments formed over the next several days. Gary responded by following several of his favorite nurses about, climbing on their laps, and accepting comforting from them.

In a dramatic turnabout, Gary slept well from his first night in the hospital, averaging between nine and eleven hours of sleep, with frequent naps during the day. He slept well whether his parents were with him or not. He always evidenced some mild distress when they left, but could accept comforting and would always lie down and nap. Surprisingly, Gary's appetite seemed poor compared to the reports from home. Throughout his hospital stay, he retained his somber demeanor and characteristically rigid facial expession. He seemed most animated and vigorous when his father appeared, or when the maternal grandfather visited.

Significantly, during the hospitalization Mrs. Ames began to verbalize her rage and anger toward her husband for his lack of involvement with the rest of the family and with her. While Gary was safely in the care and custody of the research unit nurses, she confronted Mr. Ames with her anger and asked if he wanted to "make this marriage work or leave home." Quite out of her consciousness at this moment, but reported subsequently was the realization that as an adolescent Mrs. Ames had frequently heard her mother deliver this threat almost verbatim to her father. Mr. Ames responded to his wife by trying to become more involved and available, both during the hospitalization and at home. After Mrs. Ames vented her rage at her husband, she seemed more relaxed, and Gary became dramatically less irritable with her. He fell asleep in her arms for the first time shortly after the session in which she had confronted her husband; his mother reported that this was the first time since his early infancy she could recall this happening.

Throughout Gary's hospitalization, his mother denied having any negative feelings toward him. She did say that, unlike her other children, neither Gary nor Lucy were baptized, because she had gotten into a minor dispute with her parish priest. This suggested conflict, largely unconscious, over the very existence of the twins.

Because of Gary's impressive and dramatic sleep record in the hospital, neither the neurology nor the endocrinology consultant suggested further workup. His physical examination and routine laboratory work showed entirely normal results. An overnight pass home prior to discharge was arranged, and Gary slept well, although Mrs. Ames reported that on this occasion she had fallen down a flight of stairs while holding her son in her arms. Fortunately neither was hurt, and Gary was discharged after a hospital stay of eight days.

Hospitalization had yielded several crucial pieces of data, the first being that Gary's sleep disturbance was primarily reactive in nature, with negligible organic contribution. Second, it was clear that significant marital dysfunction was being displaced and projected onto Gary. Both parents reported that they had had no sexual contact since Gary had been sleeping with them (a period of many months), and that there had been no feelings of closeness since the birth of the twins. Moreover, Mrs. Ames's affective state seemed to be intimately linked somehow with Gary's symptoms, although she had great difficulty in consciously acknowledging any negative feelings toward Gary, and focused instead only on his behavior.

Diagnostic Formulation

The study of this toddler raises complex diagnostic questions. How do we understand Gary's severe disturbance in the normal rhythm of sleep and wakefulness, or his rigidly depresed affect? It is unlikely that such pervasive symptoms result from internalized neurotic conflict. He had not achieved the degree of psychic structure formation necessary for internalized (neurotic) conflict that Fraiberg (1950) describes in her case studies of toddlers with severe sleep disturbances and phobias, nor did he show a classic primary personality disorder such as infantile psychosis.

Gary's failures in the regulation of aggression, delayed language, severe sleep disturbance, depressed mood, and acute separation anxiety, all of which were relatively long-lived, suggested at the least a critical ongoing disturbance in the development of human relationships. This disturbance, in turn, seems the result of serious impairment of the intense, mutually loving relationship between infant and caregiver one hopes to see. The lack of such a bond had significantly impaired, or distorted, the development of certain of Gary's ego functions: attitudes toward reality; the achievement of stable defenses; the organization and regulation of drive and affect; and even the development of such autonomous functions as motility, visual perception, intelligence, and speech.

Gary's case raised questions about the development of a predisposition to basic depressive mood. Anthony (1975) has suggested that for the very young child, repeated experiences of a "mother who is physically present, but emotionally unavailable, forces the child into direct conflict with her, with the result that integration *and* objective evaluation of good and bad maternal images is impaired" (p. 250). Some of Jacobson's work (1957) suggests that when the very young child encounters repeated frustration and disappointment from the love object, he experiences a severe narcissistic injury, for which he tries to compensate by overvaluing the love object, diverting the hostile, derogatory feelings toward himself. His nascent sense of self thus becomes dependent on its idealized external object rather than the real one, and this may result in an interference with his developing realistic mental representations of himself and his mother.

Mahler (1966) argues that the predisposition to a basic mood is established during the process of separation-individuation, most especially during the subphase of rapprochement (18–24 months). During this period, the young toddler, aided by maturing autonomous ego functioning, becomes not only increasingly aware of his own separateness, but also much more aware of his need for his mother's acceptance and renewed involvement. Pleasure in increased autonomy and experiences in mastery help the child gradually relinquish his demands on his caregivers to satisfy all his needs and to adjust his fantasies of omnipotence. Mahler indicates that shadowing (the caregiver), provocative darting away, continual demandingness, whininess, temper tantrums and extreme ambivalence are frequent behavioral signs alerting us to a disturbance in human relationships and a depressed mood (p. 74).

Gary illustrates such a severe developmental disturbance all too clearly. His history offers some clues about the origins of his difficulties. Although both twins were "unplanned" and unwanted, Gary was literally unexpected. As a male, he was closely identified with her husband in his mother's mind and ambivalently cathected by her. Additionally, Gary was a difficult, uncomfortable, "unreadable" infant, unrewarding and threatening to the mother's already vulnerable self-esteem. He must have experienced her as being emotionally distant and frustrating as she failed repeatedly to ease his constitutionally based predisposition to discomfort.

It appears that Gary entered the separation-individuation phase of development never having achieved a satisfactory relationship with his mother. In the months preceeding the referral, the biologically determined upsurge in aggression which occurs during the second year was coupled with Gary's panic at his increasing awareness of his separateness from his mother and the abrupt loss of his fantasies of omnipotence as a result of her emotional unavailability. Also affecting Gary were his mother's own difficulties around separateness, noted not only in her relationship to her own parents and her husband, but in the projection of her own fantasies of omnipotence and power onto Gary. Gary's precocious body mastery may have developed so rapidly, in part as an effort to compensate for the deficits into other areas of development and for the less developed, defective object relationships. His constitutional vulnerability evident in eczema, colic, neonatal infections and his failure to establish biological rhythmicity of sleep-wake cycles contributed to the onset and perpetuation of the disturbance.

Planning Intervention

How can clinicians use such a synthesis of data to fashion a meaningful, well-aimed intervention strategy for a child and his family? In Gary's case we used several modes of intervention, including both inpatient and outpatient work, direct intervention with the child, direct intervention with the parents, and, finally, what may be the most complex and poorly understood of these modalities—the meshing of parent and infant work—in which each facet of treatment influences the other and closest coordination of the parent and infant work is required.

At the completion of the external diagnostic study, the family accepted transfer from the diagnostic crisis team to the long-term treatment team, though all clinicians kept close counsel with one another as options were reviewed.[1] The new therapist, a child psychiatrist, met with Mr. and Mrs. Ames at the time of discharge from the hospital to further assess their interest in working as a couple on their severe marital distress, and also to assess and support their conscious commitment to having Gary return to their family. When the therapist gently broached the possibility of Gary's not returning home, both parents firmly maintained that they were committed to his recovery as part of the family, saying, "We brought him here to get him fixed, not give him away."

Marital Problems and Their Treatment

On the basis of these discussions at the time of discharge from the hospital, the treatment team determined that therapy directed at the severe marital problems would be the best way to begin. We hoped to reduce the marital discord and promote a reduction of Gary's tense, conflict-ridden involvement in his parents' marital strife. We guessed that on some level the parents had welcomed Gary's nightly diversions, which drew attention away from the almost total absence of intimacy in their relationship since the birth of the twins.

The parents were seen for four months in weekly couples therapy, in which they began to explore many of their conflicts and feelings about each other and their own families of origin

[1] I am greatly indebted to Drs. Jean Marachi and Kirsten Dahl, who collaborated with me in the ongoing work with this family as well as the diagnostic formulation.

and their failure to nurture one another adequately. Gary and the other children also remained an important focus of the work, both indirectly and as real concerns.

Gary's mother consistently denied ever being angry with her children, and was strongly invested in presenting herself as a dedicated, devoted mother. Gradually she expressed her anger toward her husband more openly, complaining bitterly that the *children* needed more of him. Although she could never acknowledge this directly, she was clearly irritated at Gary for always asking for his father.

Mr. Ames was overwhelmed by his wife's and his children's emotional demands, and seemed bewildered by the disappointment and anger his wife felt toward him. His usual avoidance behavior was to sit in front of the television, in a self-induced "fugue state," to distance himself from these demands. He reported that the more he tried to resolve things with his wife, the more irate and demanding she would become.

In the course of treatment, Mrs. Ames discovered that as she became less critical and angry toward her husband, he could become more available and supportive. It was clearly more difficult for her to be supportive of Mr. Ames, although rudimentary attempts did appear. For example, the couple addressed the father's complaint of feeling overwhelmed by the children at night when he arrived for dinner. They would literally surround and almost immobilize him each evening as he entered the front door. All four would tug and pull at his clothes, simultaneously demanding he do something with them "First!" Mrs. Ames finally responded to his pleas for help by firmly instructing the children to "leave your father alone" until after dinner. The result of this directive was quite striking to the parents, as all four adhered to the directive the first night.

Despite some visible repair of the marital relationship, Gary's improvement during the hospitalization gradually decayed at home. His sleep patterns, as well as his behavior during the day, fluctuated dramatically. One week the parents would report that he had slept eight hours a night for several nights the preceding week, and that he was playing well with his siblings. In the next session, they would complain that he had slept poorly all week and was biting his sisters.

Despite these vacillations, Gary did make some significant gains in several areas as the marital therapy continued. His speech developed so that by the last month of the parental work he was only slightly delayed in expressive language. He achieved toilet training at the age of 28 months, without assistance from the parents.

Another gain, a decrease in Gary's aggressive behavior, illustrates how progress in therapy may change the parents' *perception* of their child, a process which may then be reflected in the child's successful attainment of a higher developmental level. The parents noted that Gary's unprovoked attacks on his siblings and his cruel teasing of the household pets were occasionally accompanied by displays of pleasurable affect. This had led the family to conclude that Gary was a sadistic, almost alien creature, although this characterization was never directly verbalized. This behavior and its eerie effect on the family had reached their peak when Gary, then 29 months old, began collecting small toads in the backyard, bringing them inside, placing them on the kitchen floor and crushing them with his heel, with no expression of feeling. Later on, when Gary had developed enough expressive language, he was able to give his parents some reasons for what had seemed almost inexplicable primitive behavior; Gary repeated, "Bad toads, Gary No!"

The parents began bringing such "crazy explanations" to their treatment hours to discuss with the therapist, who then helped "decode" both Gary's verbalizations and his behavior: ripping up the father's sandwich was understood as wanting to feed the tuna fish sandwich to the cat, instead of wanting to destroy the father's lunch; pouring ketchup on the cat was an experiment to see if the cat liked ketchup as he did, rather than an effort to make the animal "look dead" (the parental interpretation); hitting his sister was retribution for her having taken one of his toys, and so forth. As the therapist acted as "translator" or "spokesman" for Gary, his parents began to change their view of him. They experienced him as less malicious and more normal, though not entirely likable.

After five months of marital therapy, the team reviewed the usefulness of continuing to work exclusively with the parents. Although they had become more supportive of one another and were able to communicate their mutual needs, Mr. and Mrs. Ames were still deeply divided over how to manage Gary in any consistent way. The mother reported to the therapist: "You have helped us understand what we are supposed to do to help Gary, but we just can't seem to do it on our own. We know what's right, but together we mess it up all the time."

At this stage in treatment, when Gary would awaken crying at night, the parents would argue about who was to get up and what to do. Eventually Mr. Ames would pick him up and bring him into the parental bed. His wife would then become furious and leave the bedroom to sleep on the living room couch. Gary would then wake up and begin wandering about the house. Mrs. Ames would get up to investigate what he was doing and stay up to "keep an eye on him," or hold him, for the rest of the night. Although she was clearly enraged with Gary, she professed not to feel so while she was holding him.

Mrs. Ames continued to see herself as the helpless target of his uncontrollable behavior, despite a vignette that suggests she could take charge of the situation. One evening, prior to his father's arrival home from work, Gary was whining about where his daddy was. Mrs. Ames was at the end of her rope and shrieked at him, "Get back in bed, if you know what's good for you." On the strength of this angry but clear and unambivalent message, Gary slept completely through the night and late into the next morning.

Another vignette, centered around Gary's toilet training, poignantly revealed the mother's ambivalence regarding Gary's increasing independence and separation from her. During the summer, several months after he had successfully trained himself, she encouraged Gary to urinate in the garden to avoid lengthy trips back into the house while she and the other children were outside. Gary became so pleased with this new technique that he soon refused to use the toilet inside, preferring always to urinate outside, regardless of the weather. His mother was angered by this obstinacy, and she refused to put a diaper on him even when he began to wet himself because he was not permitted to void outside. Consequently, Gary's toilet training was undone, and on one occasion he smeared himself with feces.

In taking stock of our work with the couple, we decided to directly assess the parents' views of Gary, and their interactions with him, by seeing the whole family and each parent individually with Gary. These naturalistic sessions revealed that neither parent seemed interested in, or capable of, understanding the probable thoughts or motives behind Gary's behavior. If the therapist asked Gary's parents why they thought he was doing a particular thing in the playroom, they would respond, "Because he wants to." Having hoped through extensive couples therapy to increase the Ames's sensitivity to Gary's needs and "signals" as well as to their own and each other's feelings, we found the parents' inability to engage in understanding Gary very distressing indeed.

It seemed clear that further progress was very unlikely without direct work with Gary. During this series of visits, he showed a strong interest in the therapist and responded well to attempts to try to encourage and understand his play and expressive behavior.

We decided to take Gary as well as his parents into treatment at this point. It was expected that treatment of Gary would be difficult because his language was still slightly delayed, and the parents' description of his play at age 29 months suggested that it was still quite primitive. We were not sure what degree of symbolic thinking Gary might be able to use and elaborate in direct treatment. We were also concerned about the effect on the parental work of a shift in treatment focus from the couple to Gary. Might the marital difficulties intensify? How would Mr. and Mrs. Ames react to the therapist's seeing Gary instead of them?

As the team reviewed the entire case, we concluded that parental therapy had stimulated enough beginning improvement in the couple's communication and reciprocity to bring about more stability in the family unit, evidenced particularly in the functioning of Gary's siblings. Also, Gary himself had slowly achieved modest developmental gains. Given the pervasive nature of his initial deficits, however, he could ill afford the leisurely pace of growth that continued work with the parents alone might promote. The team therefore decided that the therapist would begin working with Gary twice weekly on a trial basis, and with his parents every other week. This arrangement was a compromise, as five visits every two weeks was as many as could be expected from the family, who lived an hour's drive from the clinic.

We had hoped in the first phase of the work to explore Gary's ability to form a therapeutic alliance and to assess his capacity for symbolic play and his use of language in the therapeutic setting. We also hoped to engage Gary in play around issues of aggression and impulse control, allowing him a safe environment in which to explore these themes, and to observe his reaction to, and use of, the person of the therapist.

Gary's Psychotherapy

Not unexpectedly, two subsequent sessions were canceled. The parents seemed to be acting out their unconscious dissatisfaction with the treatment plan, despite their specific request that Gary see "their" therapist and no one else.

When work with Gary did begin, it was carried out in a standard playroom treatment setting equipped with materials appropriate to the child's developmental level. The materials included a table, two chairs, child-scale domestic furniture, water, simple nonmechanical toys, puppets, life dolls, simple animal figures, and a small collection of dress-up clothes and hats. Also important was the private storage area for each child's specially selected toys and play materials, what Mahler calls "the equivalent of the adult's associations, known only to the child and his therapist" (1966).

At the first meeting there was little difficulty in separating Gary from his mother. In fact, he hardly noted her departure. Gary avoided eye contact with the therapist and surveyed the playroom silently, with a fixed, wooden stare. He seemed drawn to the materials but unable to approach them. The therapist spoke softly to Gary, inviting him to choose something to play with, not necessarily with the therapist. Gary finally walked over to the sink and gradually began touching the water and exploring the water toys. He was allowed to do this alone until he turned his head and made eye contact with the therapist, who took this gesture as an invitation. He then sat next to Gary and began a narrative description of his play in the sink. Gary responded with a few softly uttered words. After establishing his solitary play, Gary handed a small wooden boat to the therapist. With this further invitation, some simple reciprocal play began between the two through the medium of "washing" (Gary's word).

The therapist then addressed the reason for Gary's visit, saying that he knew from talking with Gary's parents that things were "very upset at home," especially for Gary, and that he would be meeting with Gary "to try to understand and help with all the upset." He defined the "upset" as trouble with sleeping, fighting with his family, especially Mommy, and seeming to be a "very, very unhappy little boy." Gary looked wide-eyed and slightly startled as he returned the therapist's benign gaze. He said nothing, but continued to play contentedly.

The next four sessions consisted almost exclusively of

silent water play. Gary's initial uncertainty thawed, and he became increasingly comfortable and confident with the therapist, who gently persisted in attempts to broaden and elaborate his play. By the third hour, the rigid facial expression that had characterized Gary's countenance since we had first met him was obviously softening. A fleeting smile would cross the child's face whenever the therapist attempted to animate and enhance the play by introducing a small animal puppet, or "observer-companion," to the play. By the end of the fourth hour, Gary was reluctant to leave, but remained compliant. As yet, the therapist had seen no expression of the powerful aggression so troubling to his family. The therapist was uncertain whether its absence was part of a pervasive play inhibition, or was attributable to the lack of libidinal investment of the therapist as a need-satisfying object, thereby obviating the need or *wish* to be aggressive. Shortly after the fourth session, the parents noted an improvement in Gary's daytime behavior, although his sleep remained troubled.

Mrs. Ames reported to the therapist that on trips to and from the clinic she had "gotten to know Gary." He asked her questions, which she found easy to answer while she was driving, and not having to look at him directly. She disclosed that she used to think her son "hated her deeply," but he had recently told her she was "his goodest friend." Gary had also switched from constantly requesting his father to calling for her in the night. She reported she felt that "he really wasn't a nasty, mean kid," although she followed her comment with an anxious laugh.

After the introductory sessions, as he reported daily events from his family's life, Gary made increasing use of the therapist. He had also become highly invested in projective play and showed continuity of play themes from session to session. He was more verbal and more affectively available than he had been, and acted increasingly seductive with the therapist. "Gary good?" and "Gary bad?" were questions that emerged after initial limit testing began. Gary was clearly forming a therapeutic alliance.

By the second month of work with Gary (now 32 months old), his mother reported she could now distinguish among Gary's various moods. Mr. Ames reported that Gary seemed "less sadistic" and went on to say his aggressive behavior seemed to be "for reasons, now, and not crazy off-the-wall."

In Gary's sessions with the therapist, ritualized, sensory explorations in the form of clay molding and water play were mingled with rudimentary symbolic play with puppets and life dolls. Gradually Gary began to ask for paper and scissors and to cut for the last few minutes of each hour, proudly presenting his cuttings to his mother at the conclusion of the visit. Gary's attachment to the therapist became more physical and linked to nurturing: he might ask the therapist to zipper his coat, or, on other occasions, might put his arms around the therapist's neck and ask to be picked up so that he could examine the top shelf of the play cabinet. This marked a significant advance for Gary; he was now able to use the therapist's body as a kind of "affective brace" instead of a piece of mobile furniture. (Using the therapist in such a fashion signals that the child patient perceives the therapist as benevolent at a basic sensory level; it lays the groundwork for an eventual symbolic mental internalization of the therapist.) Gary exhibited increasingly positive affect in mutual play with the therapist and seemed mute and sober after missing a therapy hour.

Two parallel achievements characterized the third month of Gary's twice-weekly therapy: (a) the entry of aggression into the treatment hours, and (b) the parents' report of continuingly improved language. The theme of aggression entered through Gary's favorite ritualized play, "washing babies to get them good." Now the baby began to come under attack from several puppets, sometimes a mother life doll who "beat" the baby and held it "under" the water, and, at other times, a "fighting bear" that was similarly threatening. These episodes seemed both cathartic and intensely stimulating to Gary, and often led the therapist to set limits regarding destruction of materials and self-abusive careening about the playroom.

For the first time Gary was able to give vent to his aggressive fantasies and resentment over his disappointed longings for someone to keep him safe and not alone. When appropriate limits on the sadistic behavior were set by the therapist there followed fatigue, listlessness, and flattened affect. Interpretations made to Gary at such moments dealt with the surface limit testing, but also with the deeper motives for his acting out, particularly his fear of abandonment and annihilation. Often the therapist could only address him indirectly at such moments, as Gary needed to insulate or barricade himself after such outbursts. An interpretation might begin: "Gary wants to make sure I can control him, because if *I* can't, then he might be so *bad* I would go away and leave him all alone."

At other times, the therapist's limit setting seemed a relief, protecting Gary against retaliation fantasies and fears. Such unflinching and repetitive definition of the realities of the therapeutic alliance through limit setting and interpretation kept that alliance from being overwhelmed by Gary's fantasies of being omnipotently destructive, as in the view harbored by his parents at the outset of treatment.

During this same period, Gary reestablished sphincter control and, for the first time since the posthospitalization period, had achieved sustained, comfortable sleep. The sleep disturbance seemed to decrease after the therapist and Gary together designed some new bedtime rituals involving a snack, cuddling stuffed animals, and "reading."

During his play, Gary had been reluctant to lay a baby down horizontally in a play bed, attempting to have the baby sleep upright. He seemed both unable and unwilling to relinquish the awake, active, upright posture with all its exciting, sadistic, and stimulating interchange with the mother, perhaps because it was so critical in preserving the only truly positive side of his tie to her. Falling asleep, or even lying down, with its inherent libidinal withdrawal from the external world to the self, apparently was the equivalent of abandonment for Gary. Anna Freud (1960) describes just such a dilemma: "withdrawal of libido and of ego interests to the self becomes a prerequisite for sleep. This is not accomplished without difficulty, and the anxiety aroused by the process makes the toddler cling all the more tenaciously to his wakefulness" (pp. 157–158).

The lock on the door separating the parents' apartment from that of the grandparents broke around this time and for some reason was not repaired. Consequently, the Ames children began to visit their grandparents regularly. Gary would occasionally awaken at 2:00 or 3:00 A.M. and go up to find his grandfather, who would then hold him, read to him, or walk with him until Gary would fall back to sleep. This contact with the grandfather had a very calming effect on both Gary and his mother, who began to imitate her father's behavior, albeit with less success.

The parents now related to the therapist their secret fear that Gary might be retarded. Each had harbored this concern independently, but had never mentioned it to the other. Only when they were relatively certain he was of normal intelligence was the subject broached. Interestingly, this fear had persisted despite our telling the Ameses at the initial diagnostic evaluation that Gary was functioning at, or above, his age level in all areas except language, and showed no evidence of mental retardation.

Mrs. Ames also noted that Gary began to brag to his siblings about going to his appointments. They were all envious of his time there, not only with the therapist, but also with the mother on the drive to and from the clinic. Mrs. Ames became concerned about how this would effect Gary's siblings.

Gary's sleep continued to improve. By the end of the third month of treatment, with the help of the maternal grandfather and the rituals devised with the therapist, he slept well for three consecutive nights. At this point, however, Mr. and Mrs. Ames became worried that Gary was becoming "spoiled." The mother's distress seemed to be fueled by thinly disguised envy of Gary's positive attachment to her own father, to whom she had always felt vaguely unacceptable. She reasoned that by being treated as "special" by the grandfather, Gary was becoming stubborn with his own father.

A significant regression occurred in the treatment when Mr. Ames became infuriated one evening when Gary refused to put on his pajamas. He put Gary in his bed and told him not to leave his room, "Ever!" The result was several sleepless nights for everyone, as Gary, now prevented from seeing his grandfather, regressed to crying and screaming. His mother was, however, able to console him briefly by holding and walking him. She and Gary could now enjoy brief sustained periods of bodily contact without generating the excitation and aggressive tension that had spoiled such reciprocity earlier.

The parents and the therapist had an emergency meeting at this time. Mr. and Mrs. Ames vented their anger and frustration with Gary at a pitch not previously seen. The therapist acknowledged how trying and difficult Gary was and how hard the Ameses were trying to be good parents for him. He pointed out, however, that Gary *did* have special needs, that his special treatment was necessary for the time being, and that it was not spoiling him. The therapist explained that Gary's negativism served, at times, to help him grow in independence. On the strength of their trust in the therapist, they seemed to accept this; Mrs. Ames, in particular, expressed relief at being able to articulate her feelings. Over the next two weeks, Gary began sleeping on his own again, although he was at first successful only in his grandparents' bed.

During the fourth month of treatment, Gary used play to express and explore the relevant themes in his life more directly, greatly aided by his improving language. He began to express his aggression in more ritualized and controlled episodes; he would, for instance, build up and then knock down complex block buildings and towers. In a play session with his favorite doll, Gary carefully "fed" the baby a bottle and then stated that the bottle was "poison." He became somber, leaving the doll on the floor and avoiding further explorations, despite the invitation of the therapist. On other occasions, Gary became angry with the dolls and began beating them with his hands. When the therapist animated the doll, to inquire and protest about this punishment and mistreatment, he became glum and moved on to another play item.

During this same month, Gary said to the therapist, with a forced smile, "I don't like Gary," but he seemed unable to elaborate. This announcement was followed by several play sessions in which, with affective and verbal support from the therapist, Gary revealed multiple fearful fantasies of ghosts and monsters. He casually reported long-standing nightmares which involved his being "chased and eaten by monsters." The therapist responded by telling Gary that many boys and girls who worried about their mad and angry "baby feelings" had scary dreams about monsters. Gary seemed greatly relieved. He began using the therapist to play out the dreams with animals and life dolls with considerable relief. This play was the greatest source for Gary of what Erikson terms "satiation-comfort brought to the child through interpretive play, similar to that felt by the adult after a correct interpretation or clarification in psychoanalytic psychotherapy" (1963).

In conjunction with the exploration of these emerging themes, Gary displayed even more positive affect toward the therapist. He readily reached for his hand when walking to and from play sessions. On several occasions, he contrived for the therapist to pick him up. In so doing, he began to hug the therapist spontaneously. The therapist's acknowledgment of his affection by returning Gary's hug usually left him content, quiet, and physically relaxed.

The following month, with encouragement from the therapist, Gary's parents entered him in a regular nursery school. The therapist tried to anticipate for Mr. and Mrs. Ames some of the difficulties Gary might experience, given his tenuous toilet training, his fear of separating from his mother, his aggressive behavior with peers, and his poor social skills. Gary further elaborated in play sessions the fear that there would be "monsters at school" and the sense that he was being sent "away" to school because he was "bad." The therapist provided much reassurance and opportunities for reality testing around these issues.

In fact, Gary tolerated nursery school quite well. He quickly formed a warm, affectionate bond with the nursery school teacher, an older woman who had, coincidentally, also been his mother's nursery school teacher. Although he avoided most of the other children, Gary did play with one girl in addition to his twin sister, also in the class.

Mrs. Ames initially helped Gary by staying with him each day until he seemed comfortable. In time, however, she lost patience with him, despite the therapist's constant caution that Gary perceived his separation from her in a threatening way. Her abrupt departure from the classroom after dropping the twins at school resulted in episodes of uncontrollable tearfulness and subsequent aggressive behavior once Gary returned home.

Gary did, however, maintain most of his maturational gains and toilet training through this difficult period. Within the next two months, he was sleeping on and off between eight and ten hours a night. In one of the monthly joint sessions the therapist held with them, Gary was able to tell his mother that he was sad when she left him at school and that it was "scary for her to leave." Mrs. Ames expressed surprise and disbelief, but with the therapist's support and reiteration of Gary's statement, she did acknowledge his fear and adjust her behavior.

Despite Gary's gains, the marital situation continued to

drift aimlessly. This state of affairs represented a radical change in the previous interdigitation of the parent and child work. Until this time, ebbs and flows of progress and regression had been roughly "coupled" in the two treatments, purposefully coordinated in the monthly joint sessions with Gary and his parents. Hereafter a limited uncoupling began, permitting a parallel rather than fused therapeutic alliance between the therapist and Gary on the one hand, and the therapist and the parents on the other. What this meant, in specific terms, was that the work with the parents now was best served by more attention to them as a couple and as separate adults, and a less direct focus on their parenting behavior.

During this same period, although his parents were unable to crystalize clear therapeutic goals, Gary was busy exploring techniques in his play to protect himself from the "monsters and ghosts" that plagued his fantasy life. He involved the therapist in building elaborate block and paper constructions to sequester, incarcerate, and occasionally obliterate these nefarious forces, all the while developing and practicing more ritualized, obsessional defensive patterns which brought him greater comfort and improved organization. So important were these new architectural bulwarks against regression that Gary became quite imperious and castigating if the therapist suffered a momentary lapse of recall in the pattern of their weekly reconstructions.

With Gary's improvement, his parents returned once again to explore conflicted aspects of their relationship, especially their mutual dependency. During such periods they often temporarily stopped supporting one another. Mr. Ames began drinking more heavily but denied this behavior when confronted by his wife. Mrs. Ames expressed much concern the following month over her husband's alcohol use and "rough handling of the children," saying he was "short-tempered" with them. When, in a session with the couple, the two discussed why he had become so irritable with the children, the discussion eventually turned to Mr. Ames's own lack of fathering. The therapist then suggested that anxiety about his own failures at fathering had led him to distance himself from the family, thus unwittingly repeating his father's pattern of alienation and absence from his family. Mr. Ames became tearful and stated, in a subdued voice, that he "was only trying to prepare his children for the hard world that they would have to live in."

By the end of the following month, both parents began to raise questions about how long they would need treatment. They had worked on some of their mutual depression and helplessness and acknowledged Gary's continuing improvement. Mrs. Ames did not want to continue. She was now hopeful that Gary would sustain the gains he had made, and the one-hour trip each way was cutting more and more into her "real family time." In the spirit of supporting this move toward a less dependent status, the therapist agreed that after a carefully worked-through termination, he would be available every three months for follow-up. He noted that resumption of treatment might be necessary in the future, depending on Gary's clinical course.

Termination

To measure Gary's progress more objectively, developmental testing was performed again before termination. At 40 months, Gary functioned motorically with the physical organization typical of children two to six months older. The careless, self-abusive careening about was no longer seen. Gary's problem solving capacities (displayed in various puzzle and block designs), drawing skills, and number concepts spread into and beyond the 48-month level. The most interesting finding of the reevaluation, however, was that Gary's expressive and comprehensive language development was now excellent. His speech was usually quite intelligible, he enjoyed identifying pictures, and he showed obvious pleasure in his verbal competence and mastery. The profound language delay revealed by the initial diagnostic assessment made Gary's proficiency all the more striking.

The termination phase of treatment consisted of eight sessions. Gary preferred to deal with the termination itself through various displacement and avoidance mechanisms. A calendar was prepared with Gary so that he could follow the weekly progress toward the termination date agreed upon by parents and therapist. Following a discussion of stopping treatment, he regressed, not surprisingly, to water play, his favorite activity in the first sessions, and on one occasion urinated in his pants during the play. Rather than being upset at this, however, he appeared jubilant and content. As though compensating for such regression, in the next session he played at feeding the therapist and acknowledged for the first time that he knew his visits would end "soon."

In his last session, Gary was tearful for the first time at his mother's leaving him with the therapist in the playroom. He initially ignored the present that his therapist had given him. The therapist interpreted for him how sad they were both feeling at stopping their regular visits together. He made it clear that Gary would see him again about as often as he saw a particular uncle who visited the family several times a year. Gary responded with a sudden change of affect, gleefully opened the present, and played with the toy car until the end of the session. He exchanged hugs with the therapist as the hour ended and appeared pleased as he ran triumphantly to the waiting room to show his mother his new toy.

Discussion

Many of the difficulties in working with a preverbal or even verbal toddler emerge in this case description. We have seen Gary express his fantasies and suffering in motoric and verbal fragments which the therapist had somehow to articulate and frame, for Gary and for himself, into an accurate investigation of core conflicts. The therapist acts like a multilingual, or rather a multimodal, translator, using interpretation and clarification to highlight for Gary an understanding reached through play, intuition, and even countertransference, but primarily through extensive knowledge of intrapsychic development.

An essential developmental task for the toddler is the design and construction of a separate self. Consequently, intervention of any kind must assist the process of forming disparate memories and cognitive and sensory experiences from the here and now into that unique cohesion called "the self." The patient achieves such homogenization by using the emotionally significant relationship he forms with the therapist as a "real" person who does not feel repulsed, devalued, or enraged by the demands or suffering of the toddler. Gary was a puzzling, noncommunicative, "unreadable" little boy at the beginning of treatment, disturbing to his parents and bewildering to the therapist. His story illustrates a number of the technical problems of direct therapy with toddlers.

1. Although he began with little or no capacity for symbolic play, Gary could relate to the medium of simple sensory play, in which he could be safely active—even aggressive—and in reasonable control. This served as a safe harbor, from which Gary could eventually explore the predictable benevolence, protection, and control offered by the person, and even the body, of the therapist.

2. The value of Gary's attachment to the therapist became apparent in (a) his panic at a session's end as he feared he would not be able to return, (b) his intense wish for nurturant physical care and for affection from the therapist, and (c) the vulnerability of his fragile object relations to disappointment, demonstrated in his depressed withdrawal after the therapist had to cancel a session. With precarious ego development, including unstable defensive abilities, Gary tended to view himself and others as all good or all bad and was unable to cope with average expectable disappointments. Moreover, he was unable to handle his routine aggressive drives, and suffered in consequence of these strong impulses.

3. The role of aggression in achieving a precarious equilibrium between the disparate levels of Gary's uneven ego development and his highly conflicted family relationships was amply illustrated. Early in treatment, Gary showed endless delight and abandon in building up and knocking down, at first in isolation from, and later in partnership with, the therapist. The killing of frightening toads and the story of a baby, first helpless against Gary's attacks, later a victim of poisoning, were played out.

4. Gary's conflict around separation, evidenced in his depressed mood and clingy attempts to control his mother, faded as Gary was given support by the therapist for active mastery and control in the play. Much of the middle phase of Gary's treatment was devoted to projective dramatic and symbolic play about ritualized reunions, leave-takings, and evictions of life dolls, animals, etc. Eventually, Gary began to talk about his mother in her absence; he anticipated seeing her again, acted out what he thought she "was doing now" with the therapist, and eventually delighted in reunion with her.

5. As the treatment alliance formed, a portrait of Gary's difficulties around separation-individuation emerged. Fragments of symbolic play began to appear in which the therapist could catch fleeting glimpses of how Gary experienced himself—as a "bad," hungry and demanding baby, or as a monkey or toad, helpless in the face of overwhelming aggression. Juxtaposed with these concerns was Gary's intense longing for reunion with an "all good," need-satisfying caregiver.

Though not a complete success or "cure," Gary's treatment and that of his parents achieved some healing, maybe the most we can legitimately expect in such cases. After much intensive work, lives were deeply touched and a few possibly saved. It certainly seemed unwise to challenge the family's wish to discontinue active treatment in the face of Gary's improvement and what seemed the current limits of the couple's own capacity for change.

References

Anthony, E.J. (1975), Childhood depression. In: *Depression and Human Existence*, ed. E.J. Anthony & T. Benedek. Boston: Little, Brown, pp. 231–278.

Erikson, E. (1963), *Childhood and Society*. 2nd ed. New York: Norton.

Fraiberg, S. (1950), On the sleep disturbance of early childhood. *Psychoanalytic Study of the Child*, 5: 285–309. New York: International Universities Press.

Freud, A. (1960), *Normality and Pathology in Childhood*. New York: International Universities Press.

Jacobson, E. (1957), On normal and pathological moods: Their nature and functions. *The Psychoanalytic Study of the Child*, 12:73–113. New York: International Universities Press.

Mahler, M. (1966), Notes on the development of basic moods: The depressive affect in psychoanalysis. In: *Psychoanalysis: A General Psychology*, ed. R. Loewenstein. New York: International Universities Press, pp. 152–168.

6

The Therapist as Decoder: Psychotherapy with Toddlers

E. Kirsten Dahl, Ph.D.

My thoughts on direct psychotherapeutic intervention with toddlers have, in large measure, been shaped by my work with six very young children ranging in age from 19 to 30 months, three boys and three girls. Four of these children lived in two-parent families, one girl lived in a foster family, and one boy lived alone with his mother. Although there was no particular common psychodynamic pattern, the children manifested a remarkable similarity in their symptom pictures: five had serious eating disorders, five had severe difficulties in the regulation of aggression, four had serious sleep disorders, four showed language delays, and three showed signs of psychophysiological growth failure, although only one had been hospitalized. In spite of the severity of their symptoms, on developmental testing all demonstrated at least average intelligence and three performed significantly above age.

Judith Kestenberg (1969) has suggested that working with the very young child is ". . . like an explorer encountering a jungle tribe whose means of communication are different and strange. In order to understand the child we have to devise means to reach the inhabitant and creator of the illusory

213

land and help him grasp the intent of the outsiders who invaded it" (p. 360). I hope to illustrate some of the ways in which one can begin to "decode" the communications of the very young, frequently preverbal, child.

In general, the very young child expresses his wishes, conflicts, and fantasies in action and in word fragments. The therapist functions as a decoder or translator, gradually sharing with the child, through clarification and interpretation, the knowledge gleaned from the translation. Much of the time it is the therapist who supplies the verbalized linkages that connect the action fragments of the toddler patient into a meaningful and communicable whole. Frequently the therapist must provide a suitable medium to enable the child to express his fantasies. For example, a small child struggling with separation issues may be able to express his conflicts through a game of hiding and finding a block in a toy mailbox which has been introduced into the session by the therapist.

Not only may the therapist provide the medium for expression of a fantasy (e.g., the toy mailbox), but by her comments (e.g., "Where did the block go? Did it just disappear? There it is again! *You* found it!") she "reads" the meaning of the action and gives the child words with which he can begin to organize, and so explore, his feelings about separation from his mother.

A toddler's repetitive search for an undefined toy or listening at the playroom door may be understood by the therapist as her patient's demonstration in action of a longing for the mother. As the therapist comments on the toddler's anxious attention to "what is beyond the door," expanding her behavioral observation to include an affective statement of longing ("Where is my Mommy? I *miss* her!"), she helps the small child begin to make use of language in the service of affective differentiation and regulation.

Since the primary developmental task for the toddler is the building of an independent ego, treatment must focus on helping him achieve a meaningful integration of his memory fragments, feelings, words, concepts, and experience. This integration is achieved through the development of an emotionally significant relationship with a therapist who can be sensitive to the needs, wishes, fantasies, and conflicts of a toddler, and who can serve as an auxiliary ego to him in his struggle to integrate past and present into meaningful units. It is the therapist who connects the fragments into a meaningful whole, who clarifies the affect generating the action and the thoughts behind both. As we know, the thinking of the very young child is still very much dominated by the primary processes; a toddler's actions and words have a dreamlike quality. The therapist's work of "translation" is helped by keeping in mind the primary processes and their logic. Condensation, reversal, association by contiguity, the substitution of acting for thinking, and the magical power of thoughts and wishes are characteristic of the toddler's productions. Through the emotionally significant relationship with the therapist in which the toddler feels psychologically differentiated but not abandoned, the toddler is able to "borrow" the integrated translation of his therapist and slowly incorporate it with his own psychic structure.

The two following vignettes of psychotherapy with toddlers illustrate three basic and interrelated points: (1) the importance of working directly with the toddler, as opposed to psychotherapeutic intervention with the mother alone; (2) the role of the therapist in translating the symbolic meaning of a toddler's symptoms; and (3) issues relating to the centrality of the developmental task of separation-individuation.

Working Directly with the Toddler

One might assume that a toddler manifesting behavioral difficulties is reacting to pathological qualities in the mother-child relationship and might imagine that if the mother would change her child-rearing practices, the toddler's behavioral difficulties would vanish. This view ignores the rapidity of development in early childhood: by the time a mother is able to make significant changes in her behavior as the result of her own psychotherapy, the toddler has become an older child whose development may have been seriously compromised by the noxious mother-child relationship.

Translating a Toddler's Symptoms

Not only does the young child react to the mother's behavior, both consciously and unconsciously influenced, but his own perception of her behavior awakens and shapes his ego capacities. After 18 months, the toddler's "difficult behavior" has become symptomatic of conflict that is partially internalized. Some of the behavior represents the toddler's attempts to reach a compromise solution to this conflict. Symptomatic behavior, then, has symbolic meaning to the toddler; it not only responds to stimuli outside the child but also flows from a relatively complex inner world comprised of fantasies, wishes, and cognitions concerning himself, his significant others, and the world of inanimate objects.

Although the toddler's behavior has symbolic meaning for him, because his psychic structure is still evolving and because his use of language is still primitive and relatively idiosyncratic, much of the therapist's work may be to uncover, clarify, and organize these symbolic associations into an integrated, coherent whole. The therapist "makes sense" of the toddler's actions by drawing on her knowledge of early psychological development as well as her understanding of the particular child. The therapist's "translations" involve the linking together of wishes, fantasies, and emotions, and the ways in which these are represented in action: these formulations are then shared verbally with the child in the effort to help him achieve increased ego integration. The goal is greater reliance on secondary processes, including differentiation between thinking and doing, increased capacity to delay gratification and tolerate frustration, and a loosening of the prominence of magical thinking.

The Task of Separation-Individuation

Problems with object constancy, heightened ambivalence, destructive aggression, fantasies of omnipotence, feelings of badness, and anxiety over bodily integrity are prominent in toddlers. Pragmatically, in order to facilitate the successful negotiation of separation-individuation, one must expect to work with the toddler in the presence of his mother for quite a while, perhaps several months, in order to enable the child to master the tasks of this period successfully. While the mother is in the playroom, she may provide invaluable help to the therapist through her own observations and comments. However, the focus of the work must be on the toddler and his inner world, not on the interactional dynamics of the dyad per se.

On occasions when the mother is in the playroom for an extended period, the therapist may be able to comment, via the child, about the child's affective reactions to his mother's behavior (e.g., "Oh Mommy when you scold me and I'm just having a good time being me, I get *so* frightened!). The therapist's ability to comment on the toddler's inner world in such circumstances does not diminish the importance of parallel therapeutic intervention directly with the parents; such work may vary from counseling in child development and management techniques to psychotherapy focused on inner conflicts awakened by the parental role. Work with the parents is critical not only in developing an understanding of the toddler's day-to-day reality but in the creation of an alliance with the parents that can support and promote the young child's progressive development.

Separation from the mother for the psychotherapeutic work will only be achieved when the very young child has recreated with his therapist the earlier symbiotic, or not fully differentiated, relationship with his mother. While this will be a "real" relationship in many respects, and one in which the toddler feels nurtured and gratified, the toddler will be permitted the illusion that he is not fully differentiated psychologically from his therapist. This illusion is therapeutic and is fostered, in part, by the fruits of the "translation" the therapist is sharing with her toddler patient.

Translating the meaning of symptoms, the prominence of separation-individuation issues, and the importance of direct work with the toddler are illustrated in both of the following clinical vignettes.

Joey H., 27 Months

Joey was the very much wanted first child of a working-class couple in their twenties. The marriage had been a stormy and violent one in which Mrs. H. was physically beaten by her husband, but she experienced it as "idyllic" during her pregnancy, in spite of an enormous weight gain and developing diabetes. Both parents expected a girl but were not disappointed with a boy. Mrs. H. continued to experience the marriage as good during the neonatal period, with Mr. H. feeling proud of his son. Joey was an active, healthy, bottle-fed infant who walked at 9 months.

Early in Joey's second year, his parents' marriage began to deteriorate. Mr. H. again began to beat his wife violently and to see other women. Finally, when Joey was 18 months old and after Mr. H. had beaten his wife badly enough to knock out some of her teeth, the parents separated.

Although Mrs. H. experienced Joey as extremely active and aggressive once he began to walk, she stated that it was after the marital separation that he became unmanageably aggressive and "violent," throwing and breaking his and his mother's possessions, swearing, biting, hitting his mother, running around in a very driven way, and clinging to his mother. He also developed a sleep disturbance characterized by difficulty going to sleep and by night terrors during which he awoke crying for his father. His mother's solution to this difficulty was to take Joey into her own bed.

On intake, Mrs. H. described Joey as both "a charmer" and "a devil" and worried that he would become "just like

his rotten father." She felt overwhelmed and hopeless regarding his behavior, at the same time feeling unusually close
to him, treasuring their sleeping and showering together.

On developmental evaluation at age 26 months, Joey was
active and independent in his behavior but responded well
to firm limit setting. His cognitive capacities appeared at age
level, with Joey demonstrating many developmental successes
six months above age and two successes in the language area
a year above age. During the play sessions, however, Joey
was quite negative and angry, throwing toys around and running out of the room. He was described by his developmental
examiner as avoiding direct eye contact and exploring the
room in an independent though somewhat frenzied and joyless
manner, while maintaining a constant flow of anxious vocalization.

Joey was referred for twice-weekly psychotherapy. It was
thought that if Joey and his therapist (the "I" in this story)
could begin to understand some of the sources and meanings
of his aggressive interactions, impulsivity, and intense anxiety, he could be helped to find more adaptive ways of coping
with states of tension and unease.

When I first met him, Joey was a robust little boy with
big brown eyes, upturned nose, and shiny, shaggy brown hair.
Although engaging, he had an artificially charming, slightly
pugnacious manner which made me think of a too-cute cartoon
character, perhaps Dennis the Menace.

The early phase of treatment was colored by Joey's extreme pervasive anxiety, manifested by a great deal of tense,
apparently counterphobic behavior. For example, in an early
session Joey began to use some magic markers, commenting
excitedly and repetitively that they were "messy." He suddenly, and perhaps accidentally, marked on the table; at once
he leapt up and began to scribble wildly on the wall. It appeared that Joey attempted to ward off his anxiety about controlling the messy markers by "doing the scary thing"—that
is, by messing. However, once he had begun to be messy,

rather than experiencing a sense of mastery, Joey felt intense anxiety. This led to increasing disorganization, expressed by his explosive and provocative scribbling on the walls. The regression in ego functioning represented by this disorganization suggested that Joey needed help in reconstituting adequate ego functioning. For this reason, I removed the markers and commented that the messy markers really worried Joey and that I would put them away so that he didn't have to feel so worried. He said forcefully, "He *doesn't like* those messy markers!" In session after session, however, Joey would repetitively question me about the markers, first asking for them as though needing to be reassured that I would not allow him to become so disorganized, and then anxiously repeating while pointing to some other child's scribble, "He messed on the walls? He did this? He broke markers?"

Joey also demonstrated acute auditory sensitivity, startling every time there was a noise in the hall and then becoming disorganized and confused, repetitively asking, "Who's that?" In an effort to reduce the overwhelming intensity of Joey's anxiety I removed many of the toys which seemed to make him most anxious; he responded to this environmental manipulation, and to my comments that I put toys away because they worried him, by becoming somewhat calmer. However, at times of stress he would need to reassure himself that all the scary things were indeed put away.

In spite of the prominence of Joey's anxiety, the following themes, very much interrelated, emerged: his sense of being very bad; his anxiety that his mother would leave him because of his badness; fighting as a way of making sure his mother would stay with him; feeling that he had to be the "fixit man" and make everything all right; his longing for various surrogate fathers. A session early in Joey's treatment illustrates how these themes were presented and interconnected.

Joey was busy in the waiting room with his mother; he greeted me with a smile and then immediately exclaimed, "Fuck!" He grinned provocatively at me and then at his mother. Although he protested leaving the waiting room, he came readily when I was firm, striding ahead of his mother and me as though leading an expedition party. He ran anxiously into the wrong playroom. I commented that he needed to wait for the grown-ups so that they could help him feel safe.

At the door of his playroom, he ran in heedlessly, not waiting for the lights to be turned on, and began to cruise around the room in a manner both imperious and anxious. He picked up a toy car that could be taken apart and reassembled and put it on the table saying in a sort of garbled anxious way, "Where his knife? Fire in there. He fixit? Broken—see smoke! Fire still there. He fixit?" Although this was in part a reference to a previous actual experience of a smoking "broken" car which his mother was able to clarify, I chose to comment on Joey's affect: "Joey worries so much about that broken car and who's going to fix it." Joey became insistent that *he* had to fix it, although no matter what he did, the car remained "broken." I finally said, "Seems like a very big job to fix that broken car. Joey can't really do it all by himself. He needs help."

Joey blanched and leapt up, cruising the playroom, saying "He marked on the wall? Who made those marks? He did it?" He glanced at the closet. "You put markers away? He doesn't like those messy markers!" I said, "Joey gets so worried about things being broken that sometimes he breaks things on purpose and then he worries that they'll never be fixed." He went over to the baby doll, saying, "Baby asleep? No, baby hungry!" He started to feed the baby but then hit it violently, shouting, "Bad baby! Fucking baby!" and hurled it across the room. In a confused fashion he talked about breaking a vase at home. "He broke it. Mommy mad. He broke it?" He looked terribly worried, approached his mother anxiously and then darted away to pummel the baby. He started to throw the doll at his mother; I stopped him, holding the doll, and said, "Poor baby, he's *so* hungry and Joey says it's very naughty to be so hungry. Joey says babies get thrown away." Joey smiled, looking very relieved, and set the doll gently on the table.

He returned to the toy car, saying after examining it that it still had a fire in it. He mumbled something about Ricky, his mother's boyfriend; then he said, "Ricky not here? He go away? He not see him?" I commented that Joey missed Ricky so much; he wanted him to come back and help him fix his broken car. I said that Joey felt too little to do it all by himself. He watched me as I spoke, looking alternately solemn and anxious. When I finished, he darted away from the table, anxiously looking in the toy closet and then whirling around spitting and shouting "Fuck!" "Fuck!" at me in a very imperious way. I said that Joey got angry instead of feeling sad about the grown-up men going away. He settled down with the toy dishes and began to pretend to make coffee for his mother, emphasizing that it had lots and lots of sugar. He fed his mother coffee a number of times and although he pointed out more than once that he had a cup, somehow he was never able to feed himself anything. However, he looked quite happy as he repeatedly fed the grown-ups. When I asked him about his coffee he made a halfhearted gesture of drinking from his cup but immediately leapt up anxiously to feed his mother again.

The session was over. Joey said he didn't want to go. His mother asked him to put on his coat and hat. He refused and she looked helpless, rolling her eyes heavenward. Joey began to run around the room, giggling provocatively. I stopped him and held him firmly, putting on his jacket; he put up only a slight struggle and then seemed to enjoy my help. He went off cheerily, waving goodbye.

For the first three months of treatment Joey's mother remained in the playroom because Joey would not allow her to leave. His mother's therapist was also present, and an attempt was made to conduct parallel—and at times interlocking—treatments. The profound difficulties in the interaction between mother and son became very evident: Joey was anxiously vigilant concerning his mother's mood and the content of her talk; he continually disrupted his play in order to engage her in interaction when she was sad, anxious, or upset. At first, Joey's attempts were in the service of starting a fight, to which his mother always responded with excited rage. Gradually, as his provocative behavior was clarified and linked to his worries about his mother and his need to "do the scariest thing" when he got worried, Joey began to approach his mother in more adaptive ways: he would pretend to make coffee or food for her with "lots and lots of sugar"; he would ask for her help in putting together a toy; or he would cuddle up against her. It then became clear that his mother only acknowledged him when he became abusive toward her. Repeated attempts to offer her coffee would be ignored or only partially responded to, but a *sotto voce* obscenity from Joey would get her immediate and excited attention. She would exclaim, "See what I have to live with? He's just *bad!*" and would follow this up with a litany of Joey's wicked behavior of the week. Joey's anxious attentiveness to his mother and her rigidly rageful repetition of complaints about him dominated the sessions. Attempts to point out to both how worried Joey became about his mother's anger at him would be followed by the mother's sudden cuddling and nuzzling of Joey, behavior which was intimate and seductive, excluding both therapists. In collaborative discussions over several weeks, the two therapists made the decision to help Joey and his mother separately, in the hope that both might be able to become more productively engaged in treatment.

Separation took a total of ten sessions. The mother approached the separation by expressing great doubt that Joey would separate (and by canceling every other session). Joey responded to the separation by becoming immobilized, standing in the center of the playroom screaming and crying, conveying both great rage and intense panic.

Very slowly, however, I became able to engage Joey by reading him stories. This process began with my reading aloud, apparently to myself, as Joey stood in the middle of the room crying and surreptitiously watching me in the mirror. Session by session Joey inched closer, until one day he sat on my lap. Comments about his anger and his wanting to be the boss seemed to escalate his rigid imperiousness, while comments about how very sad and all alone he felt when Mommy went away seemed to have a calming. affect. He picked two stories which appeared to function as transitional phenomena: Margaret Wise Brown's *Goodnight, Moon*, a rhythmic, gentle bedtime story of great calmness, and Don Freeman's *Corduroy*, the tale of a lonely teddy bear who is finally adopted by a little girl.

Joey's separation from his mother was followed by a blossoming of symbolic play. In one session Joey found and named three guns: the broken one was his, a small intact one was his mother's, and a large well-functioning one was "Dr. Jim's." "Dr. Jim"—the developmental examiner—had performed Joey's diagnostic evaluation, and although the actual relationship had consisted of a brief three sessions, in Joey's inner world "Dr. Jim" had become an all-powerful, loving figure who knew just how to help Joey. Joey worried about his gun being broken and about pinching his fingers with it. He nursed from "Mommy's gun," anxiously talking about eating bullets. Then with great pleasure he announced that "Dr. Jim" let him shoot *his* gun. He hopped around the room shooting "Dr. Jim's gun" and crowing with delight.

Rather abruptly, Joey announced that the baby was very bad; he was "too hungry and he cries all the time." Nobody could help the baby and Joey said forcefully, "He's gonna get thrown away. Thrown away to *the dragons*. Dragons eat him up that bad baby!" He threw the doll away. I picked up the doll and made crying noises, saying, "I'm not bad. I'm just a little baby and I'm very, very hungry. I can't help it. I need someone to take care of me." Joey then suggested we use "Dr. Jim's gun" and shoot "all the dragons." He crept around the room pretending to shoot the dragons. After a bit, however, he said sadly, "I just can't shoot them all." I said no, it would take a long time and lots of hard work for us to figure out what to do about the dragons. Joey then went to the doll's bed and with a shy smile said, "I'm a baby. Will you cover me up?" As I wrapped a blanket around him he smiled beatifically. He wanted to take the blanket home "so the dragons don't get me," but accepted my statement that it would stay in the playroom. He went off reminding me he would be back "on Thursday" and waving exuberantly.

During these ten sessions, the psychotherapeutic work with Joey's mother helped her explore some of the sources of the anxiety which interfered with her allowing Joey to separate from her; her treatment also helped her recognize her own stake in Joey's fights with her. The fighting between the two decreased dramatically, and Mrs. H. began to acknowledge the intensity of her attachment to her son. With the support of the two therapists, and in their presence, she began to set appropriately firmer limits for her son and to withstand many of his invitations to fight.

The first year of treatment with Joey and his mother illustrates the importance of working directly with the toddler, the therapists' decoding of the affect underlying the child's behavior, and the centrality of separation-individuation issues at this stage. The treatment of Joey and his mother extended over several years and included Joey's placement in the Yale Child Study Center Therapeutic Nursery School.

Mark, 28 Months

Mark, age 2 at the beginning of treatment, was the much wanted only child of a young professional couple; his parents were very conscientious and perplexed that they had had so much trouble with their little boy.[1] During Mark's first year

[1]The author gratefully acknowledges her enormous debt to Dr. Sally Provence for her supervision; Dr. Provence's imaginative and creative understanding of very young children contributed immeasurably to the author's reconstructions of this little boy's inner world.

they had worried that he might have a milk allergy. Concern heightened toward the end of his first year as Mark's weight gain slowed down and he developed chronic, although not severe, diarrhea. In addition to this very substantial eating disorder, Mark had a serious sleep disturbance and a severe separation problem. In an effort to solve the questions about allergy, Mark was placed on a quite restricted diet for a time. He grew reasonably well until 12 or 13 months of age, at which time his weight gain decelerated. A number of dietary regimens were then tried, but with no beneficial effect on his feeding difficulty. At 15 months, after the failure of more conservative measures to improve his condition, Mark underwent an extensive pediatric endocrinological workup, which uncovered no allergy. Nothing was found regarding his endocrine, metabolic, or gastrointestinal function that might explain his difficulty. After developmental evaluation at the Yale Child Study Center, the parents accepted a recommendation for psychotherapy for Mark.

Mark was seen in psychotherapy three times a week for thirty-one sessions. When treatment was terminated because of the family's move to another city, a recommendation was made and accepted for continued psychotherapy with a clinician in the city to which the family had moved. During Mark's treatment, his parents were seen jointly for counseling, which helped them explore their feelings and reactions regarding Mark's difficulties and helped them develop better strategies for managing him.

Mark was a tiny but very attractive little boy with creamy skin and glowingly pink cheeks, thick honey-blond hair, and large sparkling eyes. His depressed, anxious facial expression was a striking contrast to his healthy good looks.

Mark began his first session without acknowledging his mother's presence; instead he explored the materials and vocalized largely in jargon, to no one in particular. He placed a mother, a father, and a baby peg person in a large yellow van and rolled it to me. When the van stopped near me, he abruptly turned away, as though not ready for closer contact. He turned then to a puzzle box and accompanied his methodical, joyless completion with a whiny "What's this?" Although he sought out neither his mother nor me for help, he would periodically complain, "I can't do it." He approached his mother only midway through the session: having taken apart some nesting cups, he placed a peg lady in the smallest one and pretended to pour tea from the peg lady into another cup; he suddenly offered this to his mother, saying sweetly, "Here's some tea." Having finally allowed himself to seek out his mother, Mark became more relaxed and playful. He began to play at washing dishes in an imaginary dishwasher, cooking, making cookies, and feeding the dolls. After filling the baby bottle with food, Mark insisted that his mother "feed the baby." The baby had to drink several bottles before Mark said, "Now he's full." He finished this first session making play-dough cookies for his mother, telling her to eat them although *he* didn't want to eat any.

I was struck by Mark's inability to use his mother for comfort at the beginning of the session, especially as this behavior contrasted with his first "recognition" of his mother around feeding her, followed by his difficulty in allowing the baby to feel nourished. I understood him as expressing concern over who was in control of eating and feeding and some awareness on his part of his being in conflict with his mother over these issues.

The next two sessions were characterized by Mark's increasingly playful animation, demonstrating a delightful ability for fantasy play. The play around feeding his mother continued: Mark pretended to make cookies and then peanut butter and jelly sandwiches. He asked, with a teasing smile, "*Who* is going to eat this?" but the only person he allowed to eat was his mother. After feeding her, he began to feed the dolls, play which was marked by the lack of any comforting or tender behavior toward the dolls and by a preoccupation with stuffing them with food because "they weren't *full*."

Mark's interest in feeding and eating play continued over the next several sessions. Although this play appeared to be fairly straightforward domestic mimicry, some aspects were noteworthy. Mark never fed himself, only his mother, and he insisted that the baby dolls could not feed themselves but had to be fed by him, and rather forcibly at that. His feeding of his mother and "the babies" was only superficially nurturing: he always continued to feed them long after they began to complain that they were full. Mark's cooking and feeding play were usually followed by an elaborate cleanup ritual; he was both imaginative and animated in his creation of the details of cleanup—the dishes were carefully put into a dishwasher, and Mark was quite concerned not only that the "garbage" be thrown away, but that it be removed to the dump by the "garbage man." These aspects of Mark's play suggested not only that he was engaged in a struggle for control over who would be "the boss" of eating, but that this struggle was colored by conflicts over "goodness" and "badness," or what was or wasn't safe to "take inside." My comments focused on Mark's wish to be the boss of eating and his worry over what to do with "all the messy garbage."

During one early session Mark sat the baby doll off in a corner and said solemnly, "She has to wait for Mommy." When I had the baby protest mildly, saying she wanted her Mommy right now, Mark looked very anxious, leaned against his mother, and stared at me as though flabbergasted that the baby would complain. Finally, he said in a low voice, "The baby comes home," and sat the baby at the table saying the baby "has to eat now"; he then began to complain that the baby wouldn't eat by herself, she had to be fed. Mark fed the baby for a long while, looking quite solemn, somehow both anxious and irritated, and then began to clean everything up quite methodically. Finally he said, "The garbage man's gonna come and take everything all away. To the dump." I said, "Mark wants that messy garbage all cleaned up." Mark grinned and nodded his head in firm agreement.

The next session also contained the apparently entwined themes of separation, eating, and control. Using the blocks, Mark made a long boat: first he stood the little family figures on it then he added some animals. He said, "They're going on a trip. They're going bye-bye." Mark and I waved goodbye to the figures; then he announced they needed food and very carefully put some play-dough in a little cup and then put this gently on the front of the boat. He grinned as though pleased with his invention. He moved the little boy figure over to the "food," made eating noises and then said to me, "You make him eat, okay?" I had the boy eat a little bit and then say, "Now I'm full." Mark looked very solemn and then said several times in a low voice, "He's full." Suddenly he said forcefully, "No, he's *not* full; he has to eat until it's *all gone!*" I mimed the little boy eating and then said, "Now I ate it all up." Mark chuckled, looking both pleased and amused. Then he said, "Now everyone eats until they eat it *all up!*" After all the figures had eaten, Mark announced, as though making a big joke, "They need a telephone so they can call home if they want to!" He got the telephone, set it next to the food, and sat back surveying the scene with satisfaction.

During the several sessions following the boat play, Mark began to follow his feeding and cleanup play with a story of cars going to get gas. Sometimes the cars would repetitively get filled with gas. When I commented that the cars never seemed to get full, Mark offered the explanation that they were broken. In a subsequent session Mark elaborated on his themes of separation from his mother, the wish to be big, and his concern with broken cars. He told a story of a little boy flying "up up up" in an airplane "all the way to Florida!" but then seemed quite anxious. I suggested that after the boy visited a little bit he wanted to go home. Mark looked surprised and then with real delight "flew" the little boy "home again!" He repeated this game several times, each time pleasurably exclaiming, "Home again!" I spoke for the boy saying, "Oh, I'm so glad to be home. It's nice to go away for a bit and then be able to come home again!" Mark then told a story of children going to school: he placed the little figures in the school bus, waved "bye-bye" to them, pushed the bus "to school" and had a teacher say "hello." Observing the scene, he commented, "Now all the boys and girls are at school." He repeated the phrase "*all* the boys and girls" several times, as if there were something particularly nice about this thought. Then all the children went home "to eat ice cream" and Mark exclaimed, "Home again!" Mark got out some small cars, saying *they* would go to school. The cars came one by one to the teacher and said sadly, "I'm broken. Please fix me." Mark was unable to say where the car was broken, but after each one was fixed by the teacher it would drive off and Mark would suddenly announce with delight, "Oh, broken *again!*" I commented, "Those cars are so worried about being broken, they get afraid nobody can help them." Mark looked at me quickly with a small smile, ducked his head down and whispered, "Yeah."

As treatment continued, Mark showed less need to begin his sessions with repetitive, anxious questions. He became more animated and began to fill his stories with imaginative detail. As he elaborated his broken car story, Mark began to manifest the delighted exuberance one expects in a 2-year-old.

At the beginning of one session, when I greeted Mark in the waiting room, he smiled broadly and hopped up and down saying excitedly, "Let's go!" For the first time, he was so eager to get to the playroom that he dashed ahead without waiting for his mother. When I urged him to wait for her, he turned around and shouted imperiously, "Hurry up!" He went up the stairs to the playroom without asking his mother to hold his hand, alternating feet for the first time. When I praised him, however, he became quite self-conscious and lost the ability. He galloped into the playroom enthusiastically and with great, crowing pleasure hopped about in front of his mother, chattering away. Finally he turned around to face me, an ear-to-ear grin on his face, and, hopping about and waving his arms expansively, crowed, "You know what? I'm wearing big boy underwear today!" I said how wonderful that must be, and his already expansive smile widened more as he jumped and hopped around the room.

For much of the rest of this session, Mark pretended to make and feed his mother cookies. Within this context, he expressed a great deal of concern about things being broken, especially the tails and legs of the animal cookies. Eventually the feeding play included feeding the dolls and, for the very first time, Mark had the dolls feed themselves. This sequence was followed by a story about people going on a trip, taking food to eat, and then all the cars becoming broken. This time Mark was clear that the cars were broken because they needed so much gas and that what would fix them was "being full."

After twelve sessions, Mark's parents reported that he was a much more animated and independent little boy; on the whole they found him much easier to "read" and to manage; the one problem remaining was his eating. The parents said that Mark still refused to sit at the table to eat a meal, ate almost nothing at mealtimes, and was very demanding of special snacks and treats between meals. It was their impression that he was driven to turn mealtimes into pitched battles in which they felt helpless and outwitted by his provocative imperiousness.

Although Mark was clearly engaged in treatment and able to convey fantasy material that seemed closely linked to his eating disorder, I was acutely aware of the short-term nature of the treatment contract due to the impending move, which could not be postponed. With only nineteen sessions remaining, I thought that the introduction of a real snack into the session might help to clarify what actually happened with Mark when he was expected to eat. Although the use of food during the therapy hour with the very young child can contaminate the treatment alliance by stimulating regression secondary to the gratification of basic needs, in this case the benefits of directly confronting the symptomatic behavior were thought to outweigh the risks.

At the conclusion of the twelfth session, Mark's mother was told that in the next session Mark would be given a snack; although standing beside his mother, Mark appeared oblivious. However, he arrived for his next appointment in an exuberant mood, making a point of demonstrating what a big boy he was. His play was a richly detailed story of a little boy going "high high high" and "up up up" in an airplane to visit his grandparents "all by himself." After repeating this game with great delight, he became briefly concerned about one of the little cars being broken and took it to the gas station to be fixed. I told him that it was snacktime and that he could return to his story when it was over. A snack of cheese, crackers, and juice had been set up at a small table with two chairs. As Mark and I sat down in the chairs, Mark invited his mother to join us, gesturing for her to sit on the floor. As she did so, he chuckled, saying, "I have a *big* chair. I *bigger* than Mommy!" Although he took both a cheese cube and a cracker, he immediately said he didn't like the cheese cube and handed it to his mother. I said, "If you don't want it, it goes on your napkin," and he took it back and put it on his napkin. A little later he said pleasantly to his mother, "If you don't want it, it goes on your napkin." Then he offered a cracker to her; before she could take it, Mark broke it in two and ate half, giving her just a crumb. During the snack, which he ate laboriously, Mark grew more solemn, at one point becoming concerned about a siren heard outside; Mark said it was an ambulance going to the hospital—"Because someone's sick; they're taking someone to the hospital." Although Mark had eaten only two crackers, and those apparently with great effort, when he announced he was going back to his story he chugged down his juice with pleasure and threw the cup away. When he returned to his story, he said the cars were "sick" and had to go to the hospital for x-rays, "to see what's wrong."

During the following sessions, over and over again Mark

told a variety of stories of cars and trucks needing to be fixed because they were "broken." He was unable to say what about them was broken, but the only way they could be fixed was by giving them gas. I commented that the cars being given gas made me think of people getting food in their tummy. Mark appeared more and more subdued during snacks. Although he didn't refuse to eat, he took a very long time, taking tiny little bites of one cracker. He drank his juice easily and with some pleasure: his trouble seemed related to actual biting.

This was a new observation. Until the introduction of the snack into treatment, Mark's eating difficulties appeared to be a gobal refusal to eat when and what his parents wanted. Now, on the basis of his observed behavior, we speculated that Mark might be specifically anxious about biting food.

Mark's mother had been in the playroom up until this point in treatment. Following his pseudoindependent attitude in the first session, Mark had turned frequently to his mother for help and comfort during the early stages of treatment. However, by the sixteenth session, he spent little time with her and clearly was actively engaged in his therapy. Parallel to this shift in Mark, his mother appeared more restless during the sessions. These seemed good indicators that both mother and son were ready to separate. During the sixteenth session Mark became interested in a toy tow truck. He had me make the two truck go "up up up" in the air and he then crowed, "Look, it's getting bigger!" With great delight he asked several times, "How did it get bigger? Why did it get bigger?" But when I turned the questions back to him, he had no answer, simply demonstrating enthusiastically that the tow truck was going "up up up" and getting "big big big!" Mark spotted a toy fire engine and announced sadly that it was broken and needed to be fixed. I asked how it could be fixed. "It needs gas!" he said forcefully. I commented that it needed gas in its tummy and it felt sad to be hurt and broken. Mark became very busy giving the fire truck gas.

Since Mark had not referred to his mother since the beginning of the session, I suggested that she leave and wait in the waiting room. Mark watched her go, a sort of neutral expression on his face, but was unable to say goodbye. After she had gone, Mark became dramatically more animated, smiling at me with conspiratorial pleasure. He found a man to "fix" the fire truck which now had "enough gas" and with great delight he had the tow truck teach the fire engine how to go "up up up" in the air and get "big big big."

At this point I suggested a snack. Smiling, Mark sat down at the table. Very solemnly he confided that he had trouble eating and that his mother had told him he wouldn't get bigger if he didn't eat but he still had trouble eating. I replied that I knew about this, but that I could see it was a very big problem for him, wasn't it? He nodded his head. I wondered if Mark would like to pour his own juice. His eyes lit up; "Oh yes!" he exclaimed and then did so with great satisfaction. Mark began to break the crackers and eat them in a snuffly, gobbly sort of way. He pointed out the crumbs all over. I said in a pleasant tone, "Yech! What a big mess!" He giggled and repeated this several times as he began to gobble raisins as well.

When he finished eating, Mark left the table, picked up a little man doll, and began tossing the man into the air, putting a lot of effort into his throws. After a bit, this game began to look less like catch and more like a fight. I said, "It looks like you and that guy are really having a fight." Mark grinned, shouted, "That's right!" and began to make grunting noises as he struggled exuberantly with the man.

The next session began with Mark asking his mother in a very hopeful voice, "When do *I* go to school?" In the room, he played out a long story about all the children going to school in the school bus except for "one little guy" who got left behind "because he's too little." After leaving the little guy behind, however, Mark changed his mind, saying, "He wants to go too," and sent the little guy off to school in a car "just his size." He followed this with a brief story of a fire truck which repeatedly broke down and constantly needed to be filled with gas, although it never seemed to get full. I commented that the fire truck's always seeming to be out of gas and needing to be full reminded me of Mark's problems around eating. Mark immediately announced in a somewhat anxious voice that the fire truck was "okay—now he's going to be full," and filled it up. At snacktime, Mark for the first time was unable to eat anything, excitedly breaking up cookies and scattering crumbs around. When I commented that he seemed to have a lot of trouble around eating today and wondered whether he didn't like making an exciting fight out of it, he looked momentarily solemn but continued to make a mess.

Mark's interest in fighting instead of eating was brought directly into the next session. He began a story in which a little boy and his mommy and daddy were going to McDonald's to eat hamburgers and french fries. Mark decided to have the family travel in the toy school bus. (Earlier in the session he had used this school bus to tell a story of "a little guy" who "smashes up all the kids that are big enough to go to school.") After putting all three in the bus, Mark solemnly removed the mother so that only the little boy and his daddy actually went to McDonald's. I asked about the mommy. "She doesn't eat," Mark said firmly. Then he abruptly picked up the boy and his daddy and began to stamp around the room. I commented that he was showing me how much he wanted to be big and also reminding me how much he and his mommy fought about eating. Mark handed me the little boy, saying "Make him fight." I had the little boy shout "I'm not going to eat!" and stamp around. Then I asked Mark what the mother should do when the little boy fought with her. Mark grinned, shouted, "She yells!" I said, "And what does the boy do?" Mark giggled, "He laughs!"

I commented that Mark seemed really to like to fight with his mother over eating, it was so exciting. Mark laughed more loudly and began to throw toys round the room, acting very big and strong. I said, "It looks as if fighting with Mommy makes Mark feel big and strong." Mark laughed in delighted agreement. I added, "But it worries you, too, because then you get afraid you won't grow big." Mark looked suddenly solemn and said that the little boy was sick. I said, "Yes, Mark worries he'll get sick from not eating." Mark said that his mother had told him that. He then began to demonstrate again what a big, strong boy he was.

At snacktime Mark drank his juice and crumbled up his crackers and then began to toss toys around, standing on a table at one point to show me he was taller than I. I commented that he was showing me how much he liked to fight with his mother. He laughed, and I said, "It looks like it's more fun to fight than eat." He agreed and climbed on the table again saying, "I'm a big boy!" I said that when he fought with Mommy he felt big and strong and that make him feel good inside, but that the fighting also made trouble for him. Mark questioned why it made trouble. I replied, "Because then you really don't eat and though you feel big and strong when you fight, you don't *grow* big and strong unless you eat food." Mark looked very startled, as though this were a new idea, and then began to gobble a peanut butter cracker, quite deliberately making a mess. I pointed out how much he enjoyed being a messy eater. He agreed, with pleasure. At the end of the session I asked if he would like to wipe off his hands and face; he said triumphantly, "No, be messy!"

The following session, Mark began kicking a ball around and then delightedly threw it in the trash. He told a story of a little car: "He doesn't eat too good," said Mark with a sad smile; "he didn't eat his dinner." He said the car couldn't eat because it was broken and then suggested we fix it by tying it to the gas pump "so it can gets lots and lots of gas." He repeated this story with another little car and then took the tow truck and said with a grin, "Even the *big tow truck* is broken! *He* doesn't eat either!" We fixed the tow truck in the same fashion, by tying it to the gas pump. Next he told a story about a little baby who didn't like to wear diapers and wanted to wear big boy underwear, but his mother made him wear diapers because he messed his pants. Mark tugged uncomfortably at his own trousers, so I asked him if he were wearing diapers. "No," he said scornfully, "I only wear diapers at night. I have on big boy underwear."

He ate his snack looking very subdued and then went to the small family dolls and said he was "the mommy" and he was going to throw the baby away "for making such a mess—he's a messy baby." Then he threw the baby in the trash. He grew quite animated and said, "Now the little girl's gonna get thrown away too!" I asked what would happen if the baby cried. He said, laughing, "The mommy will throw him away anyways. He's messy garbage." Mark threw away the little girl and the little boy. Though he grew solemn when I made the baby girl and boy cry or protest, he then laughed with real pleasure and said "I'm going to do it anyways. They're MESSY!" After he threw them all away, he showed me how big and strong he was, by moving the dollhouse and table around and then climbing on the table, saying proudly, "Look how big I am!" I said he wanted more than anything to be a big boy, to grow big. He looked quite sad.

At the end of the session, we left the playroom and Mark said anxiously, "Maybe Mommy will be gone." I reassured him that she would not, but would be waiting for him in the waiting room. Nevertheless, he had more difficulty than usual walking down the stairs, and he clutched the bannister. I suggested we change places, letting him walk on the inside, next to the wall. He smiled and looking up at me said, "Why do I feel better?" I explained he didn't feel so worried because he didn't have to look over the stairs. When he was five steps from the bottom, his mother came out of the waiting room. Mark released my hand and descended the rest of the stairs by himself. At the bottom he said with a big smile to his mother, "I'm a big boy." Then he grew somewhat silly, grinning at her and at me, nuzzling his face in his jacket and singing "Goodbye, goodbye" to me as I turned to go upstairs.

In a later session, Mark picked up the little boy doll and said he had to go to jail all by himself because he was "very, very bad." Mark couldn't say why the little boy was so bad or what he had done, but insisted he had to go to jail. When I made the little boy cry, Mark showed, for the first time in the session, his delighted smile and said, "He's going to jail anyways even if he doesn't want to and anyway he *is* a bad, bad boy." However, when I made the boy cry a second time, Mark got the mother and said they would both be in jail together; he held the two figures in his hand and made kissing sounds. He started a story about a little boy and his daddy going to McDonald's, but instead McDonald's came to them and "bashed and bashed them." A play disruption occurred; Mark began a story about a little car who wanted to go to school but wasn't old enough. Mark added with quiet delight, "But he's gonna go to school anyways. A school for cars." During snacktime Mark was very tentative about eating the cookies. I urged him to gnaw on the cookie filling. Slowly, he did, gradually becoming more and more delighted until he was gobbling and snuffling, using "great big teeth" as well as smearing his face. I asked if he wanted to wipe his mouth when it was time to go and he said enthusiastically, "NO! BE MESSY!"

Mark seemed to equate being little with being broken. Mark's pleasure in fighting with his parents over eating derived from his feeling big and strong when he fought, even though he didn't eat. As this theme emerged with greater clarity, Mark began to demonstrate how much eating stirred up his orally aggressive "gobbly feelings"; he inhibited his biting of food as a way of warding off "the gobblies." Fighting over food allowed him to feel differentiated from his mother without losing her as a result of his oral aggression.

Mark's earlier concern with being broken began to give way to more clear castration anxiety in which Mark projected his oral aggression, becoming worried that someone would bite off his penis. He showed clear perception of sexual differences and reported the fantasy that girls didn't have penises because "someone bit them off"; he added that this could happen if you were "bad." In the last month of treatment, Mark produced what seemed to be a primal scene fantasy and associated his anger over "Daddy being with Mommy" to fears that his own penis would get broken.

During this period, Mark began to offer more detailed fantasies concerning the specificity of how he was "broken." In one session he took out all the zoo animals, carefully examining each one and finally selecting the giraffe. He said with a grin that it was "the biggest." He added, "He's a little boy and he's going up up up in the airplane." Then Mark picked out the elephant, saying, "This one's big too. She's the little boy's mommy." I said, "The little boy is the biggest one of all." Mark smiled in agreement and setting the elephant and giraffe down on the table, announced that he was going to make cookies. After making several cookies with play-dough, he announced he was going to eat them; he began with tiny nibbles which progressed to his pretending to gobble all the cookies hungrily.

As Mark picked up his last "cookie," it broke. Mark's animation and amusement vanished and he looked very worried, saying, "It broke. It broke. Fix it, *please.*" Looking at me pleadingly, he clutched his genitals. I commented that Mark got very worried when the cookie broke. He nodded his head in anxious agreement and seemed to hold his genitals even more obviously, as though calling my attention to his action. "It's broken. How did it get broken? *Who* broke it?" he said in a low voice. I said yes, the cookie had broken accidentally but that I could see that Mark was so worried he wanted to hold his penis; I added, "Sometimes little boys get very worried that their penis could get broken." Mark stared solemnly at me, "Yes, your penis could get broken *off.*" Very slowly he rolled the broken "cookie" into a play-dough ball, handed it to me, and asked me to make "a girl" out of it. I said, "Yes, sometimes boys worry that their penis could get broken off and sometimes they wonder if girls had a penis which got broken off." Mark nodded and said emphatically, "Girls don't have a penis—*boys* have a penis." He then picked up the toy elephant and giraffe and with loud gobbling noises made the elephant bite the underside of the giraffe; very forcefully he said, "See, she bit it off him. She bit off his penis!" I said, "Who bit off his penis?" Mark said, "I . . . the grandma did it. *She* did it!" I asked why. "Because he's a bad boy." I said, "That little boy must feel very scared to think his penis could be bitten off." Mark moved energetically around the room, taking great strides, swinging his arms. I said, "Mark wants Dr. Dahl to see he's a *big* boy."

Mark got down the snack tray and poured out his juice, inviting me to join him. At first he seemed reluctant to eat a cracker; suddenly, he popped one into his mouth and then just as quickly took it out again, looking very worried. He took an extremely tiny bite and then became quite talkative, as though hoping to divert my attention. I said very firmly that I wanted him to eat something by biting and chewing it. He ate a few crackers rather hurriedly and without pleasure, then announced he was "full." He left the table and got out a large toy van. He said the giraffe was "sick and broken" and had to go to the hospital. After a pause he said slowly, "Remember when I used to be sick about not eating and had to go to the hospital?" I said I knew he had gone to the hospital and asked what had happened there. Mark looked very sad, but remained silent. He touched the giraffe tenderly and said, "He's so worried about being broken. He needs a play doctor."

A session toward the end of Mark's treatment demonstrates the multiple meanings his symptom had for him and the variety of defenses employed.

Mark took out the family dolls and heaped them in a pile, saying "They're all sick. The family's sick. Everyone's sick. They have to go to the hospital. Where's the doctor?" He handed me the stethoscope, saying, "You be the doctor." I asked what was the matter. Mark said slowly, "They don't eat, so they get sick and broken and they have to go to the hospital." "Why?" "I don't know why." I suggested maybe they couldn't eat because they were so worried about biting. Mark smiled slightly. "Yes," he said softly. Then he said the mommy and daddy were going to fly away in the airplane, "but the boy and girl can't go, because they are babies." I made the "babies" cry and beg to go. Mark smiled with pleasure and remained adamant, "Oh, no, they're *not* gonna go 'cause they're bad and they're babies and they *can't* go!" I made the "babies" act angry and yell "We *have* to go; we don't want to be left behind!" Mark seemed to approve of their protest but remained firm. Finally, I had one baby say, "I'm so mad, if you don't let me go with you, I'll eat you up!" Mark blanched and said anxiously, "Okay, okay, he can go. He's gonna go too."

I commented that Mark seemed scared that the baby had said he wanted to eat his mommy. Mark solemnly nodded his head in agreement. Then he picked up the mother doll and bit her feet ferociously, "I'm going to eat her up!" He looked anxious again and said, "No *you* do it." I bit the doll's foot and then explained that even if you bit very hard, you couldn't eat her up. "Why?" I said that was just the way it was and that it was the same with people, you couldn't eat them up even if you wanted to. Mark said, "You shouldn't say you'll eat her up." I said Mark didn't like to think about being so mad and threatening to eat people up.

Mark returned to the story of the sick family and said, "Why is the little boy sick? Why won't he eat?" I made the little boy say, "I *can't* eat. I'm afraid of biting food because it makes me think of biting people and that makes me think of eating up my mommy and *that* makes me so scared I can't eat. So then I get into a fight with Mommy instead." Mark looked at me intently, sighed deeply, and whispered, "Yes, that's it."

Mark then leapt up and got the snack try, saying exuberantly, "I want to eat now." He took an enormous bite of a pretzel, looked worried, spilled a little juice, paled, and said he had to clean up. Although I suggested that that wasn't necessary, he was insistent. After wiping up the juice, he said with relief, "Now that's clean. I made it okay." I commented that he was worried by his messy, gobbly feelings. He grinned and took another bit bite of pretzel. He crowed with delight and said, "All the cars are gonna eat and bite, eat and bite!" He got the giraffe, saying, "And he's gonna bite and eat, too!" Mark took a third pretzel, crouched down as though hiding, and gobbled it up. When he had finished his snack, he leapt up again, exclaiming, "The giraffe's gonna eat the school bus. No, he's gonna *ride* the school bus!" Mark began to jump exuberantly around the room, demonstrating how big he was and what fancy "tricks" he could do.

During his final sessions, Mark spoke directly of "my *great big* daddy" in a tone that suggested both admiration and envy. At one point he told me, "My great big daddy sleeps in the same bed with *my* mommy. I don't like that!" This was followed by some play with the "little boy" giraffe "who worries his penis could get broken off." As Mark explored these themes, he became able to eat without difficulty the snack provided during the session. He became expansively active and proud of his jumping, climbing, and running skills. He anticipated with pleasure attending nursery school the following fall.

During the period of Mark's treatment, his parents were seen jointly once a week in counseling focused on helping them develop more successful strategies for managing Mark and overcoming their sense of helplessness. They began by exploring some of their fears about Mark's eating difficulties, which seemed to contribute to their perception of him as fragile. They realized that Mark's failure to grow reminded them of the father's cousin, who had died in childhood of a mysterious "wasting disease"; the mother recalled that she had been a very "picky" eater as a child and that this had been a source of conflict between her and her mother. As the parents became able to evaluate their concerns more realistically, they became firmer and more consistent in their handling of Mark. This was followed by significant symptomatic improvement. The parents' greater confidence in their ability to manage Mark allowed them to observe him more empathically as well. They recognized his ambivalence, inhibitions, and counterphobic maneuvers, and decided to resume Mark's treatment with a new therapist once they had relocated.

Discussion

Although Joey and Mark differed in significant ways, certain similarities are noteworthy; these seemed the result of age-typical, although unusually intense, conflicts. A central dilemma for both was how to become psychologically separate individuals without succumbing to fears of abandonment or helplessness. Symptomatically, each boy clung imperiously to his mother without seeming to gain much comfort from her presence or to acquire the confidence to be more independent. Joey and Mark seemed unusually sensitive to the aggression (primarily their own) stimulated by the process of psychological differentiation; their conflicts concerning these aggressive, self-assertive impulses were a major contributor to the actual separation difficulties. By not accepting the child's maladaptive, frequently counterphobic efforts to cope with separation and by insisting on the mother's presence, whether or not the child appeared outwardly able to use her for support, the therapist created a psychological climate in which the conflicts surrounding separation and aggression became more evident and could be understood dynamically. The achievement of an alliance with the therapist, in which the child's inner world was responded to empathically, was followed by the developmental achievement of greater psychological separateness, manifested by the child's ability to let the mother leave the room and the appearance of richer, more imaginative symbolic play.

Leaving aside the genesis of the symptomatic behavior in each case, we could see that this behavior was linked associatively to relatively complex fantasies which were attempts to resolve conflicting feelings, wishes, and impulses. Although the boys' fantasies differed significantly, their symptomatic behavior seemed to represent an effort to ward off intense fears of being helpless, "too little," damaged, and "not separate" with counterfantasies of omnipotent control and grandiosity. The age-typical vulnerability to magical thought and the rapidity with which thought becomes action contributed to the intensity of the boys' fears and fantasies. The therapeutic work consisted of translating action into language, clarifying affects, helping the child acquire more adaptive coping strategies, and connecting action fragments to a verbalized whole. The therapist encouraged the child to lean on and borrow her ego in the service of sustaining the child's capacity to tolerate and bind anxiety sufficiently to work psychotherapeutically.

These two clinical vignettes illustrate the ways in which the very young child communicates his inner world—a world of action fragments containing memories, fantasies, wishes, and fears, associatively linked but neither integrated nor under the dominion of secondary process thought. The therapist of the very young child can use the techniques described here to help the child understand, organize, and synthesize these thoughts-in-action and go on to acquire adaptive ego functions and enlarge the ego's sphere of influence.

References

Bornstein, B., (1934). Phobia in a two and a half year old. *Psa: Quarterly*. 4:93-119.

Buxbaum, E., (1954). Technique of child therapy: a critical evaluation. *Psychoanalytic Study of the Child*. 9:297-333. New York: International Universities Press.

Fraiberg, S. (1950). On the sleep disturbances of early childhood. *Psychoanalytic Study of the Child*. 5:285-309. New York: International Universities Press.

——— (1952), A critical nervosis in a two and a half year old girl. *Psy-

choanalytic Study of the Child, 7:173-215. New York: International Universities Press.

Kestengerg, J., (1969). Problems of technique of child analysis in relation to the various developmental stages: Prelatency. *Psychoanalytic Study of the Child*. 24:358-384. New York: International Universities Press.

Mahler, M., Pine, F., Bergman, A., (1975). *The Psychological Birth of the Human Infant*. New York: Basic Books.

McDevitt, J., (1967). A separation problem in a three year old girl. Geleerd, Elizabeth (ed). 1967. *The Child Analyst at Work*. New York: International Universities Press. pp. 24-59.

Provence, S., (1966). Some aspects of early ego development. Lowenstein, Newman, Schur and Solnit (eds). 1966. *Psychoanalysis—A General Psychology*. pp. 107-123. New York: International Universities Press.

——— (1972). Psychoanalysis and the treatment of psychological disorders of infancy, ed. Wolman, Benjamin B. *Handbook of Child Psychoanalysis*. New York: Van Nostrand Reinhold Company. 191-221.

——— (1979). Application of psychoanalytic principles to treatment and prevention in infancy. *Child Analysis and Therapy*, ed. J. Glenn. New York: Jason Aronson. pp. 581-597.

Sirota, M., (1969). Urine or you're in: an ambiguous word and its relation to a toilet phobia in a two year old. *Psychoanalytic Study of the Child*. 24:252-270. New York: International Universities Press.

Sterba, Edith. 1949. Analysis of psychogenic constipation in a two year old child. *Psychoanalytic Study of the Child*. 3/4:227-252. New York: International Universities Press.

Winnicott, D.W., (1977). *The Piggle*. New York: International Universities Press.

7

Magical Thinking and Destructiveness: A Comprehensive Clinical Approach to An Infant and Mother with Multiple Affective and Developmental Challenges

Euthymia D. Hibbs, Ph.D.
Patricia Findikoglu, M.A.
Alicia F. Lieberman, Ph.D.
Reginald S. Lourie, M.D.
Robert A. Nover, M.D.
Serena Wieder, Ph.D.
Stanley I. Greenspan, M.D.

One of the important therapeutic issues in the field of clinical approaches to infants and their families is the question of whom to treat: the family, where the conglomerate of interpersonal relations may negatively affect the infant's development; the parent, whose patterns of caregiving may be a pathogenic influence on the infant; or the infant himself, who might show unfolding developmental deviations as a result of constitutional characteristics, environmental insults, and/or the interaction of these and other factors. Different clinicians have offered different answers to this question. As a result, existing therapeutic approaches in the field include individual and marital psychotherapy with the parents, family therapy,

247

parent-infant psychotherapy, and direct work with infants through cognitive stimulation, therapeutic nurseries, or individual child psychotherapy.

The cases of Amy and her mother illustrate a difficult but all too common clinical occurrence: a situation where no one therapeutic course of action was in itself sufficient to maximize the infant's chances for normal development. The potential gains that could be derived from one approach, parent-infant psychotherapy, were preempted by the mother's narcissistic absorption in herself, and her persistent inability to establish affective connections between her own experiences as a child and the experiences that, as a mother, she now gave to her children. A second approach, individual psychotherapy with the mother, was begun and continued but did not immediately result in an improvement in maternal caregiving. Still a third alternative, family therapy, was hardly a realistic possibility for a family where the only adult was a drug-abusing mother engaged in a self-defeating search for an ideal father figure for herself and her children. Finally, direct intervention with the infant, although implemented from the beginning of the treatment, was often interrupted by the mother's periodic unavailability and by the unstable arrangements for the child's daily care, which often made Amy difficult to find, as she was unpredictably switched from one baby-sitter's home to another.

This case, then, illustrates a search for optimal treatment under circumstances far from optimal. We did not have the luxury of settling on any one therapeutic course after evaluating the needs of infant and family; instead we were forced to change our plans again and again in a constant pursuit of developmental progress for the infant and affective stability for the family. Fortunately, our situation as a clinical research project of the Clinical Infant Development Unit of the Mental Health Study Center, National Institute of Mental Health, allowed us to deploy staff and other resources according to our best clinical judgment, with few external constraints.

This situation nevertheless took its toll on the therapeutic team. When the baby's welfare was at stake, as when some staff members perceived the mother as uncaring to the point of endangering her child, the professionals found themselves divided by conflicting views and deep emotions: How many chances should this mother be given to become an adequate caregiver? Were we endangering the infant by attempting to strengthen the mother-infant relationship? If we opted for foster care, would the infant really have a better chance for normal development? Last, but not least, what was our role, as an infant program, with regard to the older child, Harold, who was in urgent need of help? These questions reappeared again and again.

The approach presented here is eclectic. We moved simultaneously in different areas—treating the mother, treating the infant, making an appropriate referral for the older child and monitoring its implementation, and establishing contact with the mother's parents and with her boyfriend whenever appropriate or necessary. Throughout, we kept a careful eye on Amy's progress and were prepared to change our approach if a given plan was not translated into visible improvement after a reasonable period. This flexibility in the face of chaotic circumstances served us well. As intervention progressed, Amy's developmental adequacy increased notably in the face of formidable odds. Her older brother, Harold, acquired age-appropriate cognitive and social skills after functioning at a level of moderate developmental retardation for much of his young life. And the mother, Mrs. M., achieved a measure of psychological growth that, although still unstable and subject to regression, seemed all but unattainable during the early stages of our work.

Our work with Amy and her family lasted for more than three years and taught our staff much about the possible rewards—and the tremendous difficulty—of undertaking intensive treatment in highly unpromising circumstances. We have found our detailed case records and videotapes of Amy and her mother interacting in successive stages of the work to be dramatic teaching tools. Because of space limitations, however, this report will summarize some of our work with Mrs. M. in order to present a more detailed account of our direct intervention wth Amy.

Initial Impressions

When Mrs. M. joined the program, she was 23 years old, had a 2-year-old son, Harold, and was six months pregnant with her second child. Mrs. M. was potentially beautiful, with long blond hair and delicate features, but her appearance was marred by deep circles under her eyes and by a sad facial expression which sometimes changed to anger and suspiciousness. She was usually dressed casually in bluejeans and flat shoes. At her first meeting with the therapist, Mrs. M. was reserved but had good eye contact and was receptive to joining the program, saying that she wanted to know more about children and that she could foresee some "minor" problems with her son Harold after the birth of the baby. She anticipated that Harold, who, in her words, had "all her love and attention," would feel neglected, jealous, and abandoned when the new baby came.

At first glance Mrs. M. seemed articulate and well-organized in her thinking. She used a large vocabulary and was able to elaborate on various topics and to make coherent shifts from one topic to another. She appeared able to distinguish between fantasy and reality. She had some difficulty expressing emotions, however, and her affect was flat when she spoke about emotionally charged events, such as an abortion she had had before her present pregnancy. Mrs. M. reported that this event had been very painful for her and that her intense anxiety had triggered an attack of hyperventilation. Yet as she described the experience she seemed remote and impersonal, as if speaking of someone else.

Mrs. M.'s self-proclaimed devotion to Harold did not match the behavior observed by the therapist. Mrs. M. spoke about the many sacrifices she made for Harold, but gave as an example her not leaving him alone (at age 2) to party or go out with friends. Her tone in speaking to Harold was harsh and authoritarian, and practically no physical contact occurred between mother and son. Harold was observed playing away from his mother; whenever he turned to her or requested something, Mrs. M. responded with an abrupt rebuff or simply ignored him.

Physically, Harold was clearly suffering from severe maternal neglect. While Mrs. M. described Harold as a healthy child, she also reported incidents of colds, ear infections, and high fever, which indicated that Harold, at 2 years of age, had more than his share of illnesses. No effort had been made at toilet training. Harold's diapers were always soaked with urine; even when he had a bowel movement, Mrs. M. waited a long time before changing him. As a result, he had an almost permanent diaper rash. He looked dirty and smelled strongly of urine. He also had had several accidents: he had fallen down the stairs twice, and on one of these occasions had needed several stitches for a split lip. When Harold was 18 months old he "tried to run away" from his mother in the park. He fell and again he had to go to the hospital, this time for stitches on his eyebrow. These worrisome episodes of running away recurred often in later months.

Harold's emerging ego functions were well below age level. He used very little language, uttering only a few unintelligible and scattered words. Harold had a low frustration level: when the therapist worked on puzzles with him, he threw the whole puzzle on the floor in anger if he could not fit a piece. While playing at identifying animals and telling their names, he had temper tantrums when he could not say the right name. He often lashed out at his mother, hitting her and biting her at the slightest provocation.

Perhaps most worrisome, Harold was a sad-looking boy. He was emotionally impersonal and "inward looking" for long periods of time, isolating himself to play with his toys and often playing in a destructive manner. Whenever the therapist played with him and physically held him, Harold seemed to relax, and the tension that characterized him disappeared—something that was never observed in his interactions with his mother.

These observations raised grave concerns not only about Harold but also about the welfare of the as yet unborn baby that Mrs. M. was carrying. The therapist looked to Mrs. M.'s past for clues to her present inability to provide adequate mothering for her son.

Mrs. M.'s Past History

Mrs. M. was the oldest of four children; her parents were divorced when Mrs. M. was 5 years old. She was then sent to live with her maternal grandparents while her younger siblings stayed with her mother. This situation continued until Mrs. M. was 12 years old.

In general, Mrs. M. could not recall any events from her childhood. One of her few memories was of the anger she felt at her brothers, who were taken on a trip to Florida by her mother while she was left behind with her grandparents. Mrs. M. did not remember specific details of her stay with her grandparents, but said, in a flat tone of voice, that her grandparents were "good to her" and that her grandfather "was a father" to her. She remembered that he took her shopping and that he warmed her feet in a blanket during cold nights.

His death when she was 12 was a very traumatic event for Mrs. M. She described feeling angry at him because of this abandonment, but, characteristically, she denied deeper feelings of grief or mourning.

After her grandfather died, Mrs. M. returned to live with her mother, stepfather, and three siblings. She described herself as being the Cinderella who did all the hard domestic jobs while her sister was treated like a princess. There were violent physical fights between herself and her stepfather, which seemed to have been sexualized in her mind. She found it appalling for a "big man like him" to spank a 16-year-old in the rear, pull her hair, and hit her with, as she put it, "his hands all over her body."

Mrs. M. could not remember having any close friends during latency and early adolescence. Peer relationships at midadolescence seemed to revolve around the use of drugs: as she graphically put it, by 16, she had experimented with "all the drugs that were on the market." She had had drug-related hallucinations several times involving men entering through a window to harm her. Every time she had had these hallucinations, she had called her mother, who told her that nobody could enter through the window. Her mother did not suspect drug abuse.

Mrs. M. first menstruated at the rather late age of 18. She recalled that when she first menstruated, her mother was happy and excited, but she herself was frightened. This history became one of the first signs of Mrs. M.'s lack of confidence in her own body, which she tried to deal with by trying to keep her feelings out of conscious awareness until a crisis heightened her sense of body inadequacy or damage.

When she was 18, Mrs. M. met her future husband, a young man very dependent on his mother for even minor tasks and decisions. She married him soon after they met, to "escape" her mother's house. She first had sexual intercourse on the second night of her honeymoon. The first night, she reported, Mr. M. was not able to have an erection. Mrs. M. felt very disappointed and found intercourse itself a disappointing experience, since her husband "was not very good" or able to "turn her on."

Mrs. M. reported that during her marriage she continued to be interested in her old group of friends, the drug providers. Her husband did not participate in that milieu, and Mrs. M. found him boring and "too straight" for her. After three years of marriage, she left him. Much later, after a couple of unfortunate experiences with other men, Mrs. M. began to appreciate her ex-husband's "straightness" and "honesty" and realized that she had been too "high" to understand him earlier.

In the drug milieu, Mrs. M. met a young man named Robert. She "fell in love with him at first sight" and moved in with him immediately after leaving her husband. She was soon pregnant with Harold.

At that point, Mrs. M., age 21, started receiving Aid to Families with Dependent Children (AFDC).

Her relationship with Robert was stormy, including daily use of drugs and alcohol, as well as physical abuse. Both Mrs. M. and Robert were involved in delinquent activities such as pushing drugs and driving stolen cars.

According to Mrs. M., Robert was a carpenter and an artist, but he stopped working as soon as they began living together. Mrs. M. complained that Robert did not take care of her, and the situation deteriorated. One day while Robert was out, Mrs. M. took a friend's van, emptied the apartment of all the furniture, and moved in with Chris, a friend who had been her lover while she was still married to Mr. M.

After three weeks, Mrs. M. and Harold moved again, this time to a rented room. Mrs. M. begged Robert "to start all over again." Although he refused, the couple had sexual intercourse occasionally and a second child was conceived. After discovering this pregnancy, Mrs. M. found an apartment and urged Robert to join her. Robert did not, limiting himself to infrequent visits and some support for Harold. Despite this, Mrs. M. considered herself married to Robert and was convinced that he loved her and would, indeed, marry her one day.

When Mrs. M. was in the eighth month of her second pregnancy, Robert informed her that he was living with another woman and was planning to marry her in three months. Although she had to distort reality seriously to do so, Mrs. M. flatly denied that this could be true. She insisted that Robert was in love with her and with nobody else and that he could never marry anyone else.

As if to underscore her magical thinking and distortions of reality, Mrs. M. fantasized that the day she gave birth, Robert would see his daughter and come back to marry her and have a family with her and their children, even though Robert denied fathering the second baby. As the therapist tried to help her prepare for the new baby, Mrs. M. refused to discuss any contingency plans to allow for the possibility that Robert would in fact marry his new girlfriend. She could only think of different ways in which she would announce the birth of their new child.

In spite of these hopes, Mrs. M.'s ambivalence toward Robert was apparent in her complaints that he was not a good father to Harold because he did not buy him toys or take him out for picnics. The therapist felt that Mrs. M. was also voicing her disappointment in Robert as a provider for herself, as the "good father" she had never had and whom she sought without success in all the men in her life. Mrs. M. did not reject that interpretation.

Mrs. M.'s Present Pregnancy

Mrs. M.'s pregnancy with her second child was uneventful. She ate well and even gained 45 pounds, although when not pregnant she was usually underweight. She stopped using drugs, except for marijuana very occasionally, and had regular prenatal medical care.

Mrs. M. said that she enjoyed being pregnant and that she loved children. She also said that this pregnancy had a special meaning for her because it seemed to "make up" for the abortion her mother and Robert had forced her to have one year before.

After witnessing Mrs. M.'s abruptness and irritation with Harold, we believed that her enjoyment of pregnancy had more to do with a narcissistic satisfaction in her body's "wholeness" than with her expressed impulse to nurture children. Her adolescent worries about the late onset of menstruation and her fear of her menses lent support to this hypothesis.

Later Pregnancy and Delivery

The last months of Mrs. M.'s pregnancy were marked by quasi-delusional magical thinking involving Robert. In her fantasies, he would be there for his child's birth, and upon looking at the newborn he would realize how deeply he loved Mrs. M., the child's mother. These hopes for a "happy ending" made it very difficult for Mrs. M. to make realistic plans for the future. A large part of the therapist's work at this time involved helping her prepare Harold and herself for the new baby, including dealing with such concrete questions as who would care for Harold while Mrs. M. was in the hospital and where the baby would sleep after coming home.

As the delivery date approached, Mrs. M. started talking about the sex of the new baby. At first she said that she wanted another boy because she wanted Harold to have a brother. Only gradually did she acknowledge that she *feared* having a girl; she said she feared being as "overprotective" with a daughter as her mother had been with her. At the same time, Mrs. M. was convinced that she would, in fact, deliver a girl because she found her pregnancy different—and much harder—than her previous one.

Two things were striking in Mrs. M.'s perceptions. One was the magnitude of the protective distortion in her perception of her abandoning, neglecting mother as "overprotective." The second was her equation of womanhood with pain: her feeling that carrying a daughter was "harder" and more burdensome than carrying a son. Interestingly, this theme was elaborated during labor. Mrs. M. spoke to the therapist, who was present through labor and delivery, about her worries regarding how to handle a daughter. Between contractions she spoke about her mother slapping her hands when she touched her genitals as a child. She went on to say that she could feel close to a baby daughter but would not know how to be the mother of an older girl. It was felt that Mrs. M. was giving voice here, in this most womanly of experiences, to her unresolved conflicts about being a woman and to her fears of her own sexuality.

The delivery was fast and thoroughly normal, and, indeed, Mrs. M. gave birth to a girl. Mrs. M., who had not received any sedatives, asked to see and hold her baby. Her first comment was that the baby looked like Robert. She then asked that the therapist call her mother to tell her about her new granddaughter. Upon hearing the news, Mrs. M.'s mother asked for the baby's name and then said she was in a hurry to hang up because she was going away for the weekend. It was chilling to witness the grandmother's matter-of-factness as she pursued her weekend plans without a thought of changing them to welcome her granddaughter and to be available to her daughter in this time of need.

During her three-day stay at the hospital, the therapist was Mrs. M.'s only visitor. Mrs. M. called her friends, but everyone was too busy to visit. She made excuses to the therapist, giving reasons for the failure of friends and relatives to visit. But on the third day she broke down and said, between tears, that she felt lonely and abandoned. She was holding her baby and began breast-feeding as she promised Amy she would be a good mother, unlike her own mother.

Amy's First Month of Life

While Mrs. M. impressed hospital personnel with her apparent involvement and "bonding" with Amy, the therapist recognized Mrs. M.'s preoccupation with the fantasized return of Robert to claim her and Amy as his own. During Amy's first month we witnessed an increasingly alarming deterioration of Amy's functioning as Mrs. M.'s mothering failed to match her verbalized professions of love.

Physically, Amy was a full-term, healthy baby. On the Lipman-Parmelee Postnatal Factor Scale, Amy had an optimal score. When Amy was 3 days old, the therapist administered the Brazelton Neonatal Assessment Scale, encouraging Mrs. M. to observe while she explained the items and discussed Amy's responses with her. Amy's reflexes were normal. She had good interactive abilities and oriented well to both auditory and visual stimuli. She was able to maintain state control, showed no excessive response to stress and was relatively easy to console. On the basis of the examination, Amy appeared to be a competent and rewarding baby. Mrs. M. was very proud of her daughter's performance and said that she never knew 3-day-old babies could do so many things.

Once at home, Mrs. M. devoted an undue amount of time to nursing Amy, who spent most of her waking time at her mother's breast. When the therapist spoke about the diversity of physical and emotional needs of the baby and the different forms of interaction that were important between mother and baby, Mrs. M. could only relate the information to herself, accusing her mother for not having given her that kind of care. This was a theme that Mrs. M. returned to many times later.

Although Mrs. M. spoke of her efforts to give Amy the kind of mothering she had not had, her words were very seldom translated into concrete examples of emotional nurturing. The baby was often unclean and smelled strongly of urine. Mrs. M. did not look at the baby's eyes, smile, or talk to the baby; she never sang to her, and did not cuddle or rock her. She placed Amy on her lap or her breast as if the baby were an inanimate object. The only overt sign of affection was the kiss she routinely gave her daughter before handing her over to the therapist, saying in a flat voice, "I love my baby." Predictably, Amy also began to be very apathetic in social interactions. It took the therapist a long period of "warm-up" before Amy responded to her playing, but the therapist eventually succeeded in eliciting gazes and smiles from the baby.

The 1-month Brazelton assessment reflected clearly the developmental impact of this environment. Amy's interactive ability had deteriorated markedly. She no longer responded well to auditory and visual stimulation and did less well with animate than with inanimate stimuli. Her alertness had decreased and she was less able to maintain an alert state. While state control remained average and she still showed no excessive response to stress, Amy had become harder to console at 1 month than she had been at 3 days, and she did not cuddle as much as she had as a newborn.

The deterioration in Amy's performance in the course of the first month was extremely worrisome. While one expects to see a baby become increasingly more alert and able to sustain social interaction in the first weeks of life, Amy showed a reversal of this process. It was clear that this deterioration was due to the poor quality of Mrs. M.'s mothering, to the chaotic home environment, and to the absence of a substitute caregiver who could provide Amy the sensitive care Mrs. M. could not give.

Mrs. M. was unable as yet to make use of the therapist's suggestions for care of her children. She could use the therapist only for her own needs: to talk about her unhappy childhood and her anger at her mother, to daydream about a happy future, and ask for concrete help, ranging from diapers and formula to a ride to the well-baby clinic to advocacy with the Department of Social Services. But the therapist's intervention as an educator, who demonstrated patterns of child care and encouraged Mrs. M. to learn them, met with limited success. The therapist taught Mrs. M. how and when to change diapers, how to bathe Amy, how to hold, play, and talk with the infant. Mrs. M. performed well in the therapist's presence, but by her own admission she "kind of forgot" the rest of the week. As long as she had an audience, Mrs. M. seemed able to motivate herself to "show off" in order to gain love and approval. When she was alone with her children, however, her depletion of inner resources was unmitigated by the desire to please, and she had nothing to give.

At that time the Infant Program was growing and more people were hired. It was decided then to modify the therapeutic plan and involve, in addition to the therapist, an Infant Specialist. The latter would focus on offering concrete developmental guidance and work directly with Amy in providing age-appropriate stimulation.

We recognized that Mrs. M. was unable to "share" the therapist (the good, available mother figure) with her children. Any attempts by the therapist to focus on the children met with defensive withdrawal from Mrs. M., who regarded her children as rivals for the care and attention of the therapist. Mrs. M. often seemed ashamed of speaking with the therapist about her shortcomings as a mother and her ambivalence toward her children; any comment that might indicate that she was less than a perfect, all-loving mother was immediately followed by repeated statements about her love for her children and the sacrifices she made for them. Tentative efforts to interpret these patterns were unsuccessful, and the therapist concluded that Mrs. M.'s ego organization might well be too primitive to attempt dynamic interpretations without an initial period of ego-strengthening work. The hypothesis was that if the therapist could meet Mrs. M.'s dependency needs by being understanding and available, and by dealing with the issues that were of importance to Mrs. M., she might in turn become gradually more aware of and responsive to her children's needs. Until that occurred, we hoped that the Infant Specialist's direct intervention would help the baby attain competence in cognitive and socioaffective development.

Amy and Her Family: 1–4 Months

The general plan was explained to Mrs. M. simply and directly: the therapist would help her with her feelings about herself and about her children, while the infant specialist would work directly with Amy and would show Mrs. M. ways of caring for the baby and encouraging her development. Initially, however, both the therapist and the infant specialist felt "confused" and occasionally competitive and possessive, since there was an overlap in their respective therapeutic domains. As the work of the therapist and infant specialist became progressively more differentiated, yet better integrated, the value of this dual approach became increasingly apparent.

Our short-term intervention, however intensive and well-designed, could not reverse Mrs. M.'s deeply rooted patterns of maladaptive functioning in time to prevent the physical and emotional neglect of both Harold and Amy. The staff considered the option of foster care, but after many hours of meetings and discussion we decided to intensify our intervention program rather than seek foster care as a way to sustain the children's development. We knew from our court experience that there were no legal grounds for permanent removal, and we felt that the separation involved in a temporary removal would only compound the difficulties of facilitating the development of attachment between this mother and infant.

The infant specialist worked with Amy weekly to provide visual and auditory stimulation, to promote interest in animate and inanimate objects, and to encourage exploration of objects through eyes, mouth, and hands. All the interventions took place in the context of playful social interaction with Amy. The infant specialist remained alert and responsive to Amy's signals, so that the activity in progress was modified or discontinued if the baby seemed fatigued or uninterested. At all times, the baby's affective involvement was monitored and used by the infant specialist to choose one course of action over another. By respecting the baby's mood, we hoped to give Mrs. M. a good incentive to do the same.

Mrs. M. was present in all the sessions between Amy and the infant specialist, and modeling was an important component of the intervention. Mrs. M. followed the infant specialist's example faithfully but without much emotional involvement, like a good girl going through her homework. Carry-through after the infant specialist left was questionable.

The spontaneous interaction between mother and baby continued to be mechanical and lifeless. Feeding times reflected this quality well. The baby hung like an appendage from the mother's breast, and it was often impossible to follow Mrs. M.'s reasoning in deciding when Amy had had enough.

On the one hand, the mother seemed to be using breast-feeding in her search for the closeness that had been so harshly denied her in early years, while on the other her discomfort with intimacy was apparent from her blank look and impersonal, doll-like handling of Amy.

In spite of earnest efforts on the part of both the therapist and the infant specialist to help Mrs. M. provide better care, physical neglect continued. Amy's face was often caked with food or mucus. Her diapers were changed only sporadically and she smelled frequently of urine. Even the therapist and the infant specialist had to fight their revulsion at the baby's physical state. By contrast, however, Amy's diet seemed appropriate: fruit, vegetables, and breast milk.

While the infant specialist provided direct intervention for the baby and modeling of child care patterns for the mother, the therapist met weekly with Mrs. M., trying to help her sort out reality from the wishful thinking about Robert's return in which she continued to indulge. If the therapist attempted to discuss the children and their needs, Mrs. M. impatiently turned the subject to herself in her preoccupation with her love life.

Mrs. M.'s interest in her children during this period seemed predicated largely on their ability to secure Robert's presence. As it became clear they would not bring Robert back, Mrs. M. spoke openly of her need to take care of her own life first, which for her meant finding a man who would give her love, acceptance, and financial security.

Absorbed in herself, Mrs. M. began going to bars about once a week in search of a man. Although she criticized the men she met as "good-for-nothing drunks," she began to weave elaborate fantasies about one man to whom she was introduced. This was Peter, a 33-year-old auto mechanic whose wife had left him and their two children several years before and who lived sixty miles out in the countryside with no telephone.

As Mrs. M. wove her imagined romance, the children

deteriorated. Amy was now showing pronounced gaze avoidance in social interactions. This was particularly evident in her contacts with her mother; the baby actually turned her head away from Mrs. M. Harold's speech was increasingly delayed and he constantly got hurt by falling down the stairs, smashing his fingers in drawers or doors, or bumping his head against furniture.

Amy's 4-Month Developmental Assessment

In keeping with our program's schedule of developmental assessments, the Bayley Scales were administered to Amy when she was 4 months old. After this procedure, Amy and her mother were observed in a semistructured play situation in which Mrs. M. was asked to "do with the baby what you like to do together when you are at home."

Amy's developmental index (MDI = 99) placed her within the age-appropriate range of functioning. However, we used the Bayley Scales not only as a standardized assessment instrument but also as an opportunity for clinical observation, and in this regard Amy's performance gave cause for concern. She was a sober, quiet baby who smiled seldom and then only fleetingly. There was no cooing, laughing, or gurgling. She was visually alert, to the point that visual exploration was her predominant form of involvement with objects. She did take objects to her mouth for oral exploration, but she had very rudimentary eye-hand coordination and her grasp was so weak that objects often dropped from her hand after a very brief period. Her motor development, on the other hand, was excellent; she bore her weight well and was able to propel herself forward a few inches.

During the semistructured play interaction, Mrs. M. threw the baby in the air and turned her upside down repeatedly, as if Amy were a Ferris wheel. Although rough-and-tumble games are a regular feature of parent-infant interaction everywhere, the affective quality here was worrisome. Mrs. M. seemed sad and strained; the baby, far from enjoying the game, was very sober at its beginning and began fussing as it went on. Yet Mrs. M. continued throwing her in the air and did not stop until the fussing became very pronounced. Mrs. M. then switched to a bouncing lap game which succeeded in soothing Amy. Although not grossly inappropriate, this game also reflected sadness and self-consciousness on Mrs. M.'s part, and a sober acceptance on the part of Amy.

In general, Amy seemed to be a low-energy baby who responded with avoidance and withdrawal to the environmental stresses that surrounded her. Her patterns of gaze aversion in social interaction, which contrasted with her visual alertness to inanimate objects, told us that Amy avoided closeness. Since we knew that both her mother and grandmother also avoided closeness, we wondered if there could be a constitutional predisposition for this form of response to a neglecting affective environment. This was a question that would resurface many times during Amy's first three years.

The aggressive quality of Mrs. M.'s play with her baby during the testing had been unanticipated. During the home visits, Mrs. M. had appeared to be involved and inept rather than aggressive. This play session raised the possibility that Mrs. M.'s emotional distance from Amy was a form of protection against a powerful urge to hurt the baby. The neglecting mother might become an aggressive one.

As a result of this assessment, we intensified intervention with mother and baby. The therapist saw Mrs. M. twice a week, while the infant specialist visited the home weekly. The immediate goal of the psychotherapy with Mrs. M. was to help her become aware of her ambivalence toward her children. The first step would be to try to bring some flexibility to the rigid defenses against anger, and to enable her to make some progress toward object constancy by diminishing the primitiveness of her splitting mechanisms. Work with the baby consisted of encouraging Amy's involvement with the infant specialist through pat-a-cake, tickling games, and vocal exchanges. These interactions continued to be modeled for

Mrs. M. In addition, both the therapist and the infant specialist continued to give specific suggestions concerning feeding, sleeping, and hygiene for the children.

This intensified intervention seemed to have little immediate effect. Mrs. M. denied any ambivalence toward her children, spoke at length of her love for them, continued to neglect them both physically and psychologically, and saw no contradiction between her words and her actions. Then something happened that made possible some positive change.

The Ambivalence Emerges

At the beginning of one session, Mrs. M. announced to the therapist in a flat tone that a few days ago she had sent Harold out in the street to play and he had not come back. She searched for a long time but couldn't find him. She began running around the housing project calling his name, but there was no answer. She then saw a cruising police car. A policeman came out and asked Mrs. M. if she had lost a small boy. Mrs. M. saw Haold sitting in the back of the car and described him as looking frightened. Before the therapist had time to comment on the event, Mrs. M. said that she thought it was normal for a 2½-year-old boy to run away. She had a girlfriend, she said, who had a son who also ran away at Harold's age. She went on to say that a month ago Harold was wandering around the project when a woman found him and took him to her apartment. After many hours of searching, she said, she asked the manager to call the tenants of the project to inquire about Harold. They finally found him in the lady's apartment. Mrs. M. then reported a third incident that had taken place recently. She had left Harold in the house sleeping while she drove one of the children for whom she baby-sat to school. When she came back Harold was not there. After half an hour he was found walking toward the school. Mrs. M. thought that Harold was very smart to be able to do this: "He knew where his mother would be."

That Mrs. M. had concealed these events during two

sessions with the therapist and several telephone conversations during the past week was significant. Acting on the new information, the therapist first worked with the transference issue, speaking to Mrs. M.'s wish to please the therapist and to her fear that unless she was a "good mother" the therapist would become angry and abandon her. As Mrs. M. could agree with feeling to this interpretation, the therapist was able to use the affect now available to provide an entree into the way Mrs. M. dealt with aggressive feelings and to relate them to her earlier reactions to being abandoned. When the therapist linked these experiences to Mrs. M.'s present feelings toward her children, she commented that "sometimes parents feel they will do much better if they don't have any children." Mrs. M. then took a deep breath and said, "Sometimes I wish I was free and without children and able to do what I want. But I have so much love to give them, and when I am down or depressed it feels so good to have Harold or Amy around."

This was the first time Mrs. M. had expressed any ambivalence in her feelings about her children. It was the first breakdown in her splitting mechanisms and, after seven months of intensive intervention, the first hopeful sign of therapeutic progress.

As a result of Harold's running away, the Department of Social Services Child Protective Services became involved with Mrs. M., who became very "upset" with the agency for considering her a "bad" mother. Being "upset" was her way of expressing anxiety. Her fear that her children might be taken away seemed a projection of her own ambivalence and possibly a reliving of feelings she had experienced when separated from her mother as a child.

Mrs. M. protested Protective Service involvement, saying that she was a good mother while her mother had been bad toward her. As the therapist reminded her of her own recently acknowledged ambivalence toward her children, Mrs. M. recalled how "upset" she had been on several occasions when she had heard herself sounding like her mother: "she was talking through my mouth." She then described a dream she had when she was 7 years old: "A big ugly fish ate both her mother and father." As she spoke of this dream, Mrs. M. could remember for the first time her intense anger at feeling abandoned by them. She then said: "My mother told you once that we are a close family, but I never felt close to my mother," adding that she could never ask her mother for help in case of need. She then promised to be a better mother for her daughter: "I am sure that I would never hurt my daughter as much as my mother hurt me."

We felt that Mrs. M. was struggling with her wishes to overcome her past and be a "good" mother for Amy and her simultaneous fears that she would be unable to do so.

Flight and Rescue

In the ensuing weeks, this struggle became a melodrama that was all too real, including in the cast not only Mrs. M. and her children but the Infant Program staff as well.

With the therapist's encouragement, Mrs. M. had made contact with her father, who responded by calling and visiting. The therapist hoped that a renewed relationship with her father would help Mrs. M. toward healthier relationships with men and an enhanced capacity to care for her children. It was at about this time that the therapist announced her plans for a month's vacation.

Soon after the meeting with her father, Mrs. M. abruptly decided to become a housekeeper for Peter, the mechanic who lived in the country with his two children. Mrs. M. had made no direct agreement with Peter about duties, hours, or salary, but her fantasies were vivid. She would live in the country, run in the meadows, and go horseback riding. The children would eat fresh vegetables, eggs, and milk. Mrs. M. would begin as Peter's housekeeper and baby-sitter, but the relationship would flourish and she and Peter would marry and form a family.

In retrospect, Mrs. M.'s decision involved themes we had seen before and were to recognize many times again in our years of involvement with her. While at this particular time she might have been influenced by an unconscious need to flee from incestuous wishes awakened by the recent reunion with her father, her wish to have a man of her own was always very strong. Mrs. M. experienced the therapist's impending vacation as a rejection, likening the therapist to her mother, who had gone to Florida without taking her. Although Mrs. M. announced that someday she would go to Florida by herself, she could not carry out this wish immediately. But she could move to the country.

As Mrs. M. prepared to move, the situation in her home became chaotic. Anxious about the lack of any concrete arrangements with Peter and about the therapist's impending departure, she responded by fighting with her landlord and with every neighbor, by asking the infant program to "stay off her back" for the month that coincided with the therapist's vacation, and by taking only marginal care of the children.

Although both children had colds and Amy had had a bout of high fever, Mrs. M. was not keeping clinic appointments for her children. Amy seemed extremely thin. Mrs. M. said she was only breast-feeding Amy lately because she was too busy packing and could not be bothered preparing meals or giving Amy solids. She assured the therapist and the infant specialist that her child care practices would improve after her move. The therapist's efforts to point out the realities of the situation went unheeded. Mrs. M. could not wait to move to the country, in pursuit of the ideal life of which she dreamed. Within a week of the move, Mrs. M. realized that Peter's expectations were unrealistic and that she could not rely on his common sense to help her manage the household. Yet her anger at the therapist, about to have a vacation, left her unable to use the therapist's help in assessing the situation realistically and in dealing with pressing issues of grocery money and salary.

Mrs. M. was now living in an isolated rural section of the county, about two hours by car from the Infant Program headquarters and half an hour by car from the closest community agencies. While the therapist was on vacation, the infant specialist made a home visit in an effort to organize a program around the needs of Mrs. M. and her children. Finding Harold and Amy thin and pale and hearing Mrs. M. admit that she had been unable to arrange medical follow-up and that Peter was refusing to provide adequate money for food, the infant specialist spent many hours establishing a network of local community agency workers who would become involved with the family. Unfortunately, because of the distances involved, no public health nurse was available for home visits and Mrs. M. was unable to follow through on appointments with the local health agency.

Mrs. M.'s negative transference toward the absent therapist undermined the infant specialist's efforts and were expressed in neglect of the children that was even more pronounced than usual: feeling abandoned by her therapist, Mrs. M. "abandoned" (by her physical and psychological neglect) her own children.

The importance of a team approach in a case like this cannot be overemphasized. Without the infant specialist's involvement during this period, the children would not have had even the limited protection her visits could offer and their deterioration may have been even more pronounced.

When a second visit, two weeks later, revealed Amy looking even frailer and beginning to show pronounced developmental deficits in the affective sphere, many members of the Infant Program, including the pediatrician and the psychologist in charge of Amy's developmental assessments, urged the involvement of Children's Protective Services (CPS) in the case, or, at the very least, a serious conversation with Mrs. M., clearly outlining the Infant Program's concerns and raising the possibility of CPS involvement unless conditions improved. Many hours were spent in often heated debate about the course of action likely to prove most beneficial for the children and for Mrs. M. in the long run. Although the final decision, given the therapist's absence, rested in the hands of the case supervisor and the infant specialist, other professionals were equally vocal in their concern. That this group of competent, humane, and experienced professionals felt so intensely, not only about the welfare of Mrs. M. and her family but about the dissension that the uncertainties of their predicament aroused within the staff as well, graphically illustrates the difficulties of this case. Finally, the decision was made to continue efforts to coordinate the intervention of local social agencies on Mrs. M.'s behalf and to await the therapist's return.

An infuriated staff greeted the returning therapist: "Amy is in bad shape"; "Mrs. M. is doing worse"; "Such an intensive intervention without results!"; "You must make a contract with Mrs. M." The staff was probably voicing Mrs. M.'s anger toward the therapist who had "abandoned" her. When the therapist and the infant specialist visited Mrs. M. and her children the next day, they found a very thin, disheveled, distraught Mrs. M., and thin, sick-looking, unkempt children. But it was Amy who seemed most severely affected by the countryside experience. Although there were no facilities to weigh her at the house, she looked so wasted that nonorganic failure-to-thrive became a very plausible diagnosis. She was even more difficult to engage than at the time of the infant specialist's last visit; it took strenuous efforts to elicit the pathetic grimace that now constituted Amy's smile. Her movements were slow and she seemed to lack the energy even to cry. Instead she let out a low-grade, almost continuous whimper.

Oblivious to the children, Mrs. M. was eager only to confide her woes to the therapist, now that she had her to herself again. While the infant specialist worked with the children, Mrs. M. took the therapist to her room and told her that as soon as she had received word of the therapist's return, she had told Peter that she would be leaving in two weeks.

Although Mrs. M. talked about moving to a small town with a Navy yard in search of a "Navy man," she was able to accept the therapist's suggestion that she return to her former surroundings, where the Infant Program could be more directly helpful to her and her children. She started to call the therapist "mother" and expressed relief that the end of her countryside adventure was at hand.

Getting away from Peter proved to be less than easy. Violent fights, forcible eviction by Peter, and a "ransoming" of Mrs. M.'s belongings with two hundred dollars of her mother's money were followed by desperate attempts to reestablish a life in the city. While Mrs. M. was able to mobilize welfare and emergency housing agencies independently, she continued to use marijuana and alcohol (supplied by her friends) daily and seemed unable to attend to the children's needs.

At this point we recognized the impossibility of carrying out the therapeutic plan we would have wished—helping Mrs. M. herself provide a sustaining relationship for her children. We opted for second best and made plans to provide intensive intervention outside the home for the two children. After much searching we found a therapeutic nursery school and arranged a subsidized fee. For Amy we planned daily visits of two to three hours in our own program's playroom. Here particular attention was given to Amy's diet, since a medical checkup had confirmed that her weight placed her within range accepted for a diagnosis of failure-to-thrive. Intensive human contact encouraged Amy to express wishes and needs, and every effort was made to read her signals correctly and respond to them in a contingent fashion. Cognitive stimulation was included in the program, with the recognition that Amy's principal need was for warm, accepting, and predictable human relationships.

Mrs. M. accepted the playroom arrangement with enthusiasm. It gave her a chance to look for an apartment without worrying about baby-sitting. She also spent as many as ten or twelve hours a week during this period with her therapist, for the first time seeming interested in understanding herself and why "those things" (her disappointment with Robert, her shattered dreams of a life with Peter) kept happening to her. While pointing out connections between Mrs. M.'s early experiences and her current behavior, and proposing ways of interrupting the cycle, the therapist at the same time focused on the reality issues of housing and physical care for Mrs. M. and the children.

Amy at 8 Months: Developmental Assessment

Six weeks in the playroom produced noteworthy effects in Amy, best illustrated by her performance in the 8-month developmental assessment.

Amy's first gesture when placed at the testing table was to bang on it with one hand while looking inquisitively at the examiner, as if saying, "I'm ready!" This liveliness was later reflected in her MDI = 124 in the Bayley Scales score, which placed her one month above age level. Amy had an endearing facial expression that seemed to say "Here I am, notice me," but she was by no means a child who sought to ingratiate herself by passive means alone. On the contrary, she could be very assertive in demanding one object or another or in protesting its withdrawal. She showed an excellent capacity to reorganize after frustration, a good attention span, and respectable persistence in the face of failure.

Yet there were many reasons for concern. Amy was a sober child who did not smile once in the course of the assessment. She was goal-oriented but gave no signal of pleasure or joy in exploration or in social interaction. Physically, she looked deprived—small, thin (in spite of a weight gain of 2 pounds in the six weeks she spent at the playroom), and with sparse hair. And this physical weakness was reflected in a delay in motor accomplishments: whereas at the 4-month assessment Amy had been able to sit with support, at 8 months she was still unable to support herself in a sitting position.

During the semistructured mother-infant play interval that followed the cognitive assessment, Amy became a whiny baby. This switch in affect from sober involvement in exploration to fussiness was consistent with the observations of the playroom personnel, who had repeatedly reported that Amy smiled and even laughed with them but became very fussy when she saw her mother. Mrs. M. responded to Amy's whining by offering the breast. She consistently associated the baby's unhappiness with her desire to feed.

When asked to do with the baby the things she liked to do at home, Mrs. M. engaged in an aggressive, disorganized game, alternating throwing Amy in the air with bouncing her on the knee, without regard for the baby's startled and increasingly unhappy response. Mrs. M. laughed as the baby cried, as if pretending to herself that this was in fact a pleasurable moment for mother and baby. Only when the baby's cry became quite high-pitched did Mrs. M. stop throwing the baby around.

The most appropriate exchange observed was a sequence in which Mrs. M. encouraged Amy to crawl toward a chair. Mrs. M. seemed most invested in her baby when she could derive some narcissistic gratification from her accomplishments, but this feeling disappeared as soon as the baby made demands on her.

The 8-month developmental assessment served to provide some perspective on the results of the therapeutic intervention to date. It seemed that the intervention had succeeded in helping Amy regain her physical weight, maintain interest in social interaction and exploration, and recoup the developmental delays in cognitive functioning that had occurred as a result of the disastrous move to the countryside.

Affectively, Amy showed many of the symptoms of an institutionalized child: object hunger, promiscuous interpersonal ties, and shallow affect. But it was felt that the child retained enough interest in the world to suggest that she would profit from further therapeutic approaches.

Intervention with Mrs. M., on the other hand, had resulted in little progress. Although she seemed slightly more able to withstand and explore feelings of ambivalence, this emerging capacity was not being translated into any tangible improvement in her relationship with her children. Mrs. M. continued to get drunk and use drugs every night, often appearing dazed and disoriented during the day. The slightest fuss from Amy would bring an offer of the breast, a ringing phone would result in an abrupt end to feeding. The therapist felt that she was playing "catch-up" with Mrs. M., helping her surmount one crisis after another.

Therapeutic plans for Amy were made on this basis. Playroom attendance was clearly insufficient in itself to reverse Amy's deterioration in affectivity and object relations. The intervention staff continued to see a most worrisome pattern in the relationship between mother and children, and seemed unable to modify it soon enough to help Amy.

In an attempt to convey to Mrs. M. the seriousness of the situation, the therapist raised the possibility of foster care for the children until Mrs. M. found a house, got herself organized, and was better able to take care of the children. Mrs. M. rejected the idea violently. She berated the therapist for joining the "others" who thought she was a bad mother, and protested that she cared for her children and would not give them up.

Given Mrs. M.'s violent reaction to the suggestion of foster care, the therapist sought another solution. She proposed making a homemaker available to help Mrs. M. with the children and to work directly with the children under the supervision of the infant specialist. Mrs. M. liked this idea, and it was agreed that a homemaker would start working with the family as soon as Mrs. M. found housing.

"A Car Without Brakes"

When Mrs. M. finally found a three-bedroom house with some garden space on a side street in a low-income housing project, the long crisis of flight to the country and return was over. In a pattern we now recognized, Mrs. M. was exhausted but ready for a new start. The first week after moving to the new house, she worked hard to fix everything nicely. She decreased her intake of drugs and alcohol, renewed her search for the "straight" man who would rescue her and her children, and promised to be more careful of herself and her children in the future.

The homemaker, a warm, nurturing woman, immediately began to come to the house for four hours every day. She taught Mrs. M. about nutritional planning and physical cleanliness; under the infant specialist's supervision she worked with Amy on gross and fine motor coordination, language, and the development of social skills. Therapy with Mrs. M. consisted of reviewing and clarifying what had happened in the move to the countryside and its aftermath, and why it had happened. As usual, Mrs. M. was receptive to this kind of work, which involved much support and willingness to meet her dependency needs.

The "new start" lasted only briefly. Within five weeks of the move, Mrs. M.'s cousin, her boyfriend, and his child camped in Mrs. M.'s living room for several weeks before eviction by the rental office; Robert got married; Mrs. M. began to pick up men, whom she invited to her apartment to smoke marijuana but with whom she did not have sexual intercourse; and Mrs. M. developed an abscess on her breast, discontinued breast-feeding, developed a boil large enough to require surgery, and underwent the operation on an outpatient basis when no one—including Mrs. M.'s mother—would care for the children so Mrs. M. could be hospitalized.

Mrs. M.'s illness, which left her feeling abandoned and alone as well as physically and financially drained, signaled the onset of another period of crisis. During this period, the homemaker often spent her own money for food for the children because there was nothing to eat in the house. Amy's weight again became a source of worry. As Christmas approached, Mrs. M. became determined to find a job to supplement her AFDC income in order to give her children a "good Christmas"—one with lots of toys. She threw herself into job-seeking and for two months changed jobs an average of once a week. Mrs. M. was gone from the home twelve to eighteen hours a day, changing baby-sitters as each new sitter complained of the children's neglected condition.

The therapist pointed out, to no avail, that being available to her children was more important than giving them toys at Christmas, but recognized that Mrs. M.'s job search probably represented an attempt to escape depression and renew the search for Prince Charming. While the therapist and the infant specialist attempted to make contact with each new baby-sitter in order to monitor Amy's care, the rapid changes made it impossible for the infant specialist to see Amy, let alone work with her. Frustrated at her inability to prevent the all too predictable next crisis, the therapist thought of Mrs. M. as "a car without brakes—nothing, short of emotional disaster, can stop her."

Attempts To Deal with the Chaos

To introduce some predictability for the children in this chaotic environment, we decided to have both Harold and Amy half of each day in our playroom. With Mrs. M. virtually never at home, it made little sense either practically or therapeutically for the homemaker to continue going to the home and keeping house for Mrs. M. It was decided instead that the homemaker would continue seeing Amy in the playroom in order to provide some continuity in caregiving while allowing Amy to spend some time each day in an environment specifically designed for her age group. Mrs. M. was also urged to take Harold regularly to his therapeutic nursery school.

This plan proved difficult to implement because Mrs. M. was erratic in bringing Amy to the playroom. When she did some, Amy was only content being held by the homemaker and would not interact with anyone else. Amy's 1-year assessment, which took place about two weeks after the beginning of this arrangement, pinpointed several areas of concern. Although Amy performed at age level in the Bayley Scales (MDI = 98), she was less persistent than at the 8-month assessment and quickly lost interest in the objects presented. At the same time, she became easily upset when the objects were withdrawn. It was believed that this pattern suggested anxiety around issues of separation and an emerging attempt to defend against this anxiety by withdrawing from exploration of the objects and losing interest in them.

The semistructured mother-child interaction was also instructive. Mrs. M. engaged in a rough, abrupt bouncing game. When Amy protested, Mrs. M. attempted to console her with an empty bottle. Amy sucked on it for awhile, but soon protested again. Mrs. M. then put an end to the session by going with Amy to look for water. The symbolism of the depleted Mrs. M. attempting to satisfy her protesting daughter with an empty bottle seemed inescapable. At one year of age, Amy already needed more than Mrs. M. could give her.

Therapeutic Issues in the Work with Mrs. M. During This Period

Mrs. M.'s work as a waitress and her search for a new man provided an important therapeutic entree into Mrs. M.'s conflicts around mothering. While working as a waitress, Mrs. M. met a barman with whom she was soon smoking marijuana during work breaks and lunch hours, although she repelled his sexual advances. This episode served as a starting point for an exploration of Mrs. M.'s sexuality and her use of drugs. Although her inability for sustained introspection left the exploration incomplete, some interesting clues emerged. Mrs. M. equated sex with closeness and protection; she said that she did not care about sexual intercourse for its own sake. It seemed likely, in light of these comments, that she was nonorgasmic and might indeed fear the physical closeness involved in intercourse. This possibility was given added weight by the many instances in which she rejected sexual advances and her vague allusions to sexual dissatisfaction in her marriage. Mrs. M. also spoke, often in quick sequence, of her greater sexual satisfaction with Robert and of the violent fights they had with each other. This suggested that aggression and sexuality were so deeply fused for Mrs. M. that she could only become sexually aroused in the context of a sadomasochistic relationship.

Mrs. M.'s drug use became a simultaneous area of inquiry. She acknowledged that smoking marijuana helped her feel "full" and "high" when she was having feelings of "emptiness." The sexual imagery she used suggested to us that drug "highs" were being used as substitutes for the sexual satisfaction she could not attain in her relationship with men. Mrs. M. never spent her own money on drugs but procured them from friends (usually men) who were well supplied and generous. Smoking marijuana with them was an avenue for the intimate sharing that was closed to Mrs. M. in everyday life. The therapist spent a great amount of time in drug-related counseling, and Mrs. M. became able to stay off drugs for periods as long as two months.

As Mrs. M. began to explore tentatively the issues in her relationship to men, she was able to acknowledge how difficult it was for her to feel close to people. She was also able to see how this difficulty manifested itself in her relationship with her children. As she could tolerate an increasing awareness of her own ambivalence, the tendency to use splitting as a defense became considerably attenuated. At one point she was able to say, "I sometimes feel that I would be better off without any children, but they are there and I love them." Never before had she been so able to acknowledge her negative feelings toward her children.

Harry

Perhaps as a result of the therapeutic work, Mrs. M. found a job sorting mail which she was to keep for many months. She also became physically attracted to Harry, a man whom she met briefly at a party and pursued rather actively. Harry was a carpenter with a well-paid job who lived with his mother and father. Mrs. M. learned from a friend that he drank "a lot." Mrs. M. seemed to have an immediate need to fuse with Harry, to depend on him entirely, and to have Harry be simultaneously her father and a father to her children. A sexual relationship was apparently less important; Harry's attempts to achieve intercourse were often unsuccessful, but Mrs. M. remained kind and understanding.

During this period, Mrs. M. became openly aggressive toward Harold, seeming to displace onto her son any aggression she felt toward men in general or Harry in particular. Harold seemed to symbolize for Mrs. M. the primitive, dangerous, aggressive parts of herself. She saw Amy, on the other hand, as the poor, abandoned baby who represented Mrs. M.'s empty, lonely side. As more material emerged involving themes of emptiness and fears of body damage and loss, an important aspect of Mrs. M.'s relationship with her children became clearer. The children reassured Mrs. M. that she was complete, that her body was not as inadequate as she feared. This explained Mrs. M.'s repeated attempts to attract a man through her children; only with them as a concrete reminder did she feel at all confident of her womanhood.

New Therapeutic Dilemmas: Amy's Predicament

During these months, the therapy with Mrs. M. and her hard-won insights into herself had no apparent effect on her mothering. Harold had continued to make remarkable improvement, but this seemed due to his exceptionally good therapeutic nursery school and not to the quality of the mothering he received. Although she was now expressing feelings of guilt about doing so, Mrs. M. continued to yell at him and be very abrupt. Amy continued to deteriorate. She showed no social discrimination and went to anyone who would smile and talk to her. Mrs. M. had more difficulty acknowledging her mothering difficulties with Amy than with Harold. She professed herself proud of her daughter's "social ability."

By this time Amy was 17 months old. Given our experience with Mrs. M., we saw little likelihood that she would improve soon enough to help Amy with the developmental tasks awaiting her. Once again, the chronic dilemma posed by this case posed an acute question: what is the proper therapeutic stance when a mother cannot mother, when intensive therapeutic work results in no improvement in the quality of the mother-child relationship?

Although foster care, with the goal of terminating parental rights and placing the children permanently, seemed a tempting solution, children who have been at far greater physical and psychological danger than Amy are often returned to their homes by judges unwilling to separate parents and children related by biological ties. When children are removed and then returned by the courts, the original severe conflicts in the parent-child relationship have been greatly compounded by the trauma of separation and the inevitable correlates of guilt, self-blame, and anger in both parents and children. We feared that working toward removal would do more harm than good. And it was obvious to us that Mrs. M. would not voluntarily relinquish parental rights, no matter how deep her ambivalence toward the children.

As an alternative to removal, we designed a full-fledged therapeutic regimen to meet Amy's specific developmental needs. This program was to be implemented on a full-time basis in our new Therapeutic Infant Center, an expansion of the earlier Infant Playroom.

Amy Begins at the Therapeutic Infant Center

Since the Therapeutic Infant Center now had the staff necessary to provide consistent, full-time intervention with infants, the work with Amy took a different turn. The therapist continued psychotherapy with Mrs. M., but now we could plan for Amy to come to the Center five times a week for the whole day for at least eighteen months. The hope was that even after starting regular nursery school at age 3, Amy would continue to attend the Center twice a week for psychotherapy.

Amy was assigned two caregivers. The main caregiver would also become the child's new infant specialist, working intensively with Amy and becoming the person who discussed Amy with the mother. A second caregiver (the original home-maker, who had later worked with Amy in the infant playroom) would provide supplementary care.

Mrs. M. cheerfully accepted the idea of Amy coming into the Infant Center. For one thing, it relieved her of her baby-sitting problem. In addition, Mrs. M. did want for her children to be happy, "not to go through what I did," and was able to recognize that the program might offer something to Amy. That Harold had already made progress in the thera-peutic nursery was obvious to her.

We arranged for program staff to bring Amy to the Center in the morning. Mrs. M. would pick up the child in the afternoon to take her home. Although Mrs. M. was often late and occasionally "forgot" to pick Amy up, this arrangement had two advantages: it ensured that Amy would come to the Center, and it assured daily contact between the caregivers and Mrs. M. Often the mother was too overwhelmed with her own problems to be able to address issues concerning Amy. However, because contact occurred daily, the infant specialist was able to make good use of those days when the mother was psychologically available.

When she first started her attendance at 17 months, Amy presented a sad picture to the Infant Center staff. Her large gray eyes and fragile frame gave her a waiflike appearance. She generally arrived at the Center wet, sometimes in diapers thought to be from the night before. She had red rashes, possibly eczema, on her arms and legs. Her ill-fitting clothing added to her pitiful appearance. Going indiscriminantly to adults, with a rather flat affect, Amy bore a scary resemblance to a neglected, affect-starved orphan. Her vocabulary consisted of two or three words, and she babbled little and did not imitate adult speech. Amy was often quiet and somber, and her whininess wearied even the Center staff. She masturbated frequently with her hands in her diaper, and was almost obsessively oral, putting everything she found in her mouth.

Amy's 18-Month Assessment

The administration of the Bayley Scales when Amy was 18 months old, one month after she had begun coming to the Center, helped to document our fears concerning the extent of Amy's regression. Her MDI had dropped to 70. She was whiny, sulky, negativistic, and uncooperative. She moved slowly, with long pauses, as if severely depressed. She gave most items back to the examiner rather than trying to manipulate and explore them herself. This was in sharp contrast with the absorption in exploration of inanimate objects that Amy had shown at 8 months and, less strikingly, at 12 months.

The unstructured interactions with her mother also revealed a very whiny, unhappy child. Although Mrs. M. made several attempts to engage Amy in games or play items, Amy's only response was whining. Her mother continually attributed this to Amy's fatigue and, once frustrated, used her characteristic rough-and-tumble games to engage Amy. None of this worked. Amy, with her bottle, climbed up into the infant seat and sat there.

We knew enough of Amy's history—emotional involvement and physical care ranging from inconsistent to nonexistent, the continual environmental disruptions, the violent scenes she had probably witnessed—to expect and understand on some level Amy's difficulties. Still, a great deal remained unanswered. How did Amy feel and specifically cope with the unpredictability of her mother? How did the child view herself in this scenario? What were the conflicts with which she was struggling? What choices was she making in her attempt to deal with these conflicts? At what cost were certain defenses and coping mechanisms being employed? We hoped that intensive work with Amy would give us an answer to some of these questions.

Nature of the Intervention for Amy in the Infant Center: 17–24 months

The main direction that the Infant Center would take was clear: Amy needed an opportunity to develop and experience constancy in human relationships. As much as possible, the new infant specialist would be her main caregiver, tending to Amy's physical needs (changing, feeding, washing); comforting her in stressful situations; providing tenderness and closeness and stimulating the child to the wonders of the world. Providing such an environment would give Amy an opportunity to learn of a new kind of world, one where security and intimacy were possible. We continued to hope that as Mrs. M. progressed in her therapy she herself might come to offer such a world to her children; but meanwhile, Amy would not have to wait.

In many ways Amy thrived quickly on the very individualized attention she was receiving. She began to recognize her two main caregivers and looked specifically to them for comfort in stressful times. The driver, too, became someone Amy was genuinely glad to see. The Infant Center and office became a "home away from home," with Amy knowing all the offices, all the people, and all the places where things were kept or hung. The day was divided into indoor/outdoor, active/quiet activities, eating/sleeping periods. Amy responded well to the schedule, cooperating in the transition.

In retrospect one can see how the safety, comfort, and psychological nurturance at the Infant Center provided Amy the elements she needed to achieve the early developmental stage of homeostasis or self-regulation, an indispensable step toward forming secure attachments to her caregivers. The routine was geared to promoting homeostasis, with particular emphasis on regular eating and sleeping schedules. Soon Amy began to put some weight on her slight frame. Eating never presented a problem and she seemed to enjoy mealtime. At lunchtime Amy was ready to wash up, put her towel away, and manage a few minutes of waiting at the table by engaging in talk or song with an adult. She generally chose to sit at the same place at the table but was not upset if that place was taken. Amy used a spoon about half the time but still seemed to enjoy fingering the food. She tried most new foods and showed few dislikes, although the quantity she consumed was small. She ate slowly, as she did most things, keeping track of the other children. Sometimes she reprimanded others for banging their spoons: "No!"; "Stop!" At other times she and another child would engage in a game of feeding each other.

The nap, too, was an easy adjustment for Amy. The first couple of months she was rocked with a bottle for five minutes or so before falling asleep. Later, with the caregiver present in the room, she would lie on her cot jabbering or singing softly to herself for a few minutes before falling asleep for two hours. Often she would awaken spontaneously and go off in search of her caregiver.

From her first days at the Center, dolls were among Amy's favorite toys. She dressed them, fed them, rocked them, and diapered them. One of Amy's first words was "baby." She showed a most obvious attraction to anything having to do with babies. She even kept track of which offices had pictures of babies and made trips with the specific purpose of seeing these pictures. In the Infant Room Amy was likely to stand next to any adult who was playing with or caring for a baby. Amy was mostly gentle with the babies, bringing toys and diapers or alerting adults to a baby's crying. On one occasion Amy became visibly upset when a group of toddlers, feedings and to a large doll, got a bit overzealous and ended up gleefully dumping sand on the doll's eyes. Greatly dismayed, Amy tried to stop them by using the few words she had ("no," "baby," "eyes"). Amy sometimes displayed aggressive feelings toward babies by squeezing the dolls too tightly and hitting or pinching them, but except for later in-cidents in play therapy sessions, she rarely played aggressively with the dolls. This was interpreted as a sign that Amy was frightened of her own aggression. Later, therapy would reveal confusion around the issues of maternal care and aggression.

As the months passed, Amy learned to let her caregivers know how she felt and what she needed. When her caregivers were involved with other babies, Amy's jealousy was obvious as she squeezed into the caregiver's lap next to the baby or went to the other caregiver for a hug. The themes of ten-derness, envy, and jealousy showed us that Amy was now beginning to be capable of real human relationships, in con trast to her earlier affective promiscuity.

In time it became obvious that Amy's maternal play and interest in babies bordered on obsession. She often played with the same doll again and again and continually asked to see the baby pictures, almost to the point of ignoring other materials. One wondered about the origins of this preoccu-pation. It was known that at home Amy was still often called "baby" by her mother and her brother. And she sometimes seemed to want to be a "lap baby" again, as when she would curl up with a toy bottle in an infant seat. It is likely that Amy's preoccupation with babies represented a repetition compulsion involving earlier trauma, as well as a more adap-tive tendency to imitate new experiences. After all, much of the activity and attention that Amy witnessed daily in the Infant Center revolved around babies. Amy would continue to reveal a great deal about herself through baby play.

In addition to dolls, books were another favorite way of spending time. Amy could listen to the reading of several books in a row, and it was usually the caregiver who had to bring the sessions to a close. Amy listened intently to stories even before she could speak, seemingly enjoying the sounds of the words. She snuggled up to the reader, evidently en-joying the close bodily contact reading brings. One videotape even shows her licking the adult's arm. She seemed to take the world in through all her senses.

Amy also made good use of virtually all the materials presented to her: puzzles, blocks, push/pull toys, paints, crayons, and climbing equipment. Her overall fine motor coordination was adequate, and it could be observed in her stacking blocks, using tape, screwing lids, fitting shapes, etc. However, upon closer examination one could notice that Amy was less successful in any manipulation that required exerting force. For example, she could place pegs accurately in the holes of the pegboard, but her pegs would fall down because she could not exert enough pressure to force them into the holes. Snap beads gave her the same trouble, as did the small hammering workbench. It was an inhibition of assertion, as if Amy was hesitant about her own physical aggression. This same hesitancy revealed itself in areas of large muscle activity. It was many months before Amy could bring herself to throw a ball rather than hand it to an adult. In going up and down the slide, Amy continued to hold tightly to the railing, when she could actually let go successfully if she had allowed herself to. She seemed uneasy about body control.

This theme of inhibition of aggression appeared not only in physical activities but also in social interaction. In physical activity and object manipulation, Amy could learn to "let go" through adult encouragement and through the repeated experience of success. In the area of social interaction the situation was more complicated. The staff became worried as it became quite clear that Amy's discomfort with the overt expression of aggression was causing her to internalize a style of coping that was harmful to herself. Amy was always the most likely victim of other children's aggression. A slight push or shove from another child was likely to induce body tension, whining, and dramatic scenes that more often than not brought the attacking child back for more. Amy defended neither possessions nor her body well. If she ever hit back, she did so with little exertion, as if half-heartedly.

Amy showed a similar style in dealing with frustration and anger stemming from difficulty completing a task. When a doll did not stay put, or a puzzle piece became jammed, Amy whined, pulled at her clothes, tensed up her arms, and even had tremors. She seemed defenseless against her own anger and frustration. The acquisition of some language (something that was continually encouraged by the Infant Center staff) aided Amy somewhat, as she quickly made appropriate use of words like "stop," "stuck," and "mine" to alleviate some of the tension she felt in stressful situations. However, her difficulty in dealing with aggression actively rather than passively or by directing it toward herself continued to reveal itself in many ways.

In summary, the Infant Center intervention, with its emphasis on predictability of daily routine and constancy of human relationships, allowed Amy to achieve homeostasis and to establish genuine and rich human attachments. However, her massive inhibitions over aggression meant that she was how facing difficulties in the next developmental tasks facing her—somatopsychological differentiation and behavioral organization and initiative.

Mrs. M.'s Relationship to the Infant Center

Interaction between Mrs. M. and the Infant Center took a long time to become relatively stable. Initially, communications between the mother and the infant specialist took place through the therapist. This plan had been designed in order to ensure that all the interviewers knew what was happening and that Mrs. M. knew that the therapist and the infant specialist worked together as a team on behalf of herself and her child. In practice, the plan suffered from repeated mix-ups regarding picking-up arrangements and who said what to whom. It was strongly suspected that Mrs. M. sometimes played the therapist off against the infant specialist or vice versa in order to protect herself when she did not follow up on her word.

Communication problems worsened when the therapist went away on vacation during the second month of Amy's attendance at the Infant Center. The separation was obviously difficult for Mrs. M., and she displayed her anger at the therapist on the infant specialist and other staff members. She caused several mix-ups by failing to notify the staff of changes in her plans to pick up Amy in the afternoon. She also failed to have Amy ready in the morning and lashed out verbally at staff members over the phone.

When the therapist returned, she found herself in the middle of a growing conflict between Mrs. M. and the Center. Both Mrs. M. and the staff were angry at her. Mrs. M. rebuked her for going away, while the staff, possibly giving voice to Mrs. M.'s deeper feeling, expressed dismay that so much therapeutic intervention had not yet proven useful in helping Mrs. M. become a better mother. They went on to catalog for the therapist their complaints about Mrs. M.: her erratic behavior in bringing Amy or picking her up, her failure to keep appointments with the caregiver, her inability to follow through with the program. They asked the therapist to become firmer in her demands that Mrs. M. conform to the guidelines worked out for the intervention with Amy.

It is quite possible that the Center staff and the therapist were acting out some of the splits in Mrs. M.'s personality. The staff was reacting to the hostile, provocative, narcissistic side of Mrs. M., while the therapist was taking a protective stance toward the sad and empty little girl who asked for help. Importantly, however, Mrs. M. was showing, by her own and the staff's anger, that she was learning to protest.

To minimize Mrs. M.'s opportunities to play staff members off against each other, we decided that all communications involving Amy and the Center would be handled directly between the infant specialist and Mrs. M. The infant specialist also made clear to Mrs. M. her responsibility for arranging for Amy's pickup and sharing information about Amy's weekends. Mrs. M. responded well to her responsibilities as a mother when they were stated as simple directives.

When her own problems overwhelmed Mrs. M., Amy's

needs continued to come second. Amy was often dirty, though brief periods of improved care followed staff comments to Mrs. M. When the issue of weaning Amy from the bottle arose, Mrs. M. would comment, "I think she's ready, but first I have to get my life together."

There were moments when Mrs. M. radiated as a mother. She brightened up on being told of a newly acquired skill by Amy. The difference between Amy and Harold when he was Amy's age was readily apparent to her, and she commented on it frequently. When asked what she attributed the difference to, she reminisced about the "mess" her life was in when Harold was a baby, and spoke of how much better she was doing now. Inevitably the conversation turned to her own childhood. Her anger toward her mother was vivid.

On the other hand, it seemed that we could never be a good enough mother to Mrs. M. She was not popular with the other mothers because she remained aloof from them. She had also managed to alienate herself from most of the support staff by being rather abrupt or lashing out at them on the phone. Although the infant specialist had never displayed any anger toward her, Mrs. M. often began phone conversations by saying, "You might be angry by what I'm going to tell you but . . .". It was as if she anticipated that the anger within herself would also be encountered in others. She'd be ready by attacking first.

Often Mrs. M. witnessed angry scenes in the infant room between other mothers and their children that scared her. Once she saw another mother hit her young son in the face. She was furious and for days could talk of nothing else with the infant specialist: "What are you going to do about it? That woman is sick, she ought to be in therapy like I was last year; seeing a therapist two or three times a week—not once a week like I am doing now." She said we should keep Amy away from that woman. Eventually she confessed that she had scared herself by hitting Harold. "Boy, even Harry was surprised. I never hit . . . but at least I didn't do it in the face."

Her conflict, her anger, her concern about her loss of control, were close to the surface.

Mrs. M. continued to be only sporadically available to the children and was still prone to jump from sweetness to vituperative anger. Yet she did have more strength to build upon; guilt and the desire to be a good mother were there. She wanted to do what was right: she borrowed library books, read to the children, got them toothbrushes, asked for conferences. Between Harold's therapeutic nursery school and the Infant Program, Mrs. M. had been inundated with good modeling. She understood that there were a variety of ways to interact with children. She proved to have some observational skills and was now interested and able to talk about child development and child rearing. Although her ability to follow through after these discussions was questionable, moments of quality in Mrs. M.'s interactions with her children occurred more often than ever before.

Seeing mother and child together confirmed this impression. Amy showed no anxiety leaving home in the morning (unless her bottle was being denied or mother and she had just had an angry exchange), but she now also went willingly each afternoon with her mother. Even during the one month that Amy referred to her main caregiver as "Mom," it was always clear who the real mother was when both were present, as Amy brought items to share or looked to her mother for help. Amy was genuinely pleased to see her mother at the end of the day, running up to her crying "Mommy." Such a greeting on Amy's part brought a positive response from Mrs. M.; "Hi, pretty girl" was a favorite greeting. However, it was usually Amy who needed to initiate the greetings. When Amy was involved in play and failed to acknowledge her mother's entry, Mrs. M. usually went to the couch and addressed Amy from afar. When Harold accompanied her, the children often squabbled, with Amy screaming and whining and Harold being forced by his mother to indulge his sister in what she wanted. Even when Amy's whininess during the day had declined, it reappeared when her family was present. It was consoling to think that at least she now had more adaptive behavioral modes available to her, even if at times she reverted to the old, more pathological ones.

Harold and Mrs. M.

Communication between the Infant Program and Harold's therapeutic nursery school was excellent from the beginning. Although eighteen months earlier Harold had seemed headed for, at best, a life of borderline cognitive and affective functioning, he now was able to use language well to express his feelings (letting his grandmother know that he felt his mother did not love him and loved Amy, the "baby," more). Harold interacted appropriately with other children at school, liked his teacher, and enjoyed the school experience.

Serious problems remained for Harold at home. Mrs. M.'s inability to have Harold ready for the school bus pickup meant that he missed out on the school experience he loved and on specific opportunities for new experiences like swimming lessons in the summer. Harold still had frequent colds, stomachaches, and infections, and at 4 years of age was found to have such severe tooth decay that extractions and root canal work were necessary. Characteristically, Mrs. M. refused to believe the "quack dentist" who suggested that Harold's dental problems had been caused by her putting him to bed with a bottle and later had a very hard time keeping Harold's appointments for dental treatment.

Harold also remained the "bad" child in his mother's eyes, while Mrs. M. felt very good toward Amy. Harry had now moved into the houehold but was often harshly punitive toward the children, particularly Harold. Harold continued to be provocative and destructive, perhaps as a way of countering, in the only way he could, his constant harassment by Mrs. M. and Harry.

In Mrs. M.'s therapeutic work, new elements were added to old patterns. Mrs. M. still went through crises during which she leaned heavily on her therapist's willingness and ability to cope. However, she not only became able to identify and acknowledge dependency needs but also to become aware of angry feelings toward the therapist and her tendency to displace them for fear the therapist would punish any display of anger by leaving her. Eventually Mrs. M. was able to connect the attacks of hyperventilation she had been experiencing with her dread of separation. And as she explored these themes in close alliance with the therapist, it was clear that Mrs. M. had established an attachment that had constancy.

Amy and Her Family: 24–30 Months

AMY'S 24-MONTH ASSESSMENT

Amy's Bayley Scales performance at 24 months reflected the progress she had made in the previous six months. Gone was the passivity observed during the 12-month and 18-month assessments; Amy seemed to have reacquired the spunk and persistence that had been so impressive when she was 8 months old. The examiner described her as a "happy and easily engaged child" who functioned consistently at age level.

But semistructured interaction with her mother revealed a different aspect of Amy: she was no longer "happy and easily engaged" but whiny and unresponsive. Just before the videotaping began, Mrs. M. asked if the tapes had sound. She then proceeded to put Amy on her lap and asked her in an artificially sweet tone to sing "Jingle Bells." Amy responded with a whine. Mrs. M. then switched to throwing Amy in the air, bouncing her abruptly as she had done during previous assessments. Amy responded with fussing and whining, her face tight with tension. Mrs. M. then left (as on previous occasions) to get Amy some water, and on her return continued attempting to coax Amy to sing "Jingle Bells." She interspersed these attempts with repeated requests for hugs and kisses; Amy kissed her only once. Amy's unresponsiveness gave the distinct impression of an aggressive rejection of her mother. Indeed, Mrs. M.'s face showed unmistakable annoyance every time Amy failed to respond. The contrast between Amy's behavior toward her mother and toward the unfamiliar examiner was remarkable: as Mrs. M. watched, the examiner drew Amy quite easily into a joyful and reciprocal ball game. The little girl had become "happy and easily engaged" again.

At 2 years of age, Amy looked less fretful than ever before. Maternal care, though improved, continued uneven at best. Babyhood depression had taken its toll on Amy; extensive masturbation, possible eczema, excessive oral behavior and self-victimization were a few of the scars still present. Although Amy had improved in the last several months, she still could appear quite often as a solemn, cautious child. On the other hand, Amy had not "turned off" to the world. Curiosity, explorative behavior, and childlike humor were emerging. She could get caught up in laughing games and began to find humor in childlike incongruities (an adult trying to put on a child's jacket). In six months Amy had progressed from a pathetic, inward child, whose whininess often made liking her difficult, to an even-tempered little girl who experienced such satisfaction in interacting with trusted adults that she had endeared herself to the entire staff, who often sought Amy out for a conversation, a short game, or a hug.

INDIVIDUAL THERAPEUTIC SESSIONS WITH AMY

Observing the family functioning, coupled with seeing the child five times a week, gave Amy's caregivers a very detailed picture of what life for Amy was like. The difficulties of overcoming her history of poor physical and maternal care while continuing to cope with day-to-day upheavals were straining Amy's resources to their limit. Mrs. M.'s sporadic availability, her sudden outbursts of anger, and, at times, her outright neglect were still common occurrences in Amy's life. How did Amy view herself in this family scenario? Did she feel herself responsible for her mother's outbursts or lack of warmth? Why was she unable to exert herself physically, socially, or verbally? Why had she chosen passivity and self-victimization? How might the staff help her turn this passivity into activity? With these questions in mind, it was decided to provide individual therapeutic sessions to further enhance the work with Amy. The hope was that such sessions would facilitate the child's communication, through play and inter-action, of her dreams, fantasies, feelings, and conflicts and, as key issues were worked through, lead to an increase in her repertoire of coping mechanisms and adaptive defenses.

When Amy was 22 months old the infant specialist began seeing her, first weekly and then twice a week, for therapeutic play sessions. A strong relationship had always existed be-tween the two, and from the very beginning Amy always went willingly to her play sessions. Her mother had no objections to the therapy and in fact telephoned often to alert the infant specialist to a family crisis and to ask her to "watch and see if Amy says anything." Amy indeed said a great deal.

The play in these sessions reflected Amy's life in three ways. One form of play or behavior mirrored Mrs. M.'s be-havior closely, particularly her mothering of Amy. For ex-ample, Amy would "sweet talk" and dress a doll while handling it gently. Then she would notice that an article of clothing didn't fit right. She would then react with sudden screaming and whining, banging the doll and throwing it about. Such episodes very much resembled scenes of Mrs. M. changing Amy. A second type of episode reflected scenes of family life. Amy repeatedly played out a nighttime scene that was chaotic and exciting, with figures being woken up, moved in and out of various beds, and then sent to bed again. Finally, there was behavior that reflected Amy's unique style in dealing with her situation. Amy's play was usually cautious, methodical, and repetitive; few things were done quickly or haphazardly.

During the very first month of these sessions, Amy re-vealed scenes that would be replayed and elaborated months later. She often mouthed and bit some ferocious-looking pup-pets, laughing nervously, and waved the family figures about, having them hit her in the head. Angry wolves were eating the baby doll, and she would clearly identify with one or the other. A ferocious lion in the background was ready to get out of control. In every session Amy included moments of tender nurturing, as she gently held all the dolls in her arms and rocked them to sleep. Often, however, these moments were interrupted while everyone received a light spanking. Crying by any of the "children" met with another smack. There seemed to be a great deal of confusion around nurturing and aggression, although Amy never comfortably forgot herself in aggressive play. It is interesting that, initially, Amy chose to deal with the toy lion by hiding him behind her. When the lion did finally appear to roar, children and babies were helpless, just as they were when the mother or a doctor spanked them.

Amy seemed to be asking permission to act out. Accidentally knocking a cup off the table led Amy to knock, though gently, all the dishes on the floor, one by one, while she kept one eye on the infant specialist. She then carefully picked everything up and repeated the episode, this time throwing herself on the floor also. This scene was repeated on many occasions. Watching these scenes reminded the infant specialist of the difficulty that Amy had in the Infant Playroom exerting herself physically and emotionally. Although some of the issues around aggression with which Amy was dealing were age-appropriate, a cautiousness and compulsiveness in Amy's play indicated that she was not mastering these issues as adaptively as one would wish.

Progress went slowly, but eventually Amy was able to elaborate some of her fears and fantasies. She told the infant specialist that people were afraid at night because there were wolves, "dogs and kittycats," and bears who "jump on you," "bite you," "put fire on you," or "woof at you." Amy began to put people to sleep in "safe places," at the end of the room far from these wild things. Eventually Amy began to go over and yell, "Don't woof at my baby," or "Stay there, doggie."

She stepped on the animals and "threw fire" at them. One day she told the infant specialist that "that lion should be in a cage." She had the infant specialist help her build elaborate cages of furniture around the lion for several sessions. When the lion was allowed out, Amy told him precisely where he could "go woof." Finally the lion and bear began to walk over to sleeping figures, say "Hi!" to each other, and then leave. Amy had begun to control her lion.

Closely woven into the play theme of aggression was cautiousness. This cautiousness was revealed in ways other than Amy's hesitancy to act out. While in the play session, Amy was alert to every sound: the clicking of an exhaust fan ("What's that?"), the footsteps outside the door ("Somebody's going"), the crying of a baby ("That's Johnny"). Both in the Infant Center and play therapy Amy revealed unusual auditory and visual sensitivity to her surroundings. She always noticed if a toy was missing or in a new place. It seemed that Amy had used her alertness as a coping mechanism to prepare her for whatever her unpredictable environment might bring.

Much of the confusion and excitement that Amy experienced at home around bedtime scenes and overstimulating episodes were played out. There was a great deal of interest in clothes and what is under them in the genital region. As the play therapy continued, other sides of the child emerged: there were signs of humor (as Amy laughingly tried to fit large animals into a small bathtub) and an emerging trust in adults. Amy now asked for help from the infant specialist on difficult tasks that earlier had caused her to break down. For example, she asked the infant specialist to help stand up falling figures, or to unhook a snap on an article of clothing. She no longer resorted to whininess or to flailing her arms about as she had done before. Certainly in the Infant Room she had begun to discriminate among staff, and she had a special relationship now with her infant specialist and her other main caretaker, preferring them for physical comfort or for sharing her new successes. Amy began to extend the nurturing formerly reserved for baby dolls to concern for her peers: she tried to break up arguments between children or brought toys over to pacify a crying baby. Even her cautious style had led to some interesting consequences—a long attention span and a fine eye for detail.

At this point it appeared that Amy had been responding well to the treatment provided in the Infant Center and the play therapy sessions. Occasionally, when the infant specialist announced to Amy that it was time for a play session, Amy began talking immediately about Harry spanking her the night before or wetting the bed or getting lost in the park. She understood that this was the time to reveal her concerns. As Amy got older and worked on some of the developmental tasks confronting her, she began to use the girl or boy figure in her play, rather than the baby figure, which previously she had nurtured in every session. For many months, when toilet training was the issue, it was the boy or girl who had to "pee" or who would knock over the toilet, "make a mess," and have to clean it up, not the baby. When nursery school was about to start it was the children who were marched off under the sofa to school, not the baby. Amy referred to the nursery school as her "big school" and to the Center as "Pat's school" (the infant specialist's). Amy seemed to understand well that going to school and learning to use the toilet were changes that accompanied getting bigger.

Amy's progress can be sketched in terms of a fairly discrete developmental sequence. Given the security and availability of a few warm adults, and as themes of aggression with lions and wolves biting babies (with her in both roles) were repeatedly played out, Amy replaced her promiscuity with cautiousness in human relations, a characteristic that might well have a role in the context of Amy's functioning similar to the infant's stranger anxiety. The next step was the emergence of exploration and initiative, followed by the ability to play out the theme of aggression and "getting the lion under control." Along with these structural achievements came an increase in Amy's language development, range of affect, and ability to experience and express warmth toward others. Her interest in her body parts was age-appropriate, but also seemed an area where conflicts could be played out symbolically.

Amy and Her Family: 30–36 Months

As Amy approached 30 months there was noticeable psychological growth, some of it expected maturationally, much of it due to a sounder psychological structure. Physically Amy continued to be thin and petite, but she was cleaner than ever before, and her mother even fixed her hair up in barrettes and a ponytail. Weaning from the bottle took place uneventfully at this point. Amy was more ready to give up the bottle than her mother was to let her. The signals of Amy's readiness to move on were carefully shown and explained to Mrs. M., who only then felt comfortable in following through and helping her daughter with this developmental task.

Although Amy's fine motor coordination developed adequately, there was still an element of cautiousness in her gross motor movements. This did not prevent Amy from getting caught up in loud and active running/climbing games with her peers. The other children were important to Amy. She often asked "Where's the kids?" on arriving at the Center, and although she periodically resorted to whining in her interactions with peers there was no longer a specific child that she was afraid of or avoided. Amy sometimes even emerged as the leader in playing with the other child who came every day (Ronnie), telling him what to say, when to go to sleep, where to put his doll, etc.

At this time also, symbolic play was becoming more sophisticated, as Amy engaged in games of fireman, mother keeping house, and bedtime, even, at times, using imaginary dogs and animals.

Receptive language had been at age level for some time, although Amy spoke little. Finally, at about 30 months, her expressive language began to blossom. Just at this time, the Infant Specialist became quite sick and had to be absent for six weeks. Instead of regressing into a more infantile mode of functioning, Amy reached out to language in order to understand and cope with this loss. Taking a symbolic mode (language) and using it to control and understand an event in her life represented a momentous change in Amy's coping strategy. Language remained an important tool in helping her understand her world ("Is this school's?"; "Can I take it home?"; "I need a birthday party too"). In play therapy she occasionally stopped playing and spoke to the infant specialist about a puzzling or hurtful accident that she had experienced at home. She sometimes stuttered when she spoke about certain difficult subjects, like wetting the bed, being spanked, or fearing a puppet show. In fact, Amy's tone and loudness of speech revealed a great deal about her comfort with a particular situation.

Emotionally, Amy now showed a wide range of affect. She could be playful (naming her body parts incorrectly), scared ("Those fire engines scared me in my bed"), mad (a bit removed—"My mom called you a dum-dum"), excited ("I'm going to granddaddy's today"), concentrated (stringing three necklaces in a row), loving (bringing toys to a crying baby). Her favorite activities continued to be playing with dolls, books (including a photo album), songs and music, playdough, and water.

AMY'S 30-MONTH ASSESSMENT

At the 30-month assessment, the quality of the free play between mother and child was better than it had been six months or a year before. Mrs. M. allowed Amy to initiate the play. Since Amy was most interested in the doctor's kit, Mrs. M. helped Amy to use the stethoscope to listen to her heart and also named the other items in the bag for Amy and explained their use. During this particular session, Mrs. M. did not resort to physical, rough play (there were the usual kisses) but tried to follow Amy's lead. She was unable, however, to help Amy elaborate or enrich the play, and it was Amy who terminated each game. The assessor described Amy as a petite, sociable little girl with an evenness in developing skills (Bayley = 105). She experienced difficulty in the more complex tasks; what appeared to the examiner as a strong fear of failure affected her attempts on several items, and once again Amy's perseverance came into question. Even her mother was aware that Amy had the ability, but not the perseverance, to complete several Bayley tasks. The examiner felt the child needed repeated reinforcement for completion of tasks regardless of her success or lack of success. Becoming more confident would ensure the child would maintain her level of performance.

Amy's evaluation session with the infant specialist revealed a 2½-year-old unusually gifted in her capacities for representational elaboration and emerging differentiation. She played out the age-appropriate themes of doctors giving injections; children messing in the bathroom, exploring bottoms and the genitals; and phallic themes of "Superman" and rocket ships as well as a very organized sequence of "ghost mommy" where a baby doll was covered with a white paper and identified as a "ghost mommy" which made "eerie" sounds. "But it's just a baby," she said as the cover was taken off. Here it was clear that she reached levels of "pretend" (differentiation) and possibly a reworking of her own early relationship with an often unavailable "ghostlike" mother.

The general impression was of a youngster with precocious language and representational capacities, using them to deal with current and past conflicts. There was a slight overconcern with her "bottom," probably based on what she experienced or witnessed with her mother's boyfriend, and a slightly subdued affect, balanced by a higher than age-expected overall developmental status, curiosity, and capacities for relating to others.

NURSERY SCHOOL AND CONTINUED PLAY THERAPY

Mrs. M. and the infant specialist had often discussed future plans for Amy and the possibility of her attending nursery school. Mrs. M. had begun, and was continuing, a job as a bus aide at Harold's therapeutic nursery school and felt very positive about it. The school director had promised her a place for Amy in the school, not in the therapeutic component but in the main classroom. The staff of the Infant Program thought that this would be a good placement for Amy in the fall, when Amy would be 32 months old. Although Amy remained at risk because of her earlier development, she functioned at an age-appropriate level in most areas and would probably benefit from a nursery school experience if play therapy could continue.

In the fall Amy began attending the nursery school for five mornings a week. After spending all day, every weekday, together for eighteen months, this represented a momentous separation for Amy and for the Infant Center staff. At first, Amy spoke excitedly of going to Harold's school and riding the school bus. Eventually, however, she began asking if her caregivers would be there. For some time she stopped talking about the change altogether (although she continued to play "going to school" in the play therapy). In play sessions she got the figures and marched them off to the school, which was located under the sofa. She did not seem to know what to do with them after getting them to school and just left them there. The dog and the kittycat bit the infant specialist often during this time.

AMY BEGINS NURSERY SCHOOL

Mrs. M. was eager to bring Amy into the Center on the afternoon of the first day of school, but felt the therapy with Amy should continue only for a few weeks, until "she got used to her new school." When the infant specialist said that she thought Amy would benefit from continuing the sessions, Mrs. M. wanted to "know the truth"—did we want Amy to come just for the research or did we think Amy needed it? The infant specialist explained to Mrs. M. that Amy was a bright, competent child who often, unfortunately, did not perform to her potential. A discussion followed about the 30-month assessment and the items that Mrs. M. knew Amy could complete but had not. The infant specialist added that if Amy could be more courageous and spunky about approaching such tasks, the likelihood of her succeeding in school would be greater. Mrs. M. agreed with much feeling and went on to say that both she and her mother lacked self-confidence. She wondered if we thought that Amy was like that because she did not have a father. (Often, the key to past or future happiness for Mrs. M. was a male figure.) Following this discussion, Mrs. M. no longer questioned Amy's coming in twice a week for her play therapy sessions; she had needed to know that we wanted her and Amy for the right reasons and once this was understood a routine was quickly established. Amy came in two afternoons a week for two to three hours. Often she took a short nap on arrival, "in her old bed." A play therapy session followed, with some time in the playroom with her old friends.

AMY'S ADJUSTMENT TO THE NURSERY SCHOOL

While the therapeutic sessions continued, it was rewarding for mother and staff to see the fine adjustment that Amy had made in school. The Infant Center and the school had been in close contact. After one semester Amy's teacher described her as cooperative, intelligent, and serious. She handled transition well, shared, waited her turn, and had a long attention span. Although Amy was more involved in parallel play than in interactive play (that is, she had not yet begun involving herself in give-and-take, cooperative, symbolic play) the teacher felt that because of her age (she was the youngest in the class) this was not yet a concern. Interestingly, in her therapeutic sessions her ability for interactive, emotional representational play continued to be quite precocious in many respects, highlighting the cautiousness Amy brought to a new setting.

Mrs. M. was beaming when she shared this report with the infant specialist. She pointed out that the teacher had mentioned the word "intelligent" twice. Just as the infant specialist had decided that this was not the best of days to discuss with Mrs. M. some of the concerns that still existed about Amy (as she had planned), Mrs. M. said suddenly, "but there are some problems." She elaborated her worries about Amy's off-and-on toilet training accidents and her still somewhat excessive masturbation and concern with the genital area. As she discussed with Mrs. M. a little girl's developmental preoccupation with her body and the fear of body damage, the infant specialist recognized that she was addressing issues that were unresolved for both mother and daughter, and helping the mother heal old wounds through her daughter.

Conclusion

Work with Amy is not yet finished. In some areas her progress remains limited, partly because her mother's erratic life and sporadic availability are likely to continue affecting Amy. Mrs. M. is still unable to work with her daughter around issues of intimacy, body concerns, sexuality, and aggression. As for Amy, her difficulty in expressing aggression is still not fully resolved. She can still resort to self-victimization, and the tendency to somatization remains a possibility. Her cautiousness continues to interfere with her ability to get the most out of a situation in which social or cognitive expectations are involved. She seems to hold back affectively also: although her range of affect is wide, the depth of its expression is not so robust as one would wish. If only she could free herself to laugh harder or to cry louder!

Yet the many strengths that Amy now possesses illustrate her very significant progress. She has proved herself to be an intelligent child who is tuned in to the wonders of the world.

Although limiting in some ways, her cautiousness has paid off
in others: she has a good eye for detail, a long attention span,
and a love for books and music. Cooperative and receptive
to adult attention, Amy is well liked by almost all who interact
with her. She expresses a good deal of trust and evidences
warmth and intimacy and an age-appropriate range of affects.
Her comfortable use of language has helped her to manage
her interactions, as she reminds her mother of what she needs
for school, or "pesters" her mother to address her physical
needs. Amy can no longer be described as resembling an
institutionalized child. She has a new capacity for intimacy
fostered by her "home away from home" and her individual
therapy. One finds oneself impressed and relieved by the
resiliency of this child, with her wonderful ability to elaborate
and reason out her concerns, to maintain a warm, trusting
relationship to key adults and peers, and, slowly, to become
more assertive.

Amy has managed to separate out the two worlds in which
she lives, and has learned certain adaptive coping mechanisms
for use at home and different means to cope successfully with
the outside world. One hopes that ongoing intervention will
help Amy eventually to integrate her two worlds, as Mrs. M.
continues to become more adequate in her interactions with
Amy and as Amy's own adaptive functions become more stable
and resilient to stress.

The progress made by Mrs. M. is also noteworthy. Part
of the therapeutic work at the beginning consisted of crisis
intervention, in which the therapist allowed herself to be
viewed as the good mother who could be relied on to provide
solicitous care. After each crisis was over, a painstaking process of clarification and working through took place, and
through this process a major shift in Mrs. M.'s functioning
occurred, as she resolved her ambivalence and began to experience pride and positive feelings toward her children.

Mrs. M.'s achievements are still very vulnerable to
regression in the face of internal or external stress. But a major

shift in personality organization has been made, and there is new hope for Mrs. M.'s ability to form and sustain enduring human relationships, particularly with her children.

POSTSCRIPT: FURTHER EMOTIONAL GROWTH AND A NEW BABY BOY

Mrs. M. gave birth to a new baby boy. He was born healthy and robust with excellent state regulation and interactive abilities. Most remarkable and even surprising, however, was Mrs. M.'s ability to consolidate her gains in her nurturing of her new child. In evaluations at 3 days and 1 month, and in general observation, Mrs. M. attended to her infant's cues, was very soothing, and helped him orient and alert by varying her voice, facial expression, and gentle movements. In contrast to her flat affect when Amy was an infant, Mrs. M. bubbled with feeling, delighted in her baby's abilities, and, most important, was realistic in her planning and expectations. Her new infant had a very different start. Meanwhile, Amy and Harold continued to do well.

At the 4-month assessment, Mrs. M. and her new infant's progress were even more notable. They evidenced a solid and joyful attachment built on excellent homeostatic abilities. For example, during their free play there was clear recognition of the mother, joyful smiles, and organized visual, vocal, and motor communication, illustrated by baby Danny's "enraptured" involvement with his mother. He mimicked her mouth movements while remaining finely tuned to her voice, visual attention, and soothing handling. The enraptured affective contact and the beginning of purposeful signaling occurred during most of their free play, and home visit reports noted similar intervals in their play at home. The infant's cognitive development was in the high average to superior range with good gross, fine, and sensorimotor abilities. Most important, Mrs. M. continued to be well-organized, realistic, and optimistic; her relationship with Michael, Danny's father, was progressing to new levels of intimacy.

Particularly impressive was the degree to which Mrs. M. continued this pattern of care with only minimal help from the therapeutic team, in contrast to her pattern with her two older children. Through further therapeutic work Mrs. M.'s capacity for intimacy reached levels never anticipated, given her chaotic and deprived background. For example, she has not only dealt with increasingly more personal and emotionally relevant issues in her therapeutic relationship, but has learned to have a deep, apparently enduring relationship with the father of her new baby. She now tolerates frustration, talks rather than "acts out" in crises, and provides a consistent emotional climate for her family.

It should be noted that Amy's progress continues without individual play therapy. Her gift for using ideas to talk and play out her concerns appears to help her maintain age-appropriate levels of functioning. She is warm, trusting and focused. A good learner, she shares and interacts well with her peers. Some subtle signs of underlying affect hunger appear in playroom evaluations, suggesting Amy will continue to struggle with a difficult past. However, she seems well equipped to meet this challenge.

In addition to Amy and her mother, we have seen in six cases to date the positive impact of the treatment program on the parents' ability to care for their next child and the solid start that the children who are "second born" in the program are receiving. Regardless of the sex of the new infant, the pattern has been similar to what is described for Mrs. M., contrasting with the general trend in multirisk families toward further deterioration of both mother and infant with the birth of each subsequent child.